Waynesburg College Library
Waynesburg, Pa. 15370

D1770665

343.7304	W859d
Wolfman, Bernard AUTHOR	
Dissent without opinion TITLE	
113688	

343.7304 W859d

Wolfman, Bernard
Dissent without opinion
113688

Dissent Without Opinion

Dissent Without Opinion

The Behavior
of
Justice William O. Douglas
in
Federal Tax Cases

BERNARD WOLFMAN
JONATHAN L. F. SILVER
MARJORIE A. SILVER

University of Pennsylvania Press
Philadelphia

Copyright © 1973 by the Trustees of the University of Pennsylvania
Copyright © 1975 by the University of Pennsylvania Press, Inc.
All rights reserved

This book originally appeared in journal form in the
UNIVERSITY OF PENNSYLVANIA LAW REVIEW
whose permission for publication is gratefully acknowledged.

Photograph for cover courtesy of the Foundation of the
Federal Bar Association.

Library of Congress Catalog Card Number: 74-16827
ISBN: 0-8122-7682-5
PRINTED IN THE UNITED STATES OF AMERICA

In Memory of Zelda Wolfman and Margery S. Silver

Contents

Foreword	ix
Preface	xv
Introduction	3
I. The Record	7
Period 1. 1939-1943: The Government Years	8
Approach to the Statute	9
Attitude Toward the IRS	17
Quality of Opinions	19
Period 2. 1943-1959: The Shift to the Taxpayer	26
Approach to the Statute	28
Attitude Toward the IRS	36
Quality of Opinions	37
Period 3. 1959-1964: The Extreme Years	43
Approach to the Statute	44
Attitude Toward the IRS	52
Quality of Opinions	54
Period 4. 1964-1973: Tempered Rebellion	60
Approach to the Statute	63
Attitude Toward the IRS	67
Quality of Opinions	71
Voting Patterns on Particular Issues	74
II. Justice Douglas' Performance in Other Areas of the Law	79
Corporate Insider Regulation	79

Labor Law 94
    Approach to the Statute 96
    Attitude Toward the Labor Board 101
Welfare Law 106
III. An Attempt at an Explanation 117
    Dissatisfaction with Administrative Agencies 118
    Antipathy to the Internal Revenue Code 124
IV. Conclusion 131
Afterword 139
Appendix 141
Bibliography 177
Table of Cases 199

Foreword

Few Justices of the Supreme Court have been so well known during their own time as William O. Douglas. This is due not only to his probably unequaled production of judicial opinions, which must number over 1,000 by this time,[1] but is also due to his prolific extra-judicial writings, and particularly to the first volume of his autobiography, the recently published *Go East Young Man*. There have been a number of writings about the Justice, too.[2] But despite his unprecedently long judicial career, there have been few studies of his work there by uncommitted critics.

During the present century, we have become accustomed to the idea that the law expounded by the Supreme Court is, indeed, made by men, and that it makes a great deal of difference which men, or women, are selected for the Court. We understand, perhaps better than the Nineteenth Century did, that it is not just a question of ability, but also outlook and the Judge's conception of his own role as a Judge. For this reason, as evidenced in the

---

[1] There were approximately 600 opinions in 1959, after twenty years of service on the Court. See Book Note, *Douglas of the Supreme Court—A Selection of his Opinions*, 73 HARV. L. REV. 1040 (1960).

[2] See Frank, *Review of Douglas, Democracy and Finance*, 54 HARV. L. REV. 905 (1941).

recent past, it seems unlikely that the Senate will take a passive view of its function in confirming a Supreme Court Justice for many years to come.

Most Justices have followed a rather consistent course after taking their seats on the Court, at least after a shakedown period. Thus, we do not think of periods in the judicial careers of Chief Justice Marshall, Justices Field, Bradley, Holmes and Brandeis, or Chief Justices Hughes or Warren. All of these, and many others, have had their work carefully examined by scholars and students of the Court, and one can have a fairly clear view of where they stood and of the contributions which they made to the Court and to the law. Of course, they were not always completely consistent in their views and outlooks. Still, I believe, one never refers to "the early Hughes" or to "the later Brandeis."

It is for this reason that the study made by Dean Wolfman and his associates turns new ground. For they have shown that, in the tax field at least, there has been a very considerable change in the viewpoint of Mr. Justice Douglas during the long period of his service on the Court.

Mr. Justice Douglas took his seat on the Court on April 17, 1939. Less than a year later he wrote the opinion for the Court in *Helvering* v. *Clifford*,[3] surely one of the strongest pro-government tax cases in the books. From an Olympian point of view, the result may well have seemed desirable. But there was little, if anything, in the statute to support it. Nor was it the culmination of a series of decisions, slowly etching out a new ground in the law. Even today, it seems to have been a rather strong case of judicial law-making. Ultimately it has, on the whole, worked out quite well. However, there was at first an enormous amount of litigation. Several years later, the Treasury undertook to clarify the situation with com-

---

[3] 309 U. S. 331 (1940).

prehensive regulations.[4] Finally, in 1954, fourteen years after the *Clifford* decision, Congress enacted detailed statutory provisions, now found in sections 671-678 of the Code. These have, in fact, worked quite well. They provide clear guides for planners and draftsmen, and litigation—and administrative controversy—in this area has virtually ceased. It may well be that this result never would have been reached without the bold action of the Supreme Court in the *Clifford* case. It still remains a question whether, in a democracy, this was an appropriate judicial action. At any rate, as the following pages show, this was a product of "the early Douglas."

The present study clearly establishes that over the ensuing years there has been a steady and marked shift.[5] The existence of this shift, and the reasons for it, are never explicit, and this question has been examined by Dean Wolfman and his co-authors.

It is perhaps a fair judgment that the shift has been not only in outlook and result, but also in the care and thoroughness with which opinions appear to have been prepared. Some of them seem to have been written rather quickly, without much of the burden of legal paraphernalia. Some of the opinions in other fields seem a bit

---

[4] Treasury Decision 5488, 1946-1 CUM. BULL. 19, adding the provisions which for many years appeared in sections 29.22(a)-21, 29.22(a)-22, and 29.166-2 of Regulations 111 and the corresponding provisions of Regulations 118.

[5] This has continued through the Term which ended in July, 1974. In Snow v. Commissioner, 416 U.S. 500, decided May 13, 1974, Justice Douglas wrote the opinion for the taxpayer. In Commissioner v. National Alfalfa Dehydrating Co. 417 U.S. 134, decided May 28, 1974, Justice Douglas joined with the majority (or did not express dissent) in a highly technical decision in favor of the government involving the existence of bond discount after a reorganization. In Central Tablet Manufacturing Co. v. United States, 417 U.S. 673, decided June 19, 1974, Justice Douglas joined with three other members of the Court in dissenting against a decision in favor of the government. In Commissioner v. Idaho Power Co., 418 U.S. 1, decided June 24, 1974, Justice Douglas wrote a lone dissent in favor of the taxpayer.

bizarre, legally speaking,[6] and many of them in recent years seem to evidence an element of antipathy to the government above and beyond that usually found in the judicial process.

Why should this be? Why should Justice Douglas, a great and active administrator himself, come to take a negative view about administration, particularly in the tax field? Some of us have seen administrators at work, from the inside. Of course, there are poor and weak administrators, as well as good and strong ones. But there are many fine people in the Internal Revenue Service, carrying out an enormous responsibility, and they have, generally speaking, had good leadership. I think that most tax lawyers would feel that, on the whole, the Internal Revenue Service has been well administered. Certainly the courts cannot effectively administer the Internal Revenue System. Why, then, should there by judicial antipathy to the system, particularly when one of its serious problems arises from the fact that so few cases can come before a court with nationwide jurisdiction? Perhaps we will get more light from ensuing volumes of Justice Douglas' autobiography.

One conclusion to draw from this study is that Justice Douglas, like many others, finds no intellectual interest or challenge in tax cases—or, to put it more directly, he dislikes tax cases and does not regard them as worthy of his careful attention. Indeed, except for Justice Blackmun, it is hard to find a member of the present Court who has a real "feel" for tax law. This has done much to bring about delay and wasted litigation in the tax field. Under our system of waiting for a conflict, it often takes many years before a simple, homely problem can be resolved, and during all that time lawyers on both sides in many cases

---

[6] See, for example, Douglas, J., dissenting in Sierra Club v. Morton, 405 U.S. 727, 741 (1972).

must guard their clients' rights, take protective action, engage in numerous administrative hearings, and file suits, until the system eventually produces an answer.[7] A Court with regard for the tasks of the administrative agency, and of counsel for taxpayers and for the government, could foresee many of these problems, and bring them more quickly to a solution. Long experience has shown that this does not happen when the approach is to fend off a tax problem until a direct and articulated conflict of decisions has developed.

These are the sorts of questions which are dealt with, thoroughly and methodically, and with imagination and skill, in the present study. With this fine start, we may hope that there will be similar studies in other fields—administrative law, or criminal law, or welfare law, for example. In the meantime, we are all much indebted to Dean Wolfman and to Mr. and Mrs. Silver for the contribution which they have made here. Mr. Justice Douglas has been a great figure in the law, and he is honored by the fact that his work has stimulated their probing. This is a significant chapter in a corner of the intellectual legal history of the country.

Erwin N. Griswold
Washington, D.C.

---

[7] In United States v. Cartwright, 411 U.S. 546 (1973), a case involving the highly repetitious question of the valuation of mutual fund shares (neither very difficult nor very important), the regulation was issued in 1963. The decision from the Supreme Court as to its validity did not come until ten years later.

Preface

Justice Douglas is known well and widely for his views and his impact on Constitutional safeguards and on individual liberty. Lawyers know additionally of his work as a government administrator and of his judicial opinions affecting the securities markets and the regulation of business and free enterprise. Justice Douglas' role in the 278 federal tax cases in which he voted from 1939 to 1973 has been unique but little known and virtually unanalyzed. My interest in him in tax cases stems from one in which he voted alone, silently, in favor of my client. I thought him perceptive at the time, and I assumed that his silence reflected something like the exasperation I felt from his Brethren's failure to grasp the irresistible logic of my client's position. As the years went on, however, I became aware of what appeared to be a Douglas pattern of solitary pro-taxpayer stances. Eventually, as I became more academic in my interests and no longer a professional taxpayer partisan, I began the investigation which is reported in this book.

As my study progressed I became increasingly critical of what I saw. I interrupted my work at one time for several years, as I was uncertain of the worth of a report that might reflect adversely on a Justice because of his work in one major field, a Justice whose general social biases I tended to share and who, for many, had taken on heroic proportions. At the same time Douglas' political adversaries were seeing him as Devil and impeachable for reasons I despised. I worried, too, whether I could possibly explain Douglas' bizarre performance in tax cases and whether, even if I could, a critical diagnosis would be at all constructive. Even now, I am not certain we have the explanation for Justice Douglas' enigmatic behavior, but we have a theory and some data. We are not sure this study will prove constructive, but we are satisfied that objective and detached scholarly inquiry and analysis of the span of work of particular long-serving Justices in the major fields of the law are needed if the Justices are to be accountable.

American society is just beginning to appreciate the importance of accountability in all institutions that wield great power over people. The unrest on University campuses a few years ago may have resulted in part from the failure of administrators to account adequately to faculty, and the failure of both to account at all to students. In the world of financial institutions self-perpetuating managerial groups are starting to yield a measure of power to independent directors responsible to the public investor. The consumer movement and the critics of our health delivery systems are beginning to force an accountability on institutions and people who to a significant degree, despite their control over the welfare of millions, were all but beyond the reach of law, market forces, or public opinion.

Most judges are accountable to those on a higher court and in some instances, regrettably, to an electorate. Fortunately, all our federal judges have a constitutionally secured independence, but those on the Supreme Court are made broadly accountable only through the exposure provided by the publication of scholarly analyses and evaluations of their work. Justices should serve in the expectation of such accounting. A Justice's good heart and his good work in one or even several areas ought not deter examination in others. The Law and litigants are entitled to judging and reasoning from every Justice whatever the issue. Neither his past contributions, nor his generally lofty motives, nor his superior capacities, nor his impatience with institutions and people are warrant to any Justice to vote without judging and reasoning.

Had my co-authors, Jonathan L. F. Silver and Marjorie A. Silver, my former students, not shown their enthusiasm and shared the effort to the degree they did, it is doubtful that this work would have been completed. With humility I express to them my admiration and affection.

My collaborators and I acknowledge our debt to three people who share none of the responsibility but have participated mightily: To Christopher R. Lipsett, Article Editor of Volume 122 of the University of Pennsylvania Law Review, whose patient determination and dedication to truth helped us immeasurably; to Paul Asofsky, my research assistant in 1964-65 when he was a third-year student at the Harvard Law School; and to Toni Braemer, a third-year student at the University of Pennsylvania Law School, for her work in the preparation of the Selected Bibliography.

Philadelphia   Bernard Wolfman
December, 1974

Dissent Without Opinion

INTRODUCTION

In 1955, the senior author of this book was one of the attorneys for the losing taxpayers in a case before the United States Supreme Court involving the taxability of the two-thirds penalty portion of a Clayton Act[1] recovery.[2] Justice William O. Douglas alone, it seemed, appreciated the subtle argument of taxpayer's counsel, although his solitary dissent was without opinion. His curiosity stimulated, the author began to take notice of the frequently recurring phenomenon of Douglas' dissenting silently and alone in favor of the taxpayer. Thus began his interest in Justice Douglas' treatment of tax cases, one which grew into a comprehensive review of all tax cases in the Supreme Court[3] during Douglas' tenure.[4]

The evolution of Justice Douglas' behavior in tax cases will be developed in detail in Part I. In general, the data reveal that during his first years on the Supreme Court, Justice Douglas wrote many tax opinions for the Court,

---

[1] 15 U.S.C. § 15 (1970).

[2] Commissioner v. Glenshaw Glass Co., 348 U.S. 426 (1955).

[3] The cases considered were only those arising under income, estate, gift and excise taxes. Social Security taxes, for example, were excluded.

[4] The study was interrupted in 1965 and resumed in 1972 with the collaboration of the other authors.

usually sustaining the Government's position. Then a change occurred. He began to dissent more frequently, usually in favor of the taxpayer. And he often dissented alone, without opinion, or with only a few words. In the last decade and a half particularly, Douglas' positions in tax cases have been marked by a strong disposition in favor of taxpayers' positions, a lack of sympathy with the administration of the Internal Revenue Service, the agency charged with enforcing the tax statutes,[5] and an increasing failure to explain his votes in well-reasoned opinions.

Assisted by the statistical tables we have compiled, we will attempt to pinpoint where and how Justice Douglas changed course in tax cases. In addition, in Part II we will take a comparative look at his work in other areas of law in which the interpretation of a federal statute is involved. In Part III our effort will be speculative, groping for explanations of Douglas' approach to tax cases and his attitude toward the IRS. In Part IV we will reflect on Justice Douglas' performance in federal tax cases as a Justice of the United States Supreme Court.

In a 1948 speech on the role of dissent in the Supreme Court, Douglas said: "The judge that writes his own predilections into the law in disregard of constitutional principles or the legislative or executive edicts that he interprets is not worthy of the great traditions of the bench."[6] And similarly, speaking eleven years later "On Misconception of the Judicial Function and the Responsibility of the Bar," Justice Douglas said:

> The legislature of course passes laws that favor or disfavor certain groups. Judges who enforce these laws according to their terms, however, can not fairly have

---

[5] Before March 15, 1952, the Internal Revenue Service was known as the Bureau of Internal Revenue. T.D. 6038, 1953-2 CUM. BULL. 443. Throughout we refer only to the Internal Revenue Service (IRS) or the Treasury.

[6] Douglas, *The Dissenting Opinion*, 8 LAWYERS GUILD REV. 467, 469 (1948).

attributed to them the partiality of those who passed the laws. It is the very essence of a government of laws that the predilections of judges not carry the day, and that the law as written by the lawmakers be applied equally to all. This I had assumed to be elementary.[7]

In a sense, this book will measure Justice William O. Douglas' performance in the tax field against his own standard.

---

[7] Douglas, *On Misconception of the Judicial Function and the Responsibility of the Bar*, 59 COLUM. L. REV. 227 (1959).

I. The Record

In examining the development of Douglas' approach to federal tax cases, we have broken his tenure on the Court (from 1939 to 1973) into four separate periods.[8] Our discussion of each period begins with an analysis of statistical data presented in three tables.[9] The first of these tables (Table I) shows the number of tax cases won by the taxpayer in each period, and the number in which Justice Douglas voted for the taxpayer.[10] Table II exposes those

---

[8] The points at which the periods break were selected for the following reasons: (1) The 1943 Term marked the beginning of a clear shift in Douglas' voting pattern. (2) A radical alteration of Douglas' voting pattern began in the 1959 Term. (3) The dramatic change that began in the 1959 Term seems to have ended in the 1964 Term. (4) No events have occurred since 1964 that warrant another break.

[9] Appendix, Tables I-III, *infra*. At the beginning of the analysis of each period, the portions of Tables I, II and III relevant to that period, as well as those portions of Tables I, II and III which are relevant to prior periods, are set out in the text. Thus, for example, Table I-1 in the text contains the portion of Table I which relates to Period 1. Similarly, Table II-3 contains the portions of Table II which deal with Periods 1, 2 and 3. By doing this we hope to facilitate an understanding of the pattern which develops over time.

We have omitted criminal cases from Tables I, II, III, IV and V, since the considerations affecting judgment in such cases often differ greatly from those in other tax cases. The criminal cases are included, however, in Tables VI and VII. We have also omitted from our statistical computations and Tables I, II, III, IV, V and VI cases in which the Court disposed in a very short opinion of a case on all fours with a companion case which the Court had decided in a full opinion.

[10] In the Appendix this Table is expanded to show the number of cases in each volume of United States Reports as well.

cases, period by period, in which Justice Douglas differed with the majority of the Court, and indicates the extent to which Douglas was the sole dissenter. Subtables divide the cases into two groups, one including those which the taxpayer won, and the other, those in which the Government won. Table III indicates the way in which Justice Douglas expressed his dissenting views. The cases are again divided by period, with notation of the number of cases in which Douglas wrote an opinion, joined an opinion and dissented without opinion. (Tables IV and V, listing for comparative purposes all tax cases in which a member of the Court dissented alone or without opinion, appear with Tables I through III in the Appendix but are not reproduced in the textual discussion detailing each individual period.[11]) These compilations lay bare the fleshless pattern which led us to dig below the statistics in search of explanation.

Following this statistical analysis, our discussion of each period turns to an examination of selected tax cases which illustrate Douglas' approach to construction of the Code, his attitude toward the IRS, and the degree of attention and concern which Justice Douglas has given to tax questions as reflected in the quality of his opinions. Part I concludes with observations about Table VI, which divides the cases into various substantive categories of tax law.

Period 1. 1939-1943:

Government Years

The statistics for the years 1939-1943 disclose Douglas' strong support for the Government's positions during that period. He voted for the Government in 82%

---

[11] The Appendix also contains Table VII, which records Justice Douglas' action in every tax case in this study.

of the tax cases which the Court decided. He endorsed the taxpayer's position less often than did the Court, and registered no dissents in favor of the taxpayer.

Out of 91 cases in which he participated, Justice Douglas wrote the opinion of the Court on 29 occasions. That figure represents slightly over 30% of the cases in which Douglas voted with the majority. In only one case did he dissent without either joining or writing an opinion.

It is also worth noting that in this early period Douglas dissented in only a handful of cases (6 out of 91). He was not alone in any of those dissents.[12] Further, in 4 of the 6 cases, two other justices joined him. As the years unfold, that degree of solidarity erodes and is replaced by increased dissent, often solitary.

Our examination of Douglas' opinions in this period reveals an inclination to construe the taxing statutes favorably to the Government. In part, at least, this seems to have been due to a judicial attitude supportive of the IRS in its efforts to resolve the difficulties inherent in administering the tax system. The opinions also reflect thought and attention.

APPROACH TO THE STATUTE

Two cases in this period involved taxpayers whose hardship, due to unique factual circumstances, might have been considered compelling enough to warrant deviation from the literal command of the statute—without doing violence to the basic statutory scheme—in order to sustain their positions. Justice Douglas, writing for the Court in both cases, refused exceptional treatment.[13] In *J. E. Riley*

---

[12] During this period, Justice Roberts dissented alone 4 times; Justice McReynolds dissented alone twice; and Justices Reed and Butler each dissented alone once. Additionally, Justices Roberts and McReynolds dissented twice without opinion; Justices Black and Douglas and Chief Justice Hughes each dissented once without opinion. *See* Appendix, Tables IV-V, *infra*.

[13] Both cases were decided by a unanimous Court, but the concern here is

Investment Co. v. Commissioner[14] the taxpayer mined gold in Alaska. Because of slow mail service to and from the taxpayer's remote location, it used income tax forms from earlier years to avoid delinquency. When the tax collector sent 1933 forms to the taxpayer for use in reporting 1934 income, he did not call attention to a change in the law that had created a percentage depletion deduction,[15] and under which the taxpayer could have elected the new benefit or continued on the old cost depletion system. Unaware of the statutory change, the taxpayer made no election. Since the taxpayer had a zero basis, no cost depletion was possible. It was found that if the taxpayer had known of the new statutory alternative, it would have elected percentage depletion. The statute provided that a failure to elect the percentage depletion method for 1934 would deny the taxpayer the right to use that method later. Thus, because of tardy mail service the taxpayer failed to claim a benefit through which it would have reduced its tax liabilities substantially. In the following year the taxpayer filed an amended 1934 return, taking a deduction for percentage depletion and claiming a resultant refund. The Commissioner denied the claim on the ground that amendment was impermissible after the due date of the return.[16]

Douglas noted the taxpayer's hardship, but upheld the Commissioner. According to his interpretation, the opportunity to elect percentage depletion was "afforded as

---

not with conformity, or even the implication of "correctness" which unanimity sometimes creates. It is simply to note that Justice Douglas could plausibly have construed the statute favorably to the taxpayers and that he did not do so. This contrasts with his approach in later periods.

[14] 311 U.S. 55 (1940).

[15] Revenue Act of 1934, ch. 277, § 114(b)(4), 48 Stat. 680, 710 (now INT. REV. CODE OF 1954, § 613).

[16] Apparently the taxpayer could have sought permission of the Commissioner to amend its return in August, 1935, when it first learned of the statutory provision for percentage depletion. *See* 311 U.S. at 57, 58. The Court did not rely on that fact, however. The basis of the Court's opinion was that the Commissioner could not accept a tardy election; it did not matter whether the taxpayer's delay was or was not reasonably justified.

Table I-1 (Summary)
Tax Cases Decided by Supreme Court, 1939-1973

Period	Volumes U.S. Reports	Number of Cases	Number Won by Taxpayer	Number Douglas for Taxpayer
1 (1939-1943)	307-19	91	22½ (25%)	16 (18%)

Table II-1
Cases in which Douglas Differed with the Court

Period	Number of Cases in which Douglas Participated	Number Douglas in Minority	Percentage in Minority	Number Douglas Alone	Percentage Alone
		All Cases			
1	91	6½	7%	0	0%
		Won by Taxpayer			
1	22½	6½	29%	0	0%
		Won by Government			
1	68½	0	0%	0	0%

Table III-1
How Douglas Made His Dissenting Views Known

Period	Number of Cases in which Douglas Participated	Number Douglas in Minority	Number Wrote Dissent	Number Dissent Without Opinion	Percentage Dissent Without Opinion
		All Cases			
1	91	6½	1	1	1%
		Won by Taxpayer			
1	22½	6½	1	1	4%
		Won by Government			
1	68½	0	0	0	0%

a matter of legislative grace"[17] to be availed of only in strict accordance with the congressional requirements. Douglas recognized that the purpose of the statutory provision barring amendments was to preclude taxpayers from switching from one depletion basis to another with the benefit of hindsight. Although the taxpayer in *Riley* could not have gained from such a switch, so that the purpose of the statute was not in tension, Douglas found no authority to justify an exception. It was irrelevant to Justice Douglas that slow mail delivery had denied the taxpayer the choice Congress intended it to have. For the Justice Douglas of this early period, such hardship was perhaps "the basis for an appeal to Congress . . ." but not a "ground for relief by the courts from the rigors of the statutory choice which Congress has provided."[18]

Justice Douglas approached *Scaife Co. v. Commissioner*[19] as he did *Riley*. In *Scaife* the taxpayer's vice president had instructed its treasurer to place a value of $1,000,000 on the corporation's capital stock for purposes of the capital stock tax.[20] By mistake, the value was declared at $600,000. When the error was discovered, a new return was prepared declaring the greater value, and the taxpayer remitted the additional tax that resulted. The taxpayer sought to base its capital stock tax on the higher valuation, because the higher valuation would result in a lower taxable income for purposes of the excess-profits tax imposed by section 106(a) of the Revenue Act of 1935.[21] Like the provision in *Riley*, the statute applicable in *Scaife* required that the valuation appear on the taxpayer's return for the year of the election that fixed the value of its stock

---

[17] *Id.* at 58.
[18] *Id.* at 59.
[19] 314 U.S. 459 (1941).
[20] Revenue Act of 1935, ch. 829, § 105(a), 49 Stat. 1017, *repealed*, Act of June 21, 1965, Pub. L. No. 89-44, § 401(a), 79 Stat. 148.
[21] 49 Stat. 1019 (1935), *repealed*, Act of Nov. 8, 1945, ch. 453, § 122(a), 59 Stat. 568.

and permitted no amendment after the due date of the return for that year.[22] Finding the change untimely, the Commissioner refused to accept the new capital stock tax return and the additional sum.

Justice Douglas wrote for the Court to sustain the Commissioner's subsequent refusal to recompute the taxpayer's excess profits tax on the basis of the stock's higher valuation. Once again he recognized the harshness implicit in rejection of the taxpayer's attempt to amend its return. Nevertheless, he chose to extend[23] *Riley*, concluding that if the Court were to adopt the taxpayer's position it would be "performing a legislative, ... not a judicial, function."[24]

A second notable facet of Douglas' approach to statutory construction during this first period was his tendency to resolve ambiguity in favor of the Government; he construed narrowly the exceptions from the general rule which required all income to be reported. *Maguire v. Commissioner*[25] required a construction of section 113(a)(5) of the Revenue Act of 1928.[26] The taxpayer in *Maguire* had acquired a share of a testamentary trust established by her father. She contended *inter alia* that the basis to her of the property left by the will was its fair market value at the time the trustees delivered it to her.

---

[22] The Commissioner had statutory power to extend the due date for 60 days under appropriate regulations. He had promulgated no such regulations, however, and the taxpayer had sought no extension. 314 U.S. at 462.

[23] In *Riley* Justice Douglas said, "We are not dealing with an amendment designed merely to correct errors and miscalculations in the original return." 311 U.S. at 58.

[24] 314 U.S. at 462. On the question of whether hardship to the taxpayer is a factor to be considered in tax cases, *compare Riley* and *Scaife with* Peurifoy v. Commissioner, 358 U.S. 59, 61 (1958) (Douglas, J., dissenting), discussed at text accompanying notes 85-86 *infra*; United States v. Lewis, 340 U.S. 590, 592 (1951) (Douglas, J., dissenting), discussed at text accompanying notes 76-81 *infra*; Commissioner v. Harmon, 323 U.S. 44, 49 (1944) (Douglas, J., dissenting), discussed at notes 69-75 *infra* & accompanying text.

[25] 313 U.S. 1 (1941).

[26] 45 Stat. 819 (now INT. REV. CODE OF 1954, § 1014).

The Government claimed that the basis of property left in trust was its value (here lower) at the time the trustees received it from the executor. By her contention the taxpayer sought to avoid taxation on the amount by which the property had appreciated while in the hands of the trustees.

The statute provided that in all cases other than those specifically excepted, the basis was to be the value "at the time of the distribution to the taxpayer."[27] In the excepted cases, the basis was to be the value at the time of the testator's death. Douglas did not hold that the case before him came within one of the explicit exceptions, but he read those exceptions as evidence of a general legislative purpose to fix basis as value at the time when the property was distributed by the estate's executors. With that legislative purpose as his guide, Douglas held that the basis of the property was its value when the executors transferred control to the trustees. Thus, he ruled that the statutory phrase "distribution to the taxpayer" included a distribution to a trust of which the taxpayer was a beneficiary.

Although Justice Douglas relied primarily on his own judgment, inferentially drawn, as to what Congress must have meant, he expressed a further reason for rejecting the taxpayer's position:

> The creation of such an opportunity for manipulation of tax liability cannot be lightly presumed. Similarly, we cannot assume in absence of explicit provisions that

---

[27]Section 113(a)(5) provided in part:
If personal property was acquired by specific bequest, or if real property was acquired by general or specific devise or by intestacy, the basis shall be the fair market value of the property at the time of the death of the decedent. If the property was acquired by the decedent's estate from the decedent, the basis in the hands of the estate shall be the fair market value of the property at the time of the death of the decedent. In all other cases if the property was acquired either by will or by intestacy, the basis shall be the fair market value of the property at the time of the distribution to the taxpayer.

such as the one before the Court in *Clifford.* Justice Douglas concluded, however, that since Congress intended the definition of income to sweep broadly, its failure to adopt the Treasury's recommendations "cannot be said to have subtracted from [the definition of income] what was already there."[35] Rather, he reasoned that Congress had merely intended to refuse any per se rule regarding short term trusts, thus leaving the cases to be determined by triers of fact on a case-by-case, totality-of-the-circumstances basis. Twice, then, Douglas relied in *Clifford* on the "income" definition (or lack of definition) to reach his result.

Riley, Scaife, Clifford and *Maguire* illustrate an early tendency on the part of Justice Douglas to construe the statute against the taxpayer. The statutory provisions involved in those cases could have been construed against the Government without doing violence to the legislative purpose or scheme. At that time, however, Douglas believed in giving scope to the statute and disregarded harsh results as not within the province of the Court to correct.

ATTITUDE TOWARD THE INTERNAL REVENUE SERVICE

Two of Douglas' opinions from this first period illustrate a conscious deference to the role of the IRS. *Helvering v. Reynolds*[36] involved the retroactive applicability of a 1935 Treasury regulation interpreting the Revenue Act of 1934. The taxpayer relied upon a prior case, *Helvering v. R. J. Reynolds Co.,*[37] which squarely ruled against the retroactivity of a different regulation. Justice Douglas limited that case to its special facts. In the case before him, he noted that "[t]he magnitude of the

---

[35] 309 U.S. at 337.
[36] 313 U.S. 428 (1941).
[37] 306 U.S. 110 (1939).

task of preparing regulations under a new act may well occasion some delay," and that to refuse to apply the 1935 regulation in question retroactively would be to "introduce into the scheme of the Revenue Acts refined notions of statutory construction which would, to say the least, impair an important administrative responsibility in the tax collecting process."[38] This he would not do.

Justice Douglas' opinion in *Reynolds* reflects a willingness to defer to the Commissioner when pragmatic reasons supported the administrative action. Although it would seem to have been possible to place less weight on the practical difficulty which the Commissioner faced, Douglas chose to exercise judicial power to broaden rather than constrict the Commissioner's authority. A similar attitude is evident in *Textile Mills Securities Corp. v. Commissioner*,[39] in which the corporate taxpayer claimed, and the Commissioner disallowed, expenses incurred for publicity, nontrade advertising, and other forms of public relations in connection with a campaign for the passage of the Settlement of War Claims Act of 1928. A Treasury regulation, not the statute, stated that such expenses were not deductible as ordinary and necessary business expenses of a corporation.[40] Justice Douglas, again writing for the Court, rejected the taxpayer's argument that the regulation was contrary to statute (which allowed ordinary and necessary business expenses)[41] and hence invalid. Since there was no "clear Congressional action to the contrary,"[42] Justice Douglas ruled that the administrator's interpretation of the statutory phrase "ordinary and necessary expenses" could properly be inferred from a policy recognized in the law of contracts which opposed

---

[38] 313 U.S. at 433.
[39] 314 U.S. 326 (1941).
[40] Treas. Reg. 74, art. 262 (1931) (the pertinent portion of which is now contained in Treas. Reg. § 1.162-20 (1973).
[41] Revenue Act of 1928, § 23(a), ch. 852, 45 Stat. 799.
[42] 314 U.S. at 339.

the "business" of procuring private legislative favors. On that basis, he concluded simply, "The general policy being clear it is not for us to say that the line was too strictly drawn."[43]

QUALITY OF OPINIONS

In addition to some already discussed,[44] a number of the cases indicate that in this first period Justice Douglas devoted considerable time and thought to the writing of tax opinions. The point here is not that Douglas' conclusions were always "right." It is only to emphasize that he supported his judgments with reasoning and analysis which demanded attention and were at least arguably correct. Although several cases tempt exposition,[45] only two,[46] reasonably representative, will be discussed.

United States v. Stewart[47] involved the taxability, under the Federal Farm Loan Act of 1916[48] and the Revenue Act of 1928,[49] of capital gains resulting from transactions in certain farm loan bonds. The issue was a narrow one of statutory construction, not obviously significant to basic conceptual or schematic issues in the administration of the income tax. Douglas' opinion for a nearly unanimous Court discloses a close reading of the statute in the perspective which Congress had established, accompanied by a detailed consideration of the taxpayer's arguments.

---

[43] *Id.*
[44] *E.g., Maguire, Clifford* and *Reynolds.*
[45] *See especially, e.g.,* Helvering v. Griffiths, 318 U.S. 371 (1943); Helvering v. Gambrill, 313 U.S. 11 (1941); Guggenheim v. Rasquin, 312 U.S. 254 (1941).
[46] Virginian Hotel Corp. v. Helvering, 319 U.S. 523 (1943); United States v. Stewart, 311 U.S. 60 (1940).
[47] 311 U.S. 60 (1940).
[48] 39 Stat. 360.
[49] 45 Stat. 791.

The taxpayer had purchased the farm loan bonds with a view to their appreciation in value, and not for their interest. When the taxpayer made his purchase he relied upon statements of the Farm Labor Board which he had reasonably understood to mean that his profits on resale of the bonds would be exempt from federal income tax. Subsequently the taxpayer realized a profit on his disposition of the bonds, and the Commissioner included that profit in the taxpayer's income. After he paid the additional tax assessed, the taxpayer sued for a refund.

The applicable Revenue Act included in gross income all "gains, profits, and income derived from . . . sales, or dealings in property, whether real or personal. . . ."[50] Section 22(b)(4) of that Act specifically exempted "[i]nterest upon . . . securities issued under the provisions of the Federal Farm Loan Act," but that provision was inapposite because the taxpayer's gains were clearly not "interest." The taxpayer relied, rather, on section 26 of the Federal Farm Loan Act, which provided that

> farm loan bonds issued under the provisions of this Act, shall be deemed and held to be instrumentalities of the Government of the United States, and as such they and the income derived therefrom shall be exempt from Federal, State, municipal, and local taxation.[51]

He contended that the capital gains at issue constituted exempt "income derived" from the bonds within the meaning of section 26.

Justice Douglas noted, as a first proposition, that the term "income" was, by itself, broad enough to refer to capital gains, such as those at issue, as well as to interest received by a bondholder. He reasoned further, however,

---

[50] Revenue Act of 1928, ch. 852, § 22(a), 45 Stat. 797.
[51] Federal Farm Loan Act of 1916, ch. 245, § 26, 39 Stat. 380.
[52] 39 Stat. 756.

that the phrase "income derived therefrom" suggested a distinction between income derived from the mere fact of ownership (interest) and income realized from transactions in the bonds (capital gains). Only the first, he stated, was definitely within the statutory exemption.

Douglas found support for this view in the legislative history. Congress passed the Farm Loan Act in 1916. The same session of Congress adopted the Revenue Act of 1916,[52] which dealt with the farm loan bonds in precisely the same manner as the Revenue Act of 1928, exempting only interest.[53] Because he concluded that the exemption in the 1916 tax statute was a "legislative interpretation" of the Farm Loan Act by the same Congress which had passed that Act, Douglas ruled that "the express exemption of interest alone makes tolerably clear that capital gains are not exempt."[54]

Justice Douglas next considered five arguments which the taxpayer had advanced. First, the taxpayer relied on debates and comments in the legislative history of section 26 which referred in a general way to the importance of the exemption provision or to the fact that it created an advantage for the farm loan bonds over other investments. Douglas found these statements to be inconclusive, because they were "not sufficiently discriminating in their analysis or criticisms to throw light on the narrow issue involved."[55]

Second, Douglas found unpersuasive the taxpayer's reliance on administrative interpretations. The taxpayer referred to an unpublished memorandum by the General Counsel of the Bureau of Internal Revenue, but Justice Douglas indicated that the memorandum was not precisely on point. In any case, an administrative ruling issued two years later went directly against the taxpayer's position.

---

[53] Revenue Act of 1916, ch. 453, § 4, 39 Stat. 758.
[54] 311 U.S. at 65.
[55] *Id.* at 65-66.

The taxpayer's third argument referred to a 1938 amendment to section 26. The taxpayer maintained that this amendment, which provided that "all income, except interest, derived"[56] from farm loan bonds was includible in income, implied that prior to 1938, capital gains and other noninterest income were entitled to exemption. Douglas cited legislative materials to show that the purpose of the amendment as it was originally phrased was unrelated to the taxpayer's case. Although the form of the amendment as ultimately enacted did suggest a relevance to the taxpayer's type of transaction, Justice Douglas saw no convincing indication that the amendment was intended to change, rather than clarify, the law as it related to those transactions. He concluded that "even if a contrary implication were to be assumed, it would not override so belatedly the clear inference, based on a long series of revenue acts exempting only interest, that capital gains were taxable."[57]

Fourth, the taxpayer reviewed several other statutory exemption provisions in an effort to show that Congress had employed the word "interest" when interest was all it desired to exempt, and had reserved the word "income" for situations in which it intended to grant a broader exemption, as in section 26. Although he found this argument "suggestive," Douglas gave it little weight in view of the multitude of other factors involved in the congressional choice of phrasing and Congress' long-standing exemption of interest only in successive Revenue Acts.

Finally, Justice Douglas rejected the taxpayer's argument that he had reasonably relied on statements of the Farm Loan Board which allegedly interpreted the statutes to exempt the taxpayer's capital gain. Douglas noted that those statements were really no more specific

---

[56] Revenue Act of 1938, ch. 289, § 817, 52 Stat. 578.
[57] 311 U.S. at 68.

than the statute, but he held in any case that the Board had no authority to render authoritative opinions as to tax consequences. Taking this argument together with the taxpayer's other four arguments, Douglas found their collective force insufficient to overcome the basis for his original construction of the exemption.

The thoroughness of Justice Douglas' opinion in the *Stewart* case is impressive but in this regard it is not exceptional for this period. In later periods, however, Douglas' opinions have evidenced much less detail.

Unlike the *Stewart* case, resolution of *Virginian Hotel Corp. v. Helvering*[58] required a broad consideration of the dynamics of the statutory scheme of income taxation. The taxpayer had depreciated certain assets from 1927 to 1937 according to an estimated useful life which the Commissioner determined, in 1938, was too short. The Commissioner therefore computed a deficiency for 1938. To determine the proper basis for depreciation in 1938 and later years, the Commissioner subtracted the total amount of depreciation taken between 1927 and 1937 from the original cost of the assets.

The taxpayer had sustained net taxable losses for each of the years 1931 through 1936, and the Commissioner stipulated that as a result, "the entire amount of depreciation deducted on the income tax returns for those years did not serve to reduce the taxable income."[59] The taxpayer did not challenge the Commissioner's redetermination of the useful life of the assets. It claimed only that in computing the new basis for depreciation the Commissioner should not have subtracted the amount deducted during the loss years which was in excess of the amount which the taxpayer would have claimed if it had properly estimated the assets' useful lives, and which was

---

[58] 319 U.S. 523 (1943).
[59] *Id.* at 524.

of no tax benefit in any event. Had the taxpayer deducted depreciation at only the proper rate during the loss years, then, in computing the new depreciation basis, the Commissioner could now subtract from the original cost only the aggregate of the proper deductions. Since the taxpayer's excessive depreciation rate had not reduced his taxes during the loss years, the taxpayer argued that there was no reason in 1938 to decrease his current and future depreciation basis by the amount of the excessive depreciation originally shown. The lower basis determined by the Commissioner would result in a smaller deduction and hence a greater tax liability for 1938 and following years.

Justice Douglas' opinion for the 5-4 majority upholding the Commissioner began with an analysis of the phrasing of the statute. Section 113(b)(1)(B) of the Revenue Act of 1938[60] provided that depreciation was to be computed each year on a basis equal to the original cost of the property, less adjustments for depreciation "to the extent allowed (but not less than the amount allowable) under this Act or prior income tax laws." The parenthetical phrase, Justice Douglas explained, meant that the basis of the property must be diminished each year by at least the amount of depreciation which would be properly claimed, whether or not that amount was actually taken. Thus, depreciation could not "be accumulated and held for use in that year in which it [would] bring the taxpayer the most tax benefit."[61]

The taxpayer's argument, however, centered on the phrase "to the extent allowed." The taxpayer acknowledged that if an erroneously large deduction had saved it money, then the deduction had surely been "allowed." But it argued that when Congress used the term "allowed" it meant to encompass only cases in which the taxpayer had received a dollar benefit.

---

[60] Ch. 289, § 113(b)(1)(B). 52 Stat. 493-94.
[61] 319 U.S. at 525.

Douglas recognized the compatibility of the taxpayer's position with the purpose of the statute, but he did not believe that the meaning of the statutory language was determinable solely by its purposes.[62] Instead he based his holding first on his understanding of the dynamics of a taxpayer's claim to a deduction and our system for audit and disallowance.

> Under our federal tax system there is no machinery for formal allowances of deductions from gross income. Deductions stand if the Commissioner takes no steps to challenge them. Income tax returns entail numerous deductions. If the deductions are not challenged, they certainly are "allowed," since tax liability is then determined on the basis of the returns. Apart from contested cases, that is indeed the only way in which deductions are "allowed." And when all deductions are treated alike by the taxpayer and by the Commissioner, it is difficult to see why some items may be said to be "allowed" and others not "allowed."[63]

Then, finding no "clear and compelling" reasons for interpreting "allowed" as used in section 113(b)(1)(B) differently from its meaning in this "general setting of the revenue acts,"[64] Justice Douglas rejected the taxpayer's contention.

Virginian Hotel is a hard case. The taxpayer sought to deny the government a windfall at the taxpayer's expense. The taxpayer's position was consonant with the purpose of the statute, and four justices accepted that position because of its appeal to fairness. Douglas' judgment may or may not be more compelling than the taxpayer's argument. It is clear, however, that he rested his decision on pragmatic elements involved in the complex task of

---

[62] That purpose was "to make sure that taxpayers who had made excessive deductions in one year could not reduce the depreciation basis by the lesser amount of depreciation which was 'allowable' " *Id.* at 526.

[63] *Id.* at 527 (footnote omitted).

[64] *Id.* at 528.

administering the federal income tax, and that he carefully explained the considerations in his opinion.

The cases and statistical data permit one to form an overall picture of Justice Douglas' approach in federal tax cases during his first years on the Court. His voting record did not differ significantly from that of the Court as a whole. Although he voted for the taxpayer in a fair percentage of the cases, he generally supported a broad view of the statutory scheme, directed toward enforcement and protection of the revenue, and he rejected constrictive interpretations of the Code which taxpayers urged, as well as taxpayer pleas for exceptional treatment where a literal reading of the statutes would prove harsh. He construed special exemptions and deductions in the context of what he saw as the overriding legislative goal and schema of a progressive income tax. He gave substantial deference to the agency charged with administering the statute. His opinions reveal attention to legislative history and considerable concern for the practical necessities of administering the tax system.

Period 2. 1943-1959:

A Shift to the Taxpayer

Statistics for the lengthy second period[65] of Douglas' tenure indicate a clear shift in attitude. In this period he voted for the taxpayer in 47% of the cases in which he participated, almost three times the 18% figure for 1939-1943. Moreover, the increase did not reflect the record of the Court as a whole. The Court held for the taxpayer in only 25% of the cases, the same percentage as in the prior period. As a result, Douglas differed from the

---

[65] This second period is quite long (16½ years) as compared to the first period (4½ years); nevertheless, the number of cases is only 20% greater (116 as compared to 91).

majority of the Court in a far greater number of cases in this period than he had previously. Although he had never done so during the first period, Justice Douglas dissented in favor of the taxpayer in 29 (33%) of the 87 cases decided for the government during this second period. He was a member of the minority in over 28% of all the cases, more than four times as often as in Period 1.

The second period also witnessed a sharp decline in the percentage of cases in which Douglas explained his position in a written opinion. During these years he participated in 116 tax cases, voting with the majority in 83, but he wrote for the Court in only 10 (12%) of those cases. More significantly, in a number of cases Justice Douglas dissented without any opinion at all, or, on occasion, with only a very brief statement. In 15 of the 33 cases in which Douglas was in the minority, he failed to write or join any dissenting opinion.[66] This figure contrasts sharply with that of the first period, since in those years Douglas dissented silently in only one case.

Justice Douglas also began in this period to stand alone. In 11 cases, in 9 of which he favored the taxpayer, his vote was the only one in the minority.[67] The occasions of this phenomenon are closely linked with the incidence of his silence: of the 15 unexplained dissents, 9 were solitary, and 8 of those 9 favored the taxpayer.

Two additional factors should be kept in mind. First,

---

[66]Although the Court had overruled the court of appeals in a number of these cases, it does not seem proper to assume that Justice Douglas' silent dissents intended to indicate a reliance on the lower courts' reasoning. There are cases in which Justice Douglas stated his reliance on the court of appeals, *e.g.,* Commissioner v. Bilder, 369 U.S. 499, 505 (1962) (Douglas, J., dissenting). During this period Justice Burton dissented without opinion 4 times (3 of those with Justice Douglas); Justices Black and Jackson each dissented twice without opinion; and Justices Reed and Roberts each dissented once without opinion. *See* Appendix, Table V, *infra.*

[67]During this period Justice Roberts dissented alone 3 times; Justices Rutledge, Burton, Jackson, Black and Harlan each dissented alone twice; and Justice Whittaker dissented alone once. *See* Appendix, Table IV, *infra.*

the statistical break between Periods 1 and 2 is quite sharp. Second, as the cases suggest, the break develops progressively and continuously throughout Period 2.[68] The nature and development of the change, which seems to have begun in 1943-44, and progressed through 1958-59, is evident from an examination of the cases.

APPROACH TO THE STATUTE

Commissioner v. Harmon[69] held that a husband and wife who irrevocably elected community property treatment under an option provided by state law were not entitled to the income splitting benefits accorded by *Poe v. Seaborn*[70] to couples who lived under a mandatory community property law. Justice Douglas' lengthy dissent in *Harmon*[71] explored and criticized the distinctions on which the Court rested its decision. The basis of his argument, stated in his conclusion, was that

> ... *Poe v. Seaborn* has been carved out as an exception to the general rules of liability for income taxes. If we are to create such exceptions we should do so uniformly. We should not allow the rationale of *Poe v. Seaborn* to be good for one group of states and for one group only.[72]

This passage marks perhaps the first occasion on which Douglas articulated a philosophy leading to decisions against the Government when he finds such results

---

[68] To illustrate both factors we have broken the statistical analysis for Period 2 into two subparts in Tables I, II and III in the Appendix.
[69] 323 U.S. 44 (1944).
[70] 282 U.S. 101 (1930). Prior to Justice Douglas' tenure, the Supreme Court had held in *Poe* that a husband and wife in a state which had traditionally applied community property concepts could each report one half of their combined income, despite the fact that the entire income might have been earned by only one spouse, and thus diminish the impact of progressive rates.
[71] 323 U.S. at 49.
[72] *Id.* at 56.

Table I-2 (Summary)
Tax Cases Decided by Supreme Court, 1939-1973

Period	Volumes U.S. Reports	Number of Cases	Number Won by Taxpayer	Number Douglas for Taxpayer
1 (1939-1943)	307-19	91	22½ (25%)	16 (18%)
2 (1943-1959)	320-59	126	32 (25%)	54 (of 116) (47%)

Table II-2
Cases in which Douglas Differed with the Court

Period	Number of Cases in which Douglas Participated	Number Douglas in Minority	Percentage in Minority	Number Douglas Alone	Percentage Alone
		All Cases			
1	91	6½	7%	0	0%
2	116	33	28%	11	9%
		Won by Taxpayer			
1	22½	6½	29%	0	0%
2	29	4	14%	2	7%
		Won by Government			
1	68½	0	0%	0	0%
2	87	29	33%	9	10%

necessary in order to treat favorably those taxpayer litigants whose position he believes to be sssentially similar to that of others who have been granted favor by Congress, rejecting opportunities for nice but rational distinctions within the legislative framework. The Justice Douglas of 1941 might have accepted the Court's distinction in order to retain the broad reach of the tax statute,[73] requiring

---

[73] *Cf.* Maguire v. Commissioner, 313 U.S. 1 (1941); Helvering v. Clifford, 309 U.S. 331 (1940), both cases discussed at notes 25-35 *supra* & accompanying text.

Table III-2
How Douglas Made His Dissenting Views Known

Period	Number of Cases in which Douglas Participated	Number Douglas in Minority	Number Wrote Dissent	Number Dissent Without Opinion	Percentage Dissent Without Opinion
		All Cases			
1	91	6½	1	1	1%
2	116	33	8	15	13%
		Won by Taxpayer			
1	22½	6½	1	1	4%
2	29	4	0	4	14%
		Won by Government			
1	68½	0	0	0	0%
2	87	29	8	11	13%

that exceptions come from Congress, not the courts.[74] There are strong indications that he in fact agreed with the Court's result in *Harmon*, but was willing to reach it only by overruling, not distinguishing, *Poe v. Seaborn*, a case which he believed to be in conflict with the conceptions he had articulated in *Helvering v. Clifford*.[75] Douglas could, of course, have concurred in the *Harmon* result and still criticized the Court for its rationale, but he chose otherwise.

In *United States v. Lewis*[76] the taxpayer had reported, in the year of receipt, a bonus which he believed rightfully his. The amount of the bonus had been incorrectly computed, however, and in a later year he was required to

---

[74] *Cf.* Scaife Co. v. Commissioner, 314 U.S. 459, 462 (1941); J. E. Riley Investment Co. v. Commissioner, 311 U.S. 55, 59 (1940), both cases discussed at notes 14-24 *supra* & accompanying text.

[75] "The truth of the matter is that *Lucas v. Earl* and *Helvering v. Clifford* on the one hand and *Poe v. Seaborn* on the other state competing theories of income tax liability." Commissioner v. Harmon, 323 U.S. at 56. For the discussion of *Clifford*, see notes 29-35 *supra* & accompanying text.

[76] 340 U.S. 590 (1951).

return the portion to which he was not entitled. A deduction in the year of return would not produce a benefit equal to the tax he had paid, but the Court, in order to preserve the basic concept of the annual accounting period, held that he could not adjust the earlier year's tax. Thus the majority concluded, "We see no reason why the Court should depart from . . . well-settled interpretation merely because it results in an advantage or disadvantage to a taxpayer."[77] Justice Douglas based his dissent,[78] however, squarely on his sense of the inequity to the taxpayer: "Many inequities are inherent in the income tax. We multiply them needlessly by nice distinctions which have no place in the practical administration of the law."[79] This statement indicates an approach quite different from that in *Riley, Scaife* and other cases of the earlier period. Furthermore, Douglas' conclusion seems to be fundamentally inconsistent with his view in *Virginian Hotel*,[80] in which the problem was similar and the taxpayer's "equities" no less poignant. In both cases the taxpayer's early returns were based on excusable misconceptions of facts,[81] yet Douglas would require one taxpayer to accept the harsh consequences of his error, while eight years later he would permit the other to recoup.

Cases decided during the latter half of this period continued the trend illustrated by *Harmon* and *Lewis*. In *Arrowsmith v. Commissioner*[82] the taxpayers had liquidated a corporation in 1937. They properly reported

---

[77] *Id.* at 592.
[78] *Id.*
[79] *Id.* (Douglas, J., dissenting).
[80] For the discussion of *Virginian Hotel*, see notes 58-64 *supra* & accompanying text.
[81] The errors in both cases were in good faith, *see* United States v. Lewis, 340 U.S. 590, 591 (1951); Virginian Hotel Corp. v. Helvering, 319 U.S. 523, 531 (1943) (Jackson, J., dissenting).
[82] 344 U.S. 6 (1952).

the profits as capital gains over the years of receipt, 1937-1940. In 1944 the taxpayers paid a judgment rendered against the old corporation, as they were required to do, and they claimed an ordinary business loss deduction. Thus the taxpayers had had their profits from the liquidation taxed at the lower capital gains rates, but sought to deduct related losses from income which would otherwise have been taxable at the higher ordinary income rates. The Commissioner contended that the loss should have the same character as the profits of the earlier years, *i.e.,* that it should be treated as a capital loss (with reduced tax benefit).

The Court agreed with the Commissioner. The character of the loss was to be determined by reference to the source transaction. The source of the loss was the "exchange" of a capital asset, the stock, upon liquidation of the corporation. The Court held that it was not inconsistent with the annual accounting concept to determine the nature of the loss in that fashion, because, contrary to the taxpayer's position in *Lewis*, there was no attempt to reopen and adjust the 1937-1940 tax years. The 1944 tax would be computed according to the taxpayer's 1944 income.

Justice Douglas, dissenting,[83] did not believe that the Government's position could be accepted without violating the annual accounting concept established in *Lewis* and other cases. Rather, he stressed that "if [*Lewis*] is the law, we should require observance of it—not merely by taxpayers but by the Government as well."[84] As in *Harmon*, Justice Douglas did not take the opportunity to distinguish and thus limit a previous case with which he disagreed—*Lewis*—but voted instead to expand its scope. While there may be strong arguments against it, the

---

[83] *Id.* at 7.
[84] *Id.* at 10.

majority's treatment of the annual accounting issue was not patently meritless. Douglas' opinion did not address the majority's theory, however, and seems to rest on a somewhat personal conception of fair play between government and taxpayer.

Douglas' dissent in *Peurifoy v. Commissioner*[85] relied on his sense of hardship to the taxpayer. The Court held that construction workers who stayed at one job for periods of between eight and a half and twenty and a half months, and who maintained permanent residences elsewhere, could not deduct expenses for board, lodging and transportation at the site of their jobs. Justice Douglas dissented from the Court's refusal to rule that those expenses were necessarily incurred "away from home." Although he cited no authority for the proposition, he did "not believe that Congress intended such a harsh result [as the majority's] when it provided a deduction for traveling expenses."[86]

This concern with the statutes' harsh results sharply conflicts with Douglas' approach in *Riley*[87] and *Scaife*,[88] cases decided in the first period. In those cases it was he who said that the harshness of results in some cases was not a ground for judicial relief.

Notwithstanding the change in attitude which these opinions suggest, Justice Douglas continued to approach occasional cases of statutory interpretation as he did in the earlier period.[89] In *Equitable Life Assurance Society v.*

---

[85] 358 U.S. 59, 61 (1958).

[86] *Id.* at 62.

[87] For the discussion of *Riley*, see notes 14-18 *supra* & accompanying text.

[88] For the discussion of *Scaife*, see notes 19-24 *supra* & accompanying text.

[89] These cases, however, were perhaps not close. Of the 5 occasions during this period on which Justice Douglas wrote for the majority in favor of the Government, 4 were unanimous decisions. In the fifth, Robertson v. United States, 343 U.S. 711 (1952), (holding a prize received for winning a

Commissioner[90] an insurance company distributed what it termed "excess interest dividends" to certain policyholders who left their policies on deposit after maturity. The decision to pay these "excess interest dividends" was discretionary with the board of directors of the company,[91] but their decisions were made and announced before the year in which the payments accrued. On these facts the taxpayer claimed that, as a matter of law, the payments were deductible as "interest" paid for the use of the depositors' funds.[92] Justice Douglas, writing for the Court, held against the taxpayer since he found the payments to "have a degree of contingency which the notion of 'interest' ordinarily lacks."[93] In a passage that recalls the rationales of *Maguire* and *Clifford*, he reasoned: "If we expanded the meaning of the term [interest] to include these excess interest dividends, we would indeed relax the strict rule of construction which has obtained in case of deductions under the various Revenue Acts."[94]

In *United States v. Olympic Radio & Television, Inc.*,[95] decided near the end of this period in 1955, Justice Douglas construed section 122(d)(6) of the Internal Revenue Code of 1939[96] which allowed a taxpayer to carryback and deduct any Excess Profits Tax "paid or accrued" in any taxable year, in which the taxpayer incurred a net operating loss. The operation of

---

musical contest to be a discharge of a contractual obligation, not a gift) Justice Jackson dissented without opinion.

[90] 321 U.S. 560 (1944).

[91] The payment of "excess interest dividends" was not contingent upon any cumulation of earnings or surplus. *Id.* at 562.

[92] According to the Revenue Act of 1932, ch. 209, § 203(a)(8), 47 Stat. 225.

[93] 321 U.S. at 564.

[94] *Id.*

[95] 349 U.S. 232 (1955).

[96] Act of Oct. 21, 1942, ch. 619, § 105(e)(3)(C), 56 Stat. 807, *amending* Int. Rev. Code of 1939, § 122(d) (now INT. REV. CODE OF 1954 §172(d)).

complementary sections of the Code led him to conclude that the words "paid or accrued" did not entitle a taxpayer which kept its books on the accrual basis to compute the section 122(d)(6) deduction on the cash basis, "a basis that is inconsistent with the method of accounting which it employs."[97] Douglas' justification for the result again echoed his early approach:

> This taxpayer argues the inequity of the results which would follow from our construction of the Code. But as we have said before, "general equitable considerations" do not control the question of what deductions are permissible.... We can only take the Code as we find it and give it as great an internal symmetry and consistency as its words permit....
>
> The fact that the construction we feel compelled to make favors the taxpayer on the cash basis and discriminates against the taxpayer on the accrual basis may suggest that changes in the law are desirable. But if they are to be made, Congress must make them.[98]

---

[97] 349 U.S. at 235.

[98] *Id.* at 236. *Compare Olympic Radio with* Commissioner v. Harmon, 323 U.S. 44, 56 (1944) (Douglas, J., dissenting), reproduced at text accompanying note 72, *supra*.

See also Commissioner v. P.G. Lake, Inc., 356 U.S. 260, 265 (1958) (Douglas, J., stating that the capital gains treatment "has always been narrowly construed so as to protect the revenue against artful devices."); Alison v. United States, 344 U.S. 167, 170 (1952) (Court authorizing taxpayers, victims of embezzlement, to take deduction for loss in year of discovery, rather than year of theft; finding loss "sustained" in that year, in accord with Regulation requiring that deduction be taken in year of theft ordinarily but not always. "An inflexible rule is not needed; the statute does not compel it.") (Douglas J., dissented.) *But see* Lewyt Corp. v. Commissioner, 349 U.S. 237, 240 (1955) (Douglas, J., writing for the Court) a companion case to *Olympic*, holding for the taxpayer on a related issue:

> But the rule that general equitable considerations do not control the measure of deductions or tax benefit cuts both ways.... [W]here the benefit claimed by the taxpayer is fairly within the statutory language and the construction sought is in harmony with the statute as an organic whole, the benefits will not be withheld from the taxpayer though they represent an unexpected windfall.

The six cases discussed demonstrate an unsteady change in some areas of statutory construction during this period. Some cases suggest that Douglas wanted to avoid "inequitable" consequences to the taxpayer at bar, and thus gave weight to considerations which did not influence him during his first five years on the Court.[99] At the same time he continued to construe the Code against the taxpayer in cases in which the results apparently did not offend his sense of fairness.

ATTITUDE TOWARD THE INTERNAL REVENUE SERVICE

Justice Douglas' opinions during this period only infrequently expressed his attitude towards the Internal Revenue Service. A comparison of two cases, however, suggests that his conception of the proper deference owed the agency was in a state of flux.

Robertson v. United States,[100] decided in 1952, involved a taxpayer who had written a symphony during the years 1936-1939, for which he received a prize in 1947. He computed his 1947 tax as though the income had been received ratably over the period 1937-1939. The Commissioner did not object to spreading the income, a technique authorized by section 107(b) of the Internal Revenue Code of 1939,[101] but claimed that the amount should be spread over the three-year period ending with the receipt of the prize, 1945-1947. The Treasury regulation which construed section 107(b)[102] supported the Commissioner's interpretation. Justice Douglas, writing for the Court, surveyed the legislative history, found that it supported the Commissioner's position, and held for the

---

[99] *See also* Merchants Nat'l Bank v. Commissioner, 320 U.S. 256, 263 (1943) (Douglas, J., dissenting) (construing charitable deduction for estate tax).

[100] 343 U.S. 711 (1952).

[101] Revenue Act of 1939, ch. 247, § 220, *adding* Int. Rev. Code of 1939, § 107(b) (now INT. REV. CODE OF 1954, § 1302).

[102] Treas. Reg. 111, § 29.107-2, 8 Fed. Reg. 15010 (1943).

Government. He also noted simply: "That is the construction given by Treasury Regulations . . . ; and while much more could be said, it seems to us that that construction fits the statutory scheme."[103]

On the other hand, his dissent in *United States v. Korpan*,[104] decided in 1957, suggests a less deferential attitude toward the Service. In *Korpan* the critical issue was whether pinball machines constituted "slot machines" for the purpose of application of a special tax on gaming devices.[105] A Treasury regulation[106] stated that pinball machines of the type in question were subject to the tax, and the Court agreed that the legislative history sustained the Government's position. Justice Douglas' two-line "dissent from the conclusion that . . . pinball machines are games of chance within the meaning of the statute"[107] did not address the regulation at all.

QUALITY OF OPINIONS

Several factors suggest that Douglas did not devote as much attention to tax cases in this period as he had previously. As mentioned earlier, he failed to give any indication of his views in almost half of his dissents. In a number of the instances in which he did express his dissenting views, his opinions were not as thorough as those in the earlier period.[108] In *Arrowsmith*, for example, he simply failed to join issue with the majority's analysis. In *Lewis* and *Korpan* as well, his short dissents cited no authority, and failed to explain his thinking. Furthermore, despite an apparent conflict with the

---

[103] 343 U.S. at 715-16.
[104] 354 U.S. 271 (1957).
[105] INT. REV. CODE OF 1954, § 4461.
[106] Treas. Reg. 59, § 323.22, 7 Fed. Reg. 10835 (1942).
[107] 354 U.S. at 277.
[108] *But see, e.g.,* Allen v. Trust Co., 326 U.S. 630 (1946) (Douglas, J., writing for the Court in favor of a taxpayer); Commissioner v. Harmon, 323 U.S. 44, 49 (1944) (Douglas, J., dissenting), discussed at notes 69-75 *supra* & accompanying text.

orientation of his majority opinion in *Virginian Hotel*, his *Lewis* opinion ignored the earlier case. This tendency is most apparent, however, in Douglas' treatment of two sets of companion cases, *Tank Truck Rentals, Inc. v. Commissioner*[109] and *Commissioner v. Sullivan;*[110] *General American Investors Co. v. Commissioner*[111] and *Commissioner v. Glenshaw Glass Co.*[112]

In *Tank Truck* the taxpayer sought to deduct fines paid as penalties for violations of a state law[113] which set a maximum weight limit for trucks using the state's highways. It was established that profitable operation of the taxpayer's business required that it violate truck weight limitation. Accordingly, the taxpayer argued that the fines were deductible as ordinary and necessary business expenses.[114] Justice Clark's opinion for a unanimous Court rested on the proposition "that a State [should] not be thwarted in its policy."[115] He reasoned that

> [c]ertainly the frustration of state policy is most complete and direct when the expenditure for which deduction is sought is itself prohibited by statute. If the expenditure is not itself an illegal act, but rather the payment of a penalty imposed by the State because of such an act, as in the present case, the frustration attendant upon deduction would be only slightly less remote, and would clearly fall within the line of disallowance.[116]

The deduction was denied.

---

[109] 356 U.S. 30 (1958).
[110] 356 U.S. 27 (1958).
[111] 348 U.S. 434 (1955).
[112] 348 U.S. 426 (1955).
[113] No. 142, § 1, [1945] Pa. Laws 328, *as amended*, PA. STAT. ANN. tit. 75, § 903 (1971).
[114] *See* Act of Oct. 21, 1942, ch. 619, § 121(a), 56 Stat. 819, *amending* Int. Rev. Code of 1939, § 23(a)(1)(A) (now INT. REV. CODE OF 1954.
[115] 356 U.S. at 35.
[116] *Id.* (citation omitted).

Justice Douglas wrote a shorter opinion, also for a unanimous Court, *upholding* a taxpayer's deduction in *Sullivan*.[117] But read in light of Justice Clark's *Tank Truck* opinion, Justice Douglas simply fails to illuminate the crucial issues. The taxpayer in *Sullivan* had leased premises and paid employees to conduct a gambling enterprise illegal under Illinois law. The state had outlawed not only the operation of the enterprise, but also, and more significantly, the payment of rent for premises used to carry on the enterprise.[118] The chief question before the Court was whether the taxpayer could deduct his rental payments as ordinary and necessary business expenses.[119] Justice Douglas' opinion relied on a Treasury regulation[120] which permitted a taxpayer to deduct the federal excise tax on wagers.[121] This regulation, he held,

> seems to us to be recognition of a gambling enterprise as a business for federal tax purposes. The policy that allows as a deduction the tax paid to conduct the business seems sufficiently hospitable to allow the normal deductions of the rent and wages necessary to operate it.... That is enough to permit the deduction, unless it is clear that the allowance is a device to avoid the consequences of violations of a law, as in ... *Tank Truck Rentals, Inc. v. Commissioner, supra,* or otherwise contravenes the federal policy expressed in a statute or regulation, as in *Textile Mills Corp. v. Commissioner* ....[122]

But this argument ignores the thrust and the scope of

---

[117] 356 U.S. 27 (1958).

[118] ILL. REV. STAT. ch. 38, § 336 (1945).

[119] *See* Act of Oct. 21, 1942, ch. 619, § 121(a), 56 Stat. 819, *amending* Int. Rev. Code of 1939, § 23(a)(1)(A) (now INT. REV. CODE OF 1954. § 162).

[120] Treas. Reg. 118, § 39.23(a)-1, 1954-1 CUM. BULL. 51.

[121] Revenue Act of 1951, ch. 521, § 471(a), 65 Stat. 529-30, *adding* Int. Rev. Code of 1939, §§ 3285(d), 3290.

[122] 356 U.S. at 28-29. For a discussion of Justice Douglas' *Textile Mills* opinion, written in Period 1, see text accompanying notes 39-43 *supra*.

the *Tank Truck* opinion which was handed down the same day as *Sullivan*, and which he joined. Douglas wrote that the payments in *Sullivan* were deductible because the enterprise was recognized as a "business for federal tax purposes"; the deduction sought did not amount to the federal government's paying a portion of a state imposed fine; and the deduction was not contrary to a federal policy expressed in a statute or regulation. None of these considerations, however, suffices to reconcile *Sullivan* with *Tank Truck*. The second is contrary to the terms of *Tank Truck*. Justice Clark's words, that the "frustration of state policy is most complete and direct when the expenditure for which deduction is sought is itself prohibited by statute,"[123] appear to render *Sullivan* an *a fortiori* application of *Tank Truck* because the rental in *Sullivan* was manifestly illegal under state law. Additionally, since *Tank Truck* itself was built on deference to *state* policy, Justice Douglas' third consideration, the effect on *federal* policy, further confuses the scope and rationale of that case.[124]

Apparently Douglas intended to distinguish the cases largely on the basis of the Treasury regulation which he cited. But that regulation was irrelevant to the stated issue, which was the possible frustration of state policy by allowance of the rental and salary deductions. First, the act of paying the federal excise tax, unlike the taxpayer's payment of rent, is lawful conduct. Second, for the federal government to subsidize a payment of excise taxes to itself does not involve a frustration of *state* policy. Moreover, as Douglas employed it in deriving his first consideration, the regulation demonstrates only that the enterprise was a "business for federal tax purposes." There was nothing in

---

[123] 356 U.S. at 35.

[124] Justice Douglas' treatment of these last two considerations is unsatisfying in another way; he does not deal with the question why they would or would not apply to the case at hand.

Tank Truck, however, to suggest that that taxpayer's trucking enterprise was not also a "business for federal tax purposes."

The result is somewhat bewildering. Although *Sullivan* and *Tank Truck* may be distinguishable, Justice Douglas' opinion does not reconcile the cases and fails seriously to address the issues. As a result the reader is left with only a confused sense of the law.[125]

A comparison of *Glenshaw Glass*[126] and its companion case, *General American Investors*,[127] presents a similar enigma. *Glenshaw Glass* raised the question whether a taxpayer must include in income amounts received as punitive damages for fraud and violations of the federal antitrust laws. *General American Investors* involved the taxability of "insider profits" recovered by a corporation under section 16(b) of the Securities Exchange Act of 1934.[128] Chief Justice Warren wrote a full opinion for the Court in *Glenshaw Glass*, concluding that the receipts there involved were taxable income. The Chief Justice wrote a very brief opinion in *General American Investors*, holding that *Glenshaw Glass* controlled. He said that the Court could find no relevant difference between the receipts in *Glenshaw Glass* and those involved in *General American Investors*. Justice Douglas dissented without opinion in *Glenshaw Glass*,[129] but concurred in the result in the *General American Investors*[130] case. He offered no explanation as to the

---

[125] It is the authors' belief that the Douglas result in *Sullivan* is more compatible with the statute than the one he agreed to in joining Justice Clark's opinion in *Tank Truck*. *See* Wolfman, *Professors and the "Ordinary and Necessary" Business Expense*, 112 U. PA. L. REV. 1089, 1111-12 (1964), *cf.* Commissioner v. Tellier, 383 U.S. 687, 692-94 (1966).

[126] 348 U.S. 426 (1955).
[127] 348 U.S. 434 (1955).
[128] 15 U.S.C. §§ 78a et seq. (1970).
[129] 348 U.S. at 433.
[130] *Id.* at 436.

basis on which he, alone among the members of the Court, was able to distinguish the cases. One is left only to guess at his reasoning.[131]

This second period marks a substantial and significant shift in Douglas' attitude toward the congressional plan of income taxation. He frequently voted for the taxpayer in cases which the Court decided for the Government, an event which never occurred in the 91 cases of Period 1. His early concern that Congress, not the Court, should be the arbiter of "fairness" in issues of tax policy weakened early in Period 2, and continued to diminish in strength. There was an accelerating tendency for him not to state the reasons for his votes, accompanied by an increased frequency of dissents overall. A greater proportion of his opinions fails to satisfy the student who asks, "Why?"

Another event of note occurred near the end of this period. In 1958 Justice Douglas wrote the opinion for the Court in *Commissioner v. P. G. Lake, Inc.*[132] That opinion sustained the Commissioner's position. In the more than fifteen years that have elapsed since then, Justice Douglas has not written a tax opinion for the Court that supported the Government.[133] Indeed, he has written

---

[131] Taxpayer's counsel in *Glenshaw Glass* had offered the Court a possible basis for distinguishing *General American Investors*. In granting certiorari because of a presumed conflict between the two cases as decided below, the Court implicitly denied the distinction, which was argued for at that early stage. Brief for Respondent, William Goldman Theaters, Inc., In Opposition to Certiorari at 2, Commissioner v. Glenshaw Glass Co., 348 U.S. 426 (1958). The Warren opinion for the Court thought so little of it, that it was ignored. Justice Douglas' position could be explained by an acceptance of that distinction, but again one can only speculate. *See* Brief for Respondent, William Goldman Theaters, Inc. at 16-17, *id.*

[132] 356 U.S. 260 (1958).

[133] Justice Douglas did, however, write concurring opinions in support of the Government's position. *See* Appendix, Table VII, *infra. But cf.* Federal Power Comm'n v. Memphis Light, Gas & Water Div., 411 U.S. 458 (1973) (decision in which Justice Douglas delivered the opinion of the Court, holding for the Commission and construing the 1963 Tax Reform Act as permitting the Commission to abandon flow-through valuations of the property of the respective utilities).

for the Court in only one tax case since *Lake*.[134]

Period 3. 1959-1964:

Extreme Years

The statistical data for the years 1959-1964 are extraordinary. The trends which began and developed in the second period, sixteen years long, accelerated dramatically during these six years. This period, involving only 35 cases, and substantially shorter than the preceding two periods, is marked off because it demonstrates an extremity in Justice Douglas' voting pattern that is not seen in any other series of Court Terms. The statistics for the fourth and final period, 1964-1973, indicate a blunting of the extreme tendencies which distinguish this third period.

In the years 1959-1964, Douglas voted for the taxpayer in 73% of the tax cases, as compared with 47% in Period 2 and 18% in Period 1. Furthermore, the Court's judgments lend added significance to that datum. A majority of the Court held for the taxpayer only 17% of the time (in 6 out of 35 cases), the lowest percentage of taxpayer success in any of the four periods. Thus Douglas differed from the majority of the Court in 54% of the cases in this period, as compared with 28% in the preceding period. In every one of his dissents Justice Douglas voted for the taxpayer. This contrasts sharply with the first period, when each of his dissents favored the Government.

The frequency of opinionless and nearly opinionless dissents also grew significantly, as did the percentage of

---

[134] Nash v. United States, 398 U.S. 1 (1970) (holding for the taxpayer). In May, 1974, Douglas wrote his second post-1958 opinion for the (unanimous) Court, Snow v. Commissioner, 416 U.S. 500 (1974) (holding for the taxpayer). This study concluded with cases decided in the Term ending June, 1973.

Table I-3 (Summary)
Tax Cases Decided by Supreme Court, 1939–1973

Period	Volumes U.S. Reports	Number of Cases	Number Won by Taxpayer	Number Douglas for Taxpayer
1 (1939-1943)	307-19	91	22½ (25%)	16 (18%)
2 (1943-1959)	320-59	126	32 (25%)	54 (of 116) (47%)
3 (1959-1964)	360-76	35	6 (17%)	24 (of 33) (73%)

occasions on which Justice Douglas was the lone dissenter. No other justice joined Douglas in 9 of the 18 cases in which he dissented. Those solitary stances were in cases representing more than 27% of the tax cases in which Douglas participated. In 6 of those 9 solitary dissents, he dissented without opinion.[135] In 2 others he wrote brief dissents, totaling twelve lines, which failed to explain his views in any detail. In the remaining one, Justice Douglas relied on the opinion of the court of appeals below. Douglas produced 3 full dissenting opinions, but all were in cases in which one or two other justices joined him.

Justice Douglas wrote no opinions for the Court during this period, although he wrote 2 concurring opinions. Consequently there are few opinions to help explain the extreme shift in his voting pattern.

APPROACH TO THE STATUTE

In *Knetsch v. United States* [136] the question was whether certain payments made by a sixty-year-old taxpayer to an insurance company constituted deductible

---

[135] He, together with Justice Black, also dissented without opinion in one other case, United States v. Patrick, 372 U.S. 53 (1963). Justice Black also dissented alone in one case during this period. No other Justice dissented alone or without opinion during this period. *See* Appendix. Tables IV, V, *infra*.

[136] 364 U.S. 361 (1960).

Table II-3
Cases in which Douglas Differed with the Court

Period	Number of Cases in which Douglas Participated	Number Douglas in Minority	Percentage in Minority	Number Douglas Alone	Percentage Alone
		All Cases			
1	91	6½	7%	0	0%
2	116	33	28%	11	9%
3	33	18	54%	9	27%
		Won by Taxpayer			
1	22½	6½	29%	0	0%
2	29	4	14%	2	7%
3	6	0	0%	0	0%
		Won by Government			
1	68½	0	0%	0	0%
2	87	29	33%	9	10%
3	27	18	67%	9	33%

Table III-3
How Douglas Made his Dissenting Views Known

Period	Number of Cases in which Douglas Participated	Number Douglas in Minority	Number Wrote Dissent	Number Dissent Without Opinion	Percentage Dissent Without Opinion
		All Cases			
1	91	6½	1	1	1%
2	116	33	8	15	13%
3	33	18	8	7	21%
		Won by Taxpayer			
1	22½	6½	1	1	4%
2	29	4	0	4	14%
3	6	0	0	0	0%
		Won by Government			
1	68½	0	0	0	0%
2	87	29	8	11	13%
3	27	18	8	7	26%

"interest paid . . . on indebtedness" within the meaning of the Internal Revenue Code.[137] The transaction was extremely complicated:

> On December 11, 1953, the insurance company sold Knetsch . . . 30-year maturity deferred annuity savings bonds [with a life insurance provision, in the total amount of $4,000,000] and bearing interest at 2-1/2% compounded annually. The purchase price was $4,004,000. Knetsch gave the Company his check for $4,000 and signed [nonrecourse notes of] $4,000,000 . . . for the balance. The notes bore 3-1/2% interest and were secured by the annuity bonds. The interest was payable in advance, and Knetsch on the same day prepaid the first year's interest, which was $140,000. Under the Table of Cash and Loan Values made part of the bonds, their cash or loan value at December 11, 1954, the end of the first contract year, was to be $4,100,000. The contract terms, however, permitted Knetsch to borrow any excess of this value above his indebtedness without waiting until December 11, 1954. Knetsch took advantage of this provision only five days after the purchase. On December 16, 1953, he received from the company $99,000 of the $100,000 excess over his $4,000,000 indebtedness, for which he gave his notes bearing 3-1/2% interest. This interest was also payable in advance and on the same day he prepaid the first year's interest of $3,465. In [his] return for 1953, [Knetsch] deducted the sum of the two interest payments, that is $143,465, as "interest paid . . . within the taxable year on indebtedness,' under § 23(b) of the 1939 Code.
>
> The second contract year began on December 11, 1954, when interest in advance of $143,465 was payable by Knetsch on his aggregate indebtedness of

---

[137]INT. REV. CODE OF 1954, § 163(a).

$4,099,000. Knetsch paid this amount on December 27, 1954. Three days later, on December 30, he received from the company cash in the amount of $104,000, the difference... between his then $4,099,000 indebtedness and the cash or loan value of the bonds of $4,204,000 on December 11, 1955 [less $1,000]. He gave the company appropriate notes and prepaid the interest thereon of $3,640. In [his] return for the taxable year 1954 [Knetsch] deducted the sum of the two interest payments, that is $147,105, as 'interest paid... within the taxable year on indebtedness,' under § 163(a) of the 1954 Code.[138]

The taxpayer and the insurance company repeated these transactions in succeeding years, the taxpayer again claiming "interest" deductions. In form, then, the sixty-year-old taxpayer contracted for receipt of monthly annuity payments beginning when he reached ninety, or alternatively, for an insurance death benefit should he die before that age. In fact, however, his subsequent annual borrowings "kept the net cash value, on which any annuity or insurance payments would depend, at the relative pittance of $1,000."[139] The taxpayer expected to benefit under the arrangement from the "interest" deduction claimed for his payments. He expected to profit only because his losses on the transaction were less than his anticipated tax benefits.[140]

---

[138] 364 U.S. at 362-63.

[139] *Id.* at 366.

[140] The taxpayer expected a deduction for interest paid in excess of $140,000 although he would retain untaxed the $100,000 he had borrowed. Increases on the cash surrender of the bonds, compounding at 2½%, would be taxed only when the bonds were surrendered or sold. (Even then they might be taxable only at the lower rate for capital gains. *See* Blum, *Knetsch v. United States: A Pronouncement of Tax Avoidance*, 1961 SUP. CT. REV. 135, 137, 40 TAXES 296, 297 (1962).) Thus, through the arrangement, Knetsch meant to turn a taxable amount of $143,465 (in the first year, increasing each year) into a presently non-taxed $100,000 (in the first year, increasing each year).

The Commissioner disallowed the deductions for both years, however, and the lower courts, viewing the transactions as sham, upheld him. Justice Brennan, for the Supreme Court, held that the propriety of the interest deduction depended on "whether what was done, apart from the tax motive, was the thing which the statute intended." [141] He then found that the taxpayer had no stake as insured or annuitant since the repeated annual borrowing on the bonds consistently depleted their net cash value. As the Court saw it, the transaction was devoid of economic reality, but for the presumed tax benefits. On that basis, Justice Brennan called the transaction a sham, and the deduction was disallowed.

Justice Douglas, dissenting, [142] refused to decide "whether what was done . . . was the thing which the statute intended." Because he thought that the Court could not consistently apply its definition of "interest" in future cases, Douglas did not feel obliged to seek out the Congressional purpose underlying the deduction provision as it might apply to the case before him. Rather, he said that he would require Congress to "particularize" abuses of the deduction which it intended to proscribe. Thus, although he acknowledged that the taxpayer never intended to come out ahead in his investment apart from the income tax deduction, Justice Douglas voted to sustain that deduction. That result was required, he thought, because "[t]he insurance company existed; it operated under Texas law; it was authorized to issue these policies and to make these annuity loans," [143] and because the documents spoke in terms of borrowed money and interest.

Douglas' view in *Knetsch* of the relationship between the Court and Congress contrasts most sharply with the

---

[141] 364 U.S. at 365, *quoting from* Gregory v. Helvering, 293 U. S. 465, 469 (1935).
[142] 364 U.S. at 370.
[143] *Id.*

view he expressed as a young Justice in *Helvering v. Clifford.*[144] The issue in *Clifford* was "whether the grantor after the trust has been established may still be treated, under this statutory scheme, as the owner...."[145] Although Douglas considered only the face of the transaction in *Knetsch*, his premise in *Clifford* was that "[t]echnical considerations, niceties of the law of trusts or conveyances, or the legal paraphernalia which inventive genius may construct as a refuge from surtaxes should not obscure the basic issue."[146] Significantly, Justice Roberts, dissenting in *Clifford,*[147] had argued that the problem was one of "drawing a line" which only Congress should draw, precisely the approach which Justice Douglas took in *Knetsch*. In *Clifford*, however, Justice Douglas found that "the failure of Congress to adopt... [a] rule of thumb"[148] merely left the issue to the courts for a case by case determination of when to look beyond the formalities of the trust.

Several other opinions indicate Douglas' willingness during this third period to decide statutory questions in favor of the taxpayer while affording only a vague hint of the process by which he construed the statute. The plainest example is *United States v. Gilmore,*[149] an important case interpreting section 23(a)(2) of the 1939 Code[150] which permitted a deduction for expenses incurred for the conservation of property held for the production of income. Justice Douglas' brief dissent[151] in favor of the taxpayer found the majority's reading of the

---

[144] 309 U.S. 331 (1940).
[145] *Id.* at 334.
[146] *Id. See also* Commissioner v. P.G. Lake, Inc., 356 U.S. 260, 265 (1958) (Douglas, J., stating for the Court that the capital gains treatment "has always been narrowly construed so as to protect the revenue against artful devices.").
[147] 309 U.S. at 343.
[148] *Id.* at 338.
[149] 372 U.S. 39 (1963).
[150] 53 Stat. 12 (now INT. REV. CODE OF 1954 § 212).
[151] 372 U.S. at 52.

deduction provision "unjustifiably narrow" but did not explain how or why it was to be more "broadly" interpreted.

Three cases involving the exclusion of gifts from the recipient's gross income further illustrate Douglas' tendency in this period to construe the Code without telling why or how he arrived at his interpretation. The Court's opinion in *Commissioner v. Duberstein* [152] disposed of two cases, *Duberstein*, and *Stanton v. United States*. Those cases posed the question whether certain transfers of property to a taxpayer were gifts excludable from income under section 22(b)(3) of the 1939 Code.[153] The Court considered various suggested constructions of the statutory term "gift," deciding finally that a gift is that which, under all the circumstances, was given with a "detached and disinterested generosity, out of affection, respect, admiration, charity or like impulses."[154] Turning on an examination of all the attendant facts, the Court's approach would yield a result primarily factual in character. That rendering of the statutory term "gift" followed the one originally employed years earlier in *Bogardus v. Commissioner*.[155] The Court simultaneously reaffirmed the doctrine of *Dobson v. Commissioner*,[156] however, rejecting the broad scope of review in "gift" cases which *Bogardus* had earlier suggested.

Applying *Bogardus*, as refined by *Dobson*, the Court saw evidence and findings of fact in *Duberstein* sufficient to support the Tax Court's conclusion that there had been no gift; but in *Stanton* it remanded to the district court for more specific findings. Douglas' dissent [157] treated both cases alike, holding for the taxpayer in both as a matter of

---

[152] 363 U.S. 278 (1960).
[153] 53 Stat. 10 (now INT. REV. CODE OF 1954, § 102).
[154] 363 U.S. at 285 (citations omitted).
[155] 302 U.S. 34, 43 (1937).
[156] 320 U.S. 489, 498 n.22 (1943).
[157] 363 U.S. at 293.

law. It reads: "MR. JUSTICE DOUGLAS dissents, since he is of the view that in each of these two cases there was a gift under the test which the Court fashioned nearly a quarter of a century ago in *Bogardus v. Commissioner.*"[158] In the third case, however (*United States v. Kaiser*[159]), decided the same day as *Duberstein*, Justice Douglas attempted in his concurring opinion[160] to articulate his conception of the gift exclusion.

Applying the *Duberstein* rationale, a majority of the Court in *Kaiser* upheld, as not clearly erroneous, a jury's finding that the transfer in question was a gift.[161] Citing *Bogardus*, Justice Douglas concluded that the transfer was a gift as a matter of law, "since my idea of a 'gift' within the meaning of the Internal Revenue Code is a much broader concept than that of my Brethren."[162]

But Douglas' concurrence in *Kaiser* merely stated his conclusion that the gift exclusion should be "broader," without an examination of legislative history, and without apparent appreciation of the difficulties which had confronted the Service and the lower courts. Like his dissent in *Duberstein*, it failed to expose his understanding of the *Bogardus* test on which he relied. In neither opinion did he explain why he differed with the Court, except that his conception of a gift was "broader." It would seem that Justice Douglas' position in *Duberstein* and *Kaiser* rested on warrantless imposition of personal inferences from the evidence.[163]

---

[158] *Id.*

[159] 363 U.S. 299 (1960).

[160] *Id.* at 325.

[161] Three justices, however, also basing their approach on *Duberstein*, found as a matter of law that there was no gift. *See* 363 U.S. at 327, 328 (Whittaker, J., dissenting, with whom Harlan and Stewart, JJ., joined).

[162] *Id.* at 326.

[163] There is some suggestion in the *Kaiser* concurrence as well that Justice Douglas' conclusion was based on his own perception of the facts: "[T]he whole setting of the case indicates *to me* these payments were welfare, plain and simple." *Id.* at 326 (emphasis supplied).

ATTITUDE TOWARD THE INTERNAL REVENUE SERVICE

Two of Douglas' opinions in this period suggest a reversal of his earlier sympathetic attitude towards the Service.[164] *Commissioner v. Lester*[165] involved the deductibility of payments made by a taxpayer to his former wife. The statute [166] permitted a divorced husband to deduct certain payments to his ex-wife, but not those "which the terms of the ... written [divorce] instrument fix[ed]" as child support. It required further that any amounts deductible for the husband would be taxable to the wife. The taxpayer's settlement agreement provided for the wife's custody of the couple's three children and for payments to the wife which would be reduced by one-sixth upon the emancipation or marriage of each child. The Commissioner contended that the words of the divorce settlement identified a sum for the support of minor children with sufficient clarity to render that sum nondeductible.

The issue was a close one of statutory interpretation.[167] Seeking a rule that would lead to negotiating certainty for divorcing spouses, the Court held that payments were deductible to the husband (and taxable to

---

[164] These cases do not conflict directly with Justice Douglas' earlier decisions involving the weight to be given to Treasury regulations or the deference due the administrative considerations of the IRS. They do strongly indicate, however, that Justice Douglas' early apparent sympathy with IRS positions had completely dissipated by this time. *But cf.* Cory Corp. v. Sauber, 363 U.S. 709 (1960), in which Justice Douglas voted with the majority in a per curiam decision to uphold the validity of Treasury rulings interpreting an excise on air conditioning units. Three justices dissented. The majority result favored the taxpayer, however.

[165] 366 U.S. 299 (1961).

[166] Int. Rev. Code of 1939, ch. 1, §§ 22(k), 23(v), 56 Stat. 816-17 (now INT. REV. CODE OF 1954, §§ 71, 215).

[167] The Commissioner contended that he was supported by administrative interpretation, and, as the Court noted, "[T]here was such a contrariety of opinion among the Courts of Appeals that the Commissioner was obliged as late as 1959 to issue a Revenue Ruling" which was itself inconclusive. 366 U.S. at 305-06.

the wife) unless the agreement "expressly specif[ied] or 'fix[ed]' a sum certain or percentage of the payment for child support...."[168] Since the agreement did not do that in so many words, the husband-taxpayer was held to be entitled to the deduction.

Justice Douglas' concurrence severely criticized the Government for seeking relief from the courts rather than from Congress. He said that because of the complex and intricate nature of the revenue laws, the Government should turn "square corners" in moving against the taxpayer. This, he thought, had not been done with Mr. Lester. It was clear to the Court, Justice Douglas implied, and thus should have been to the Commissioner, that the language of the statute permitted the taxpayer the deduction he sought. Therefore Douglas believed that the Commissioner was trying to use the Court to change the meaning of the statute. He was alarmed for fear that the Government's "purse" and "endurance," longer than those of any taxpayer, would be the decisive factor in such litigation. But Douglas' chastisement of the Government in this case is strange, since the Court's result, though well reasoned, was not manifest on the face of the statute or its history.

Justice Douglas' dissent in *Rudolph v. United States*,[170] which involved the deductibility of expenses connected with a taxpayer's attendance at a convention of insurance salesmen, emphasizes his mistrust of the IRS. He complained that the Service had discriminated against the taxpayer because it had permitted other professionals and businessmen to deduct convention expenses. He relied particularly on a Commerce Clearing House report stating that " 'the Commissioner has recently withdrawn his objections in two Tax Court cases to the deduction of

---

[168] *Id.* at 303.
[169] *Id.* at 306.
[170] 370 U.S. 269, 278 (1962).

convention expenses incurred by two IRS employees.' "[171] "It is odd, indeed," Douglas argued, "that revenue agents need make no accounting of the movies they saw or the nightclubs they attended in order to get the deduction, while insurance agents must."[172] He did not acknowledge the possibility that the Commissioner might be making tooled judgments based on factual differences in individual cases, nor did he indicate the source of his information about the movies and nightclubs.

QUALITY OF OPINIONS

The statistical data show that although Douglas was more frequently in dissent during this period, he chose less frequently to state the basis of his disagreement with the majority. Additionally, as the cases already discussed have indicated,[173] when he did write, his positions were often unexplained or poorly explained.

Justice Douglas' opinion in *Rudolph*[174] was utterly reckless. The taxpayer had sold insurance from a base in Texas. Because he sold a large amount of insurance, his insurance company offered him and his wife the opportunity to attend its convention in New York City, together with 150 other qualifying employees and their spouses, all at company expense. The group travelled on special trains and stayed together in one hotel. The trip took a week, two and a half days of which were spent in New York. Only one morning in New York was devoted to company business, however. The taxpayer and his wife were on their own for the rest of the time.

The Commissioner included the value of the trip as

---

[171] *Id.* at 284. Justice Douglas also quoted language in the circular to the effect that the National Association of Internal Revenue Employees had announced its belief that the Commissioner's action set a precedent which all IRS employees could rely upon in deducting convention expenses. *Id.*
[172] *Id.*
[173] *See* notes 136-63 *supra* & accompanying text.
[174] 370 U.S. 269, 278 (1962) (Douglas, J., dissenting).

income to the taxpayer, not subject to a business expense deduction. Having lost in his contest of that position in the district court and the court of appeals, the taxpayer secured a writ of certiorari. The district court had found that the trip was offered by the company chiefly in the way of a bonus or award for work previously done, and was accepted by the Rudolphs primarily as a pleasure, not a business, trip. The Supreme Court subsequently noted the agreement of the parties that the tax consequences of the trip turn upon the "Rudolphs' 'dominant motive and purpose' in taking the trip and the company's in offering it."[175] Since the resolution of the controversy as thus presented turned solely on issues of fact, subject to review only according to the "clearly erroneous" test, the Court dismissed the writ as improvidently granted.[176]

Justice Douglas dissented from dismissal of the writ,[177] arguing that receipt of the trip was not income as that term was defined in the Code and regulations, but that if the value of the trip did constitute income, it was "plainly deductible." The first part of his argument seems to be two-pronged. First, Douglas asserted that the benefits were not provided as compensation for services rendered. It is not clear, however, whether he meant that they were not added compensation for services already performed, or that they were not compensation for services rendered during the week of the convention itself, or both. At one point Douglas said: "On this record there is no room for a finding of fact that the 'expenses paid' were 'for services' rendered."[178] The only finding below to which that statement could conceivably have referred

---

[175] Id. at 270.
[176] Id. Justice Harlan, obviously responding to Justice Douglas' dissent, wrote a full concurring opinion in support of the correctness of the decision below. Id.
[177] Id. at 278.
[178] Id. at 279.

was the trial court's finding that the trip was a bonus for work already performed. If Justice Douglas meant to attack that finding, then he failed to offer any support from the record for his conclusion, and failed to state why the district court's conclusion was wrong.[179] If, on the other hand, Douglas intended simply to say that the convention expenses were not paid as compensation for services rendered during the week of the trip, then his point is of questionable relevance. The district court had not found or even suggested that the expenses were paid in return for contemporaneous services; and neither Justice Harlan's opinion[180] nor the Government's briefs[181] proffered that basis of decision. Thus, the first prong of Justice Douglas' effort to show that the payments were not income was unjustified or irrelevant, or both.

In the second prong of his argument that the paid convention expenses were not income to the taxpayer, Douglas relied upon a Treasury regulation which provided that:

> [o]rdinarily, facilities or privileges (such as entertainment, medical services, or so-called 'courtesy' discounts on purchases), furnished or offered by an employer to his employees generally, are not considered as wages subject to withholding if such facilities or privileges are of relatively small value and are offered or furnished by the employer merely as a means of promoting the health, good will, contentment, or efficiency of his employees.[182]

---

[179] Furthermore, Justice Douglas agreed with the district court that the taxpayer qualified for the trip solely on the basis of the success of his earlier work. *Id* at 279. With that, there should have been no room for a finding that the trip was not offered as a bonus for the taxpayer's employment.

[180] *Id.* at 270.

[181] Brief for the United States in Opposition to Certiorari, Rudolph v. United States, 370 U.S. 269 (1961); Brief for the United States, *id*.

[182] Treas. Reg. § 31.3401(a)-1(b) (10) (1955).

He relied on this regulation even though on its face it had no relevance to the case. The regulation exempted fringe benefits only from the wage *withholding* requirement, not from inclusion in the taxpayer's income, and withholding was not in issue in the case. The section of the Code [183] under which the regulation was promulgated does not determine whether the benefits furnished by the employer constitute income. Indeed, it assumes that they are income, because it is only particular "income" which the regulation relieves from the withholding requirement.

In the second part of his opinion Justice Douglas argued that even if the value of the trip was income, that value was "plainly deductible" as an ordinary and necessary business expense. In reaching this result he ignored the findings below that the convention's business activity was limited to a single morning in New York. [184] He thus asserted implicitly that those findings were clearly erroneous, but he did not criticize or discuss the evidentiary basis of the district court's conclusions. In place of the facts found below, Douglas asserted that more than one-half of the week was devoted to business activity. He based that conclusion on his own finding, again without citation to the record, that the four days of travel time to and from New York were arranged as a professional seminar.

Douglas also concluded that the company's payment of the wife's expenses (if income to Rudolph) was deductible, because her presence on the trip was for a bona fide business purpose. [185] The district judge had found it unnecessary to reach this factual issue because he found the trip's primary purpose to be personal. [186] Rather than suggest a remand, Justice Douglas apparently concluded

---

[183] INT. REV. CODE OF 1954, § 3401.
[184] Rudolph v. United States, 189 F. Supp. 2, 3 (N.D. Tex. 1960).
[185] *See* Treas. Reg. § 1.162-2(c) (1958).
[186] 189 F. Supp. at 5.

that the record permitted only one finding. In support of his conclusion, he cited the testimony of an insurance executive who indicated that the convention program included reference to the wife's role in her husband's work, and that without the wife's presence the convention might have degenerated into a stag party. That testimony may say something about salesmen's conventions. To Justice Douglas it said that a rational person could conclude only that the expenses of Rudolph's wife were ordinary and necessary business expenses for Rudolph, and not personal.

It is hard to believe that Douglas took his lengthy *Rudolph* dissent seriously. He seems to have reacted to an unsubstantiated belief that the Commissioner and the courts were treating insurance conventions differently from all other professional meetings. He seemed particularly incensed by the Commissioner's withdrawal of objections in the tax court cases which permitted two IRS agents to deduct convention expenses. Yet he made no effort to examine, analyze or distinguish away those cases. Justice Douglas' anger comes through. His willingness to base judgment on a hunch about the real world of professional meetings and on an arbitrariness of the Commissioner in dealing with them also comes through. His principle of law does not.

The *Rudolph* opinion most forcefully illustrates Douglas' increasing tendency during the second and third periods to apply the statute from a viewpoint most sympathetic to the taxpayer before him. The opening statement of his concurring opinion in *Commissioner v. Lester* also reflects the shift which had taken place between the first period cases, *Riley*[187] and *Scaife*,[188]

---

[187] For the discussion of *Riley*, see notes 14-18 *supra* & accompanying text.
[188] For the discussion of *Scaife*, see notes 19-26 *supra* & accompanying text.

and the cases decided in the third period:

> In an early income tax case, Mr. Justice Holmes said 'Men must turn square corners when they deal with the Government.' The revenue laws have become so complicated and intricate that I think the Government in moving against the citizen should also turn square corners.[189]

In *Riley* and *Scaife* Justice Douglas told the taxpayers that the Court was the wrong forum in which to obtain equitable relief from the revenue laws as the Commissioner and Court were construing them. In *Lester*, as in *Knetsch*, it was the Commissioner whom he told to seek relief elsewhere. The opinions in these cases portray a Justice Douglas not recognizable by reference to the portrait formed by the cases in the first period. Concurrently, *Rudolph* and the gift exclusion cases [190] illustrate another disturbing development: an apparent tendency to disregard the facts found by the factfinder. In this period Justice Douglas did not seem to perform as a Justice in tax cases, at least insofar as the role calls for reasoned opinions and the suppression of one's own impressions and predilections in face of the facts as found.

This period was therefore an extreme one. Douglas was more alienated from the Court than in any other period, this by reference both to the percentage of cases in which he dissented and to those in which he dissented alone. And the positions he took were the least justified of any period.

One wonders why this extreme behavior occurred at this time. It is possible that Douglas' attention was focused on the congressionally sanctioned inequities that pervade the tax code which result in privilege for some and undue

---

[189] 366 U.S. 299, 306.
[190] United States v. Kaiser, 363 U.S. 297, 325 (1960) (Douglas, J., concurring); Commissioner v. Duberstein, 363 U.S. 278, 293 (1960) (Douglas, J., dissenting), both cases discussed at notes 152-64 *supra* & accompanying text.

burden on others. It was in this period that Louis Eisenstein wrote his famous indictment of the tax system. *The Ideologies of Taxation*.[191] That book, which Douglas read and reviewed,[192] may have forced to the surface of Justice Douglas' thinking a deep-seated conviction that so rotten a system as Eisenstein describes, replete with special favors, ought not be supported in the way that the Court supports it when it decides for the Government against a taxpayer (big or little) who has not been effective in the congressional lobbies.

Period 4. 1964-1973:

Tempered Rebellion

The data for this period, though not projecting as extreme a picture as that drawn in the preceding five years, continue to reveal a decidedly protaxpayer bent. Justice Douglas voted for the taxpayer in 23 of the 38 cases (59%), while the Court decided that way only 10 times (26%). Justice Douglas differed with the Court in 35% of the cases. All of his dissents favored the taxpayer, as they did in Period 3, but the percentage of his solitary and mute dissents decreased significantly. Douglas was alone in only 6 of the 38 cases or 16% of the time. He dissented without opinion only twice; on both occasions he stood alone.[193]

These statistics serve in part to emphasize the extreme nature of the preceding period. It is difficult to explain the lowered incidence of solitary and, particularly, silent dissents in this latest period. The ratio of silent dissents to total cases for this period is lower than those for both

---

[191](1961).

[192] Douglas, Book Review, N.Y. Herald Tribune, Sept. 24, 1961, § 6 (Books), at 13, col. 1. *See* text accompanying notes 439-44 *infra*.

[193] These figures remain higher than those for any other member of the Court, however. During this period Justice Black dissented once without opinion, and Justices Black, Blackmun and Harlan each dissented alone once.

Table I-4 (Summary)
Tax Cases Decided by Supreme Court, 1939–1973

Period	Volumes U.S. Reports	Number of Cases	Number Won by Taxpayer	Number Douglas for Taxpayer
1 (1939-1943)	307-19	91	22½ (25%)	16 (18%)
2 (1943-1959)	320-59	126	32 (25%)	54 (of 116) (47%)
3 (1959-1964)	360-76	35	6 (17%)	24 (of 33) (73%)
4 (1964-1973)	377-413	38	10 (26%)	22½ (59%)

Table II-4
Cases in which Douglas Differed with the Court

Period	Number of Cases in which Douglas Participated	Number Douglas in Minority	Percentage in Minority	Number Douglas Alone	Percentage Alone
		All Cases			
1	91	6½	7%	0	0%
2	116	33	28%	11	9%
3	33	18	54%	9	27%
4	38	13½	35%	6	16%
		Won by Taxpayer			
1	22½	6½	29%	0	0%
2	29	4	14%	2	7%
3	6	0	0%	0	0%
4	10	0	0%	0	0%
		Won by Government			
1	68½	0	0%	0	0%
2	87	29	33%	9	10%
3	27	18	67%	9	33%
4	28	13½	48%	6	21%

Table III-4
How Douglas Made his Dissenting Views Known

Period	Number of Cases of which Douglas Participated	Number Douglas in Minority	Number Wrote Dissent	Number Dissent Without Opinion	Percentage Dissent Without Opinion
		All Cases			
1	91	6½	1	1	1%
2	116	33	8	15	13%
3	33	18	8	7	21%
4	38	13½	10	2	5%
		Won by Taxpayer			
1	22½	6½	1	1	4%
2	29	4	0	4	14%
3	6	0	0	0	0%
4	10	0	0	0	0%
		Won by Government			
1	68½	0	0	0	0%
2	87	29	8	11	13%
3	27	18	8	7	26%
4	28	13½	10	2	7%

Periods 2 and 3. Some of his writing can perhaps be explained on the basis suggested by the statistics for the prior period,[194] that he will write when he is not alone. That will not, however, explain all the cases. Eighty-three percent of his writing occurred in the later part of the period, when it was clear that the personnel of the Court was in a state of flux.[195] Perhaps Douglas felt compelled to state his positions in writing to inform his new colleagues on the Court of his viewpoints in tax cases, or

---

[194] *See* text accompanying note 135 *supra*.

[195] Of the 12 opinions he wrote, 8 were after April, 1969. At that point it was clear that President Nixon would soon appoint new Justices to fill the seats of both Chief Justice Warren and Mr. Justice Fortas.

perhaps he believed that written opinions might persuade some of them.[196]

APPROACH TO THE STATUTE

The bare statistics and whatever rationalization aside, the content of Douglas' opinions in this period reflects the same attitudes and trends exhibited in Period 3. His approach to statutory construction, as in Period 3, often focused on what he considered unfairness to the taxpayer at bar, and frequently ignored larger issues of statutory design and congressional purpose.

Justice Douglas' separate dissent in *United States v. Skelly Oil Co.*[197] set the tone for his interpretation of the Code in this period. In a prior tax year Skelly had received X dollars for sale of depletable oil, and had taken the 27-1/2% oil depletion deduction,[198] thus effectively reporting only 72-1/2% (X). In the year under review the taxpayer had refunded a portion of those X dollars to its customers. It sought to deduct the full amount of that refund,[199] notwithstanding the fact that it had effectively reported only 72-1/2% of that sum as taxable income in the prior tax years. The Court concluded that, absent a clear congressional mandate, it should not read the statutory scheme to permit such a "double deduction" and, accordingly, held in favor of the Commissioner. Justice Douglas accepted the technical construction of the statute which Justice Stewart advocated in dissent,[200] but added his own statement to emphasize his difference with

---

[196] Justice Douglas' opinions reflect a judicial awareness of the Court's altered makeup. In his dissent in SEC v. Medical Comm. for Human Rights, 404 U.S. 403, 411 (1972), for example, he identified a number of decisions as representing "the present Court's" approach to certain issues.

[197] 394 U.S. 678, 687 (1969) (Douglas, J., dissenting).

[198] INT. REV. CODE OF 1954, § 613.

[199] According to *id.* § 1341(a)(4).

[200] 394 U.S. at 692 (Stewart, J., dissenting).

the majority's approach. Douglas read the Court's opinion as an attempt to inject "equity" into the taxing statute. He rejected that approach, saying "we do not sit to do equity in tax cases."[201] He disdainfully detailed the great number of special favors which Congress had deliberately placed in the Code, concluding that it was not the Court's role to alter the meaning of statutory schemes in the interest of equity. But it is clear from the majority's opinion that its concern was not with "equity" as the Justices might perceive it, but with the result most reasonable in light of the statutory plan that Congress had fashioned. Douglas did not address the merits of the Court's inferences as to legislative intent.[202] Since his opinion makes it implicitly clear that he personally deplored the special tax favors embedded in the Code (such as percentage depletion[203]), it is puzzling that he voted in *Skelly* to increase their effect, despite the rational and acceptable, if not compelling, arguments that supported the Court's construction to the contrary.[204]

Douglas also asserted in *Skelly Oil* that the Supreme Court should generally avoid tax cases, and accept them only in the rare case of a clear conflict in the circuits. Tax law should be made and modified only by Congress, he said, because inequities could be "quickly corrected" by that body, and because the Supreme Court lacked sufficient expertise in the field to discover the congressional intention.[205] Perhaps Justice Douglas voted

---

[201] 394 U.S. at 687. This position is akin to that reflected in Justice Douglas' dissent in Knetsch v. United States, 364 U.S. 361, 370 (1960), discussed at notes 136-48 *supra* & accompanying text.

[202] *Cf.* United States v. Stewart, 311 U.S. 60 (1940) (Douglas, J.), discussed at text accompanying notes 47-57 *supra*.

[203] *Cf.* text accompanying notes 439-42, 445-49 *infra*.

[204] *Cf.* Arrowsmith v. Commissioner, 344 U.S. 6, 9 (1952) (Douglas, J., dissenting), discussed at text accompanying notes 82-84 *supra*; Commissioner v. Harmon, 323 U.S. 44, 49 (1944) (Douglas, J., dissenting), discussed at notes 69-75 *supra* & accompanying text.

[205] Cohn, *Mr. Justice Douglas and Federal Taxation*, 45 CONN. B. J. 218, 236 n.72, 241-42 (1971) suggests that the contrary is true.

and spoke as he did in *Skelly Oil* because he felt that Court-sanctioned double deductions might rip the tax system apart and force Congress to start anew with a statute free of special favors. This would be a plausible explanation only if Douglas' view were shared by the majority. As things were, perhaps he just would not lend his judicial support to a tax system he believed unworthy.

Douglas' dissent in *United States v. Generes* [206] repeats the view that the Supreme Court should avoid the resolution of ambiguities in the Code. The issue was whether a now worthless debt owed by a closely held corporation to a shareholder-officer could be treated by the shareholder-officer as a business bad debt, rather than a nonbusiness bad debt. [207] Characterization as a business bad debt would afford the shareholder-officer a greater tax benefit. [208] The issue arose because of the taxpayer's dual status in the corporation. As a salaried officer with duties to perform, his relationship to the corporation was, for purposes of the statute, "business," but as an investor in the corporation his relationship was "non-business." The relevant Treasury regulation [209] specified that the debt was a business bad debt if the "loss resulting from the debt's becoming worthless" bore a "proximate" relation to the taxpayer's trade or business. At trial the district court had charged the jury that the loss was "proximately" related if the taxpayer's assumption of the debt had a "significant" business motivation. Applying that test, the jury found the necessary relation and returned a verdict for the taxpayer. The Government had argued, however, that the debt could bear a proximate relation to business only if that "business" (maintenance or enhancement of the *employee* relationship) was the taxpayer's "dominant" motive in incurring the debt, and that the jury should have

---

[206] 405 U.S. 93, 113 (1972).
[207] *See* INT. REV. CODE OF 1954, § 166(a),(d).
[208] *See* 405 U.S. at 94-95.
[209] Treas. Reg. § 1.166-5(b)(2) (1959).

been so charged. A majority of the Court held for the Government.

Douglas' dissent in favor of the taxpayer rested on two grounds. First, he said that the trial court had charged the jury with the exact words of the regulation, and the jury found the debt not proximately related. But thi description of the trial below wholly ignored the trial judge's additional instruction which defined "proximate" for the jury. Justice Douglas' second ground echoed the basis of his view in *Skelly Oil*:

> I protest now what I have repeatedly protested, and that is the use of this Court to iron out ambiguities in the Regulations or in the Act, when the responsible remedy is either a recasting of the Regulations by Treasury or presentation of the problem to the Joint Committee on Internal Revenue Taxation which is a standing committee of the Congress that regularly rewrites the Act....[210]

Apparently finding this sufficient, Douglas did not address the majority's analysis or the derivation of its principle.

Justice Douglas also said that had he originally voted to grant certiorari in *Generes*, he would have voted to dismiss the writ as improvidently granted. That comment serves to emphasize an apparent inconsistency with his position in the *Rudolph* case,[211] decided in Period 3. Perhaps it is significant that in *Rudolph*, where the Court's dismissal of the writ preserved a judgment for the

---

[210] 405 U.S. at 114-15. [On June 24, 1974, Douglas, dissenting alone, wrote an opinion for the taxpayer in Commissioner v. Idaho Power Co., 418 U.S. 1 (1974), in which he seems to acknowledge a significant judicial role for the Court in tax cases, in apparent retreat from his recently expressed views in *Generes* and in *Skelly Oil* 394 U.S. 678 (1969). In doing so, he relies on 62 Stat. 991, enacted in 1948. Proofs of the initial manuscript of this study were mailed to Justice Douglas a number of weeks before *Idaho Power* came down.]

[211] 370 U.S. 269 (1962).

Government, Douglas dissented from the dismissal, and spoke to the merits in his opinion. In *Skelly Oil* and *Generes* Justice Douglas advocated a limitation on the Court's role that in those cases would have resulted in affirming lower court decisions for the taxpayers.

ATTITUDE TOWARD THE INTERNAL REVENUE SERVICE

Cases in the final period continue to reveal a certain hostility to the Service. In his separate dissent in *Skelly Oil* Douglas chastised the Service for its practice of taking inconsistent positions in the lower courts, hoping to produce a conflict in the circuits which would require Supreme Court resolution. Similarly, the *Generes* dissent echoed Justice Douglas' protest in *Commissioner v. Lester,* [212] a Period 3 case, that the government works an unfair hardship on the taxpayer when it fails to resolve ambiguities in the Code in favor of the taxpayer and instead litigates—using the procedures which Congress has laid out for disposition of tax controversies.

Douglas' mistrust of the IRS, which seems stronger in this period even than at the time of the *Lester* case, is evident as well in *United States v. Powell.* [213] The IRS had issued a summons to the taxpayer requiring him to produce records relating to four- and five-year-old tax returns. The Code[214] sets a three-year statute of limitations on the Commissioner's power to challenge a tax return, unless he alleges fraud. Another section of the Code [215] prohibits the Service from subjecting a taxpayer to "unnecessary examination or investigations." The taxpayer argued that those provisions, taken together, prevented a district court from enforcing the IRS

---

[212] 366 U.S. 299, 306 (1961) (Douglas, J., dissenting). For discussion of *Lester*, see text accompanying notes 165-69 *supra*.
[213] 379 U.S. 48 (1964).
[214] INT. REV. CODE OF 1954, § 6501(a),(c)(1).
[215] *Id.* § 7605(b).

summons unless the Service demonstrates a reasonable basis for suspecting fraud. Justice Harlan, writing for the Court in upholding the Commissioner perceived that Congress intended to put a lesser burden on such inspections. From an examination of legislative history he concluded that the extent to which Congress wanted to protect the taxpayer was satisfied by the requirement that a superior official in the IRS approve the inspection, and thus that the district court should not inquire into such an administrative determination of necessity, absent some abuse shown by the taxpayer.

Justice Douglas dissented,[216] apparently mistrustful of allowing IRS officials, rather than a district court, to determine whether a sufficient basis existed to warrant an inspection. He reasoned that the purpose of the congressionally ordained statute of repose required that the Service come forward and convince the district court that it had a reasonable basis to believe that the taxpayer had engaged in fraud.[217]

Two additional opinions, *Commissioner v. Stidger*[218] and *United States v. Correll*[219] suggest an almost complete reversal of Douglas' early willingness to defer to the reasonable administrative needs and judgment of the Commissioner. *Stidger* posed the question whether a military officer's expenditures for meals at a "permanent" duty post[220] to which his dependents were prohibited

---

[216] 379 U.S. at 59.

[217] Ryan v. United States, 379 U.S. 61 (1964), a companion to *Powell*, supports the conclusion that distrust of the IRS lay at the basis of his position. Justices Stewart and Goldberg, who had joined Justice Douglas' opinion in *Powell*, voted in favor of the Commissioner in *Ryan*, believing that "a sufficient showing was made that the Government was not proceeding capriciously." *Id.* at 63 (Stewart and Goldberg, JJ., concurring in result). But Justice Douglas again dissented.

[218] 386 U.S. 287 (1967).

[219] 389 U.S. 299 (1967). *See also* Bingler v. Johnson, 394 U.S. 741, 758 (1969) (Douglas, J., dissenting on basis of court of appeals' opinion, 396 F.2d 258 (3d Cir. 1968), holding invalid Treas. Reg. § 1.117-4(c) (1956)).

[220] The designation of a duty post as "permanent" is a question of

from accompanying him, were deductible as business travel expenses incurred "away from home."[221] Concluding that such a post constituted the taxpayer's "home" within the meaning of the statute, the Court held the expenses nondeductible. The majority found it unnecessary to consider whether the Commissioner's interpretation of "home" as meaning "place of business" was always correct. Rather, two considerations relating specifically to military service formed the basis of its opinion. First, the Court relied on the fact that the Commissioner's position with respect to military personnel, that an officer's home was his permanent duty post, was of long standing and had been upheld in the Tax Court in 1948,[222] and that neither the courts nor Congress had rejected it since that time. Second, the Court found that Congress had provided a "special system of tax-free allowances for military personnel,"[223] which was "designed to provide complete and direct relief from [the particular financial problems of military families] as opposed to the incomplete and indirect relief which an income tax deduction affords to a civilian business traveller."[224]

Douglas[225] thought that the Court's result was unnecessarily harsh. He cited a passage from Eisenstein's book[226] to illustrate the seemingly irrational distinctions often made in the Code. The Court, he said, should not add to the harshness of the tax law unless Congress has plainly called for an arbitrary classification. He thought it plain that "home" as used in the statute meant the taxpayer's "residence," as opposed to his place of business.

---

military terminology derived from "the language and policy of the statutory provisions prescribing travel and transportation allowances for military personnel." 386 U.S. at 292.

[221] INT. REV. CODE OF 1954, § 162(a)(2), reproduced at note 229 *infra*.

[222] Bercaw v. Commissioner, 165 F.2d 521 (4th Cir. 1948).
[223] 386 U.S. at 294.
[224] *Id.* at 295.
[225] *Id.* at 297 (Douglas, J., dissenting).
[226] *See* text accompanying note 191 *supra*.

Since such a definition did not lead to a harsh result, Douglas said that his definition should be accepted without further inquiry.

Chief Justice Warren's opinion for the Court discussed questions of fairness but concluded that Congress had dealt with the problem of servicemen's expenses elsewhere. Justice Douglas, however, in dismissing the two foundations of the majority's argument, offered neither discussion of the overall congressional scheme nor any attempt to persuade the reader that his position was consonant with that scheme.

In *Correll*[227] the Court sustained a long-standing position of the Commissioner (the "overnight rule"[228]), which restricted application of the deduction for meal expenses incurred on business travel "away from home"[229] to only those meals taken on trips during which the taxpayer had to stop for sleep or rest. Although the Court recognized that the "overnight rule" was somewhat arbitrary, it found that the Commissioner's interpretation had "achieved not only ease and certainty of application but also substantial fairness."[230] The court of appeals had nevertheless held the Commissioner's interpretation invalid as contrary to the statute's plain language. The majority of the Court rejected this objection, explaining in some detail that "[t]he language of the statute—'meals and lodging ... away from home'—is obviously not self-defining."[231] In any case, the Court held, there was strong evidence that Congress had accepted the Commissioner's inter-

---

[227] 389 U.S. 299 (1967).
[228] *Id.* at 302 n.10.
[229] INT. REV. CODE OF 1954, § 162(a)(2):
There shall be allowed as a deduction all the ordinary and necessary expenses paid or incurred during the taxable year in carrying on any trade or business, including
. . . .
(2) traveling expenses (including amounts expended for meals and lodging ...) while away from home in the pursuit of a trade or business.
[230] 389 U.S. at 303.
[231] *Id.* at 304.

pretation: Congress failed to alter the rule throughout its long life, despite its opportunity to do so in the major 1954 revision. Hence, the Court accepted the Commissioner's position as a reasonable implementation of the congressional design.

Much could be offered in criticism of the Court's opinion in *Correl*, but Justice Douglas' dissent [232] against the majority's "shrunken" interpretation of the statutory language occupies only half a page. It begins and ends with the assertion that "away from home can have nothing to do with overnight." He argued:

> 'Overnight' injects a time element in testing deductibility, while the statute speaks only in terms of geography. As stated by the Court of Appeals: 'In an era of supersonic travel, the time factor is hardly relevent to the question of whether or not travel and meal expenses are related to the taxpayer's business and cannot be the basis of a valid regulation under the present statute.' [233]

But Justice Douglas' reliance on the court below missed the issue. As the majority opinion noted, the question was not whether meal expenses in travel not requiring an overnight stop are related to business; [234] the question was whether such expenses are for "meals and lodging... away from home." Nor did Douglas' opinion address either of the majority's considerations at all. Rather, he failed again to explain why his result was the more consistent with the statutory scheme.

QUALITY OF OPINIONS

Correll and *Generes*, cases already discussed, stand as examples of Douglas' failure during this period to explain

---

[232] *Id.* at 307.
[233] *Id., quoting* Correll v. United States, 369 F.2d 87, 89-90 (6th Cir. 1966).
[234] *Id.* at 305 n.19.

his votes. Not all of his opinions reflect this carelessness,[235] but one additional case deserves attention.

In *United States v. Davis*[236] a corporation redeemed some of the stock owned by the taxpayer, its sole shareholder. The issue was whether that distribution was "essentially equivalent to a dividend," and hence taxable as ordinary income, or was not equivalent to a dividend, and thus taxable only as capital gain.[237] Justice Marshall's majority opinion reviewed the legislative history at length, concluding that Congress had intended, in enacting section 302 in the 1954 revision, to change prior case law as it had developed under the 1939 Code. Thus, the Court held that such a redemption of some of a sole shareholder's stock "is always 'essentially equivalent to a dividend,'" notwithstanding any showing that the transaction was motivated by a bona fide business purpose.

Justice Douglas, without citation to or discussion of the legislative history, concluded that the business motive was sufficient to sustain a holding that the distribution was not equivalent to a dividend.[238] He stated his reliance on the reasons given by the courts below,[239] which had held for the taxpayer. But those courts had relied in part on cases arising under the 1939 Code,[240] and had not

---

[235] *See, e.g.,* Commissioner v. Estate of Bosch, 387 U.S. 456, 466 (1967) (Douglas J., dissenting). *Cf.* Wolfman, Bosch, *Its Implications and Aftermath: The Effect of State Court Adjudications on Federal Tax Litigation*, 3d ANN. INSTITUTE ON ESTATE PLANNING, ch. 69-2 (1969) (critical of the majority position).

[236] 397 U.S. 301 (1970).

[237] *See* INT. REV. CODE OF 1954, § 302.

[238] 397 U.S. at 313 (Douglas, J., dissenting).

[239] Davis v. United States, 408 F.2d 1139 (6th Cir. 1969), *aff'g* 274 F. Supp. 466 (M.D. Tenn. 1967).

[240] Revenue Act of 1950, ch. 994, § 208(a), 64 Stat. 931-32, amending Int. Rev. Code of 1939, § 115(g) (now INT. REV. CODE OF 1954, § 302). The district court opinion, Davis v. United States, 274 F. Supp. 466 (M.D. Tenn. 1967) relied primarily on Keefe v. Cote, 213 F.2d 651 (1st Cir. 1954), decided under the 1939 Code. In determining that the tests for application of the 1939 and 1954 Codes were identical, the district court relied on Kerr v. Commissioner, 326 F.2d 225 (9th Cir. 1964), a case which did not consider the legislative history found persuasive by Justice Marshall.

considered the legislative materials which formed the basis of Justice Marshall's opinion.[241] Additionally, Justice Douglas concluded that the majority's rule constituted statutory "revision," of a sort best left to Congress; but this ignores the thrust of Justice Marshall's analysis, which found that Congress had made the revision in its adoption of section 302. Thus, Douglas' treatment of this statutory issue of major significance was cursory if not cavalier.

Although one might see in the statistics for this period an indication that the themes which developed during the second and third periods were weakening, the cases do not seem to support that conclusion. Justice Douglas was still hostile to the Service. There is no evidence of a return to the approach to statutory construction used in Period 1. Despite somewhat increased written participation, his opinions were still wanting in reasons to support their conclusions. Furthermore, Douglas' opinion in *Skelly Oil* called on the Court virtually to retire from the tax scene.

That sentiment of withdrawal is perhaps the natural outgrowth of the trends already observed. The statistics and opinions suggest that in the later periods Justice Douglas has approached tax cases predisposed to vote in favor of the taxpayer. Not often, however, has the majority of the Court decided the cases his way. His silent dissents and careless opinions demonstrate an indifference to the law in tax cases. It is little wonder that one so minded, and at the same time ineffective with his Brethren, would prefer that tax cases appear on the Court's docket as infrequently as possible.

The court of appeals' opinion, Davis v. United States, 408 F.2d 1139 (6th Cir. 1969) did not consider explicitly whether the applicable test had changed with the advent of the 1954 Code. In support of its consideration of the taxpayer's business motive, it cited cases decided under the 1939 Code, *e.g.,* Phelps v. Commissioner, 247 F.2d 156 (9th Cir. 1957); Keefe v. Cote, 213 F.2d 651 (1st Cir. 1954), as well as 1954 Code cases.

[241] S. REP. NO. 1622, 83d Cong., 2d Sess., 44, 234 (1954).

Voting Patterns on Particular Issues

The preceding chronology indicates that as Justice Douglas' votes in tax cases tended increasingly through Periods 2 and 3 to favor the taxpayer, his opinions reflected an altered approach to applying the taxing statutes, a growing distrust of the Revenue Service, and a greater incidence of careless and silent dissents. Although the figures since 1964 imply a blunting of Justice Douglas' pro-taxpayer attitude, his opinions during the final period continued to reflect his changed approach toward both the Code and the IRS. Furthermore, although the incidence of opinionless dissents decreased in the last period, his opinions were often strident and unreasoned.

A look at Douglas' votes with reference to substantive tax issues presented in the cases permits several observations. The statistics for this purpose are set out in Table VI in the Appendix, a summary of which is reproduced on the next page. Although the data in Table VI provide no basis for comprehensive or conclusive generalization, we note the following: [242]

1. Justice Douglas has generally (5 out of 6 cases) voted for the taxpayer in construing the income tax exclusion for "gifts."

2. Justice Douglas has only rarely supported the beneficiaries of the percentage depletion allowance, even in the periods when he generally voted for the taxpayer. [243]

---

[242] The Court has decided a number of corporate income tax cases during Justice Douglas' tenure, but his votes in those cases do not seem to fall into any particular pattern.

Justice Douglas' votes in estate tax cases, taken as a whole, follow his general pattern. He has voted consistently (in 6 out of 7 cases) in favor of the taxpayer in deduction cases under the estate tax. However, there are insufficient cases to delineate a pattern regarding any more narrowly defined an issue.

[243] Justice Douglas voted for the taxpayer in 2 out of the 9 cases. One of those was the fourth period case, United States v. Skelly Oil, 394 U.S. 678, 687 (1969) (Douglas, J., dissenting), discussed at notes 197-205 *supra* &

3. In contrast to the observation in Item 2, Justice Douglas' votes on depreciation (8 cases) seem to have followed his overall pattern of development.

4. Justice Douglas' votes in section 162 cases (construing the deduction for business expenses) have also followed his general pattern. [244]

5. As in the depletion area, Justice Douglas has tended to support the Government (although less strongly than the Court as a whole) in cases where the issue involves capital gains, even in periods when he otherwise supported the taxpayer far more than did the Court. In his most extreme anti-Government period (1959-64), however, there were only two such cases, and in both he dissented without opinion in favor of the taxpayer.

6. The statistics as to cases involving tax accounting show an early swing away from the Government, one which continued throughout his years on the Court, although he supported the Government's position in the single case decided in the last period.

7. Justice Douglas has always shown a pro-taxpayer inclination in the area of procedure and enforcement. That tendency has increased as his general attitude altered. This fact is consistent with Douglas' decisions in other fields of the law,[245] where he seems consistently to favor pro-

---

[244] Justice Douglas' votes in all the cases involving deductions from gross income (including depreciation, depletion and business expenses) have followed the overall pattern as well.
accompanying text. The other, Commissioner v. Southwest Exploration Co., 350 U.S. 308 (1956), presented 2 cases with similar facts. Two taxpayers, one an owner of land adjacent to offshore drilling, and the other an offshore driller, each claimed the percentage depletion allowance on the amount of oil which the driller paid as rent to the landowner. Although he had taken inconsistent positions in the courts below (and lost in both cases), the Commissioner contended in the Supreme Court that the landowner was entitled to the deduction. The Court agreed. Justice Douglas dissented without opinion. *Id.* at 317. He thus voted against the government's position but against a taxpayer as well.

[245] In the areas of criminal and constitutional law, for example.

Table VI (Summary)
Votes Broken Down by Period and Type of Case

Type of Case	Period	Number Cases Douglas Participating	Number Cases Court for Taxpayer	Number Cases Douglas for Taxpayer
Gifts	1	1	1	1
	2	2	0	1
	3	3	1	3
	4	0		
	Totals	6	2	5
Percentage Depletion	1	1	0	0
	2	4	1	1
	3	2	0	0
	4	2	0	1
	Totals	9	1	2
Depreciation	1	3	1	1
	2	1	1	1
	3	2	0	2
	4	3	1	2
	Totals	9	3	6
Business Expenses	1	7	0	0
	2	9	2	3
	3	3	0	3
	4	5	1	4
	Totals	24	3	10
Capital Gains and Losses	1	8	0	1
	2	3	0	1
	3	2	0	2
	4	6	1	2
	Totals	19	1	6
Accounting	1	1	0	0
	2	11	3	7
	3	4	1	4
	4	1	0	0
	Totals	17	4	11
Procedure & Enforcement	1	13	7	8
	2	24	6	12
	3	5	2	4
	4	14	3	12
	Totals	56	18	36

cedural safeguards that restrict the reach and exercise of governmental power.

It therefore appears that Justice Douglas' affinity for the taxpayer has its deepest roots in the areas of the gift exclusion, depreciation, business expense deductions and tax accounting. The taxpayers' positions in cases involving percentage depletion and capital gains have seemed less attractive to Douglas. The relevance of these trends will be examined in Part III.[246]

---

[246] *See* text accompanying note 449 *infra*.

II. Justice Douglas' Performance In Other Areas of the Law

Douglas' extreme behavior in the tax field is special. Since it is not unrelated to his conduct in other areas of the law, however, there may be some value in examining his decisions in several of the other fields in which federal legislation establishes policy for an agency to administer. We have chosen our sample from the areas of labor law, welfare law and corporate insider regulation.[247] The sharpest contrasts to Justice Douglas' approach to tax cases are found in his opinions involving corporate insider regulation. This result may stem from the fact that he was deeply involved in the work of the Securities and Exchange Commission, and became its Chairman, before he joined the Court.

Corporate Insider Regulation

Justice Douglas' opinions in cases involving statutes which regulate the activities of corporate insiders have

---

[247]While the SEC is not an original party in every action brought under the statutes regulating insiders, it frequently intervenes or participates as amicus curiae in actions brought by private parties. As the respective footnote citations *infra* demonstrate, the SEC participated as amicus curiae or party litigant in each of the cases discussed in the text, with the exception of American United Mut. Life Ins. Co. v. Avon Park, 311 U.S. 138 (1940).

received comprehensive analysis elsewhere.[248] The treatment here simply illustrates that Douglas' general approach to the controlling statutes in these cases, as contrasted with those in tax cases, has been consistent throughout his tenure on the Court.[249] His statements as Chairman of the SEC reflect an early awareness of and commitment to the purpose and breadth of the congressional regulatory plan. That commitment, largely developed prior to Douglas' appointment to the Court, formed the touchstone of his judicial approach from the beginning, and it is reflected in even his most recent opinions which continue to cite broad philosophical language from his early cases.[250]

Several of Douglas' speeches as Chairman of the SEC reflect two of the primary tenets which he attributed to the statutory scheme to regulate insider trading. First, he thought that Congress intended those statutes to begin a thorough reform of "both the organization and the management of business and a resetting of the laws under which it operates."[251] Strong measures were needed to

---

[248] *See generally* Countryman, *Justice Douglas: Expositor of the Bankruptcy Law*, 16 U.C.L.A. L. REV. 773 (1969); Hopkirk, *William O. Douglas—His Work in Policing Bankruptcy Proceedings*, 18 VAND. L. REV. 663 (1965); Jennings, *Mr. Justice Douglas: His Influence on Corporate and Securities Regulation*, 73 YALE L.J. 920 (1964). All three articles are important reviews of Justice Douglas' work in this area. Hopkirk's general thesis is that throughout his career Justice Douglas "manifested a continuity of approach to bankruptcy problems emphasizing functional analysis." Jennings contends that Justice Douglas has been a major architect of the present rules which govern the manager-investor relationship. Countryman's analysis seems to be that Justice Douglas decided cases so as to insure the effective operation of federal regulation, and that he frequently accomplished that end by a broad construction of the congressional delegation of power to courts and agencies. *See also* Epstein, *Economic Predilections of Justice Douglas*, 1949 WIS. L. REV. 531 (1949).

[249] *See e.g.,* Hopkirk, *supra* note 248, at 698: "William O. Douglas' major contributions to the field of bankruptcy law are marked by a high degree of continuity in approach and in solutions."

[250] *See, e.g.,* Caplin v. Marine Midland Grace Trust Co., 406 U.S. 416, 435, 439 (1972) (SEC, supporting petitioner, participating as "unnamed respondent," *id.* at 419 n.8), *citing* Pepper v. Litton, 308 U.S. 295 (1939).

[251] W. Douglas, DEMOCRACY AND FINANCE 11 (1940) [hereinafter cited as DEMOCRACY AND FINANCE].

halt the abuses which insiders were committing by virtue of their positions, abuses which he thought to be contributing causes of financial disorder.[252] Second, Douglas believed that Congress intended the SEC to have broad discretionary powers[253] to insure fair and equitable dealing. His position regarding the stock exchanges is a prime example.[254] Although he preferred reform initiated by the exchanges themselves to reform which the Commission could impose directly, there is no doubt that the exchanges cooperated largely because he made clear a willingness to act in their breach. Characterizing his view of the proper relationship of the SEC to the exchanges, Douglas said, "Government would keep the shotgun, so to speak, behind the door, loaded, well oiled, cleaned, ready for use but with the hope it would never have to be used."[255]

American United Mutual Life Insurance Co. v. City of Avon Park[256] illustrates an early judicial application of Justice Douglas' views as to the purposes of the acts regulating insiders.[257] In that Bankruptcy Act[258] case, the lower court approved the city's plan for composition of its debts, a plan developed by the city's fiscal agent, Crummer & Company. In an apparent effort to ensure the

---

[252] *Id.* 8-14, 16.

[253] This is of course consistent with reading a statute narrowly in order to achieve the congressional purpose. *See, e.g.,* Emil v. Hanley, 318 U.S. 515 (1943) (limiting power of trustee in bankruptcy). Thus, Professor Countryman has said in connection with the bankruptcy cases, "On ... [occasion], the Justice has deemed it appropriate to use both limiting and broadening interpretations to resolve difficulties which the draftsmen could hardly have anticipated." Countryman, *supra* note 248, at 775.

[254] *See generally* DEMOCRACY AND FINANCE *supra* note 251, at 79-91, 244-64.

[255] *Id.* 82.

[256] 311 U.S. 138 (1940).

[257] For a similar approach in other early corporate regulation cases, *see, e.g.,* Connecticut Ry. & Lighting v. Palmer, 311 U.S. 544, 562 (Douglas, J., dissenting, advocating a pragmatic approach to valuation of a 999-year lease); Pepper v. Litton, 308 U.S. 295, 312 (1939) (requiring bankruptcy court, in exercise of its equity jurisdiction, to "undo" fraudulent scheme "[n]o matter how technically legal each step in that scheme may have been").

[258] 11 U.S.C. §§ 401-03 (1970).

statutorily required assent to the plan by two-thirds of the city's creditors, Crummer acquired more than one-third of the claims which others held. There was no showing, however, that Crummer had disclosed its own status as a creditor when, acting as the city's agent, it solicited the assents of other bondholders. Justice Douglas wrote for the Court, reversing approval of the plan. More significant than the mere holding, however, is Douglas' approach to an issue treated solely because it would have to be addressed on remand. To protect outsiders, the statute[259] prohibited Crummer from participation in a future vote on confirmation of the plan if its claims were "controlled" by the city. Justice Douglas looked to the fundamental purposes of the Act and defined "control" broadly:

> The abuse at which the Act is aimed is not confined to those cases where the holder of the claims is an agent of the city within the strict rules of *respondeat superior*. Rather, the test is whether or not there is such close identity of interests between the claimant and the city that the claimant's assent to the plan may fairly be said to be more the product of the city's influence and to reflect more the city's desires than an expression of an investor's independent, business judgment.[260]

That kind of approach to statutory interpretation fits perfectly with the views Douglas voiced as chairman of the SEC.

Cases decided during what we have termed Douglas' second period, in which his attitude toward the tax system seems to have shifted, demonstrate a continued dedication to the implementation of the broad purposes of the insider regulation statutes. This is true, for example, in *Brown v.*

---

[259]*Id.* § 403(d).
[260]311 U.S. at 148.

Gerdes[261] and *Leiman v. Gutman*,[262] in which the Court, Justice Douglas writing, consolidated exclusive control over the permissible litigation fees of the bankrupt's attorneys in the bankruptcy court itself, rather than allow the attorneys and the estate to agree on fees. It is more useful, however, to examine the opinions written in later periods when, according to the statistics and our examination of the cases, Douglas' strong preference for the taxpayer replaced a consistent approach to the tax statutes.

General Stores Corp. v. Shlensky,[263] decided in 1956, illustrates Douglas' continued strong support for the policies of the Bankruptcy Act.[264] The petitioner instituted Chapter XI proceedings, and proposed an arrangement of its debts. The SEC, together with a single stockholder, moved for a dismissal of those proceedings unless the debtor also complied with the more drastic requirements[265] of Chapter X. The sole issue was the propriety of the district court's selection of Chapter X as

---

[261] 321 U.S. 178 (1944) (SEC amicus curiae). *See, e.g., id.* at 181:

Sec. 77B, like § 77 of the Bankruptcy Act, had as one of its purposes the establishment of more effective control over reorganization fees and expenses... in recognition of the effect which a depletion of the cash resources of the estate may have on both the fairness and feasibility of the plan of reorganization.... And Ch. X of the Chandler Act which took the place of § 77B set up an even more comprehensive supervision over compensation and allowances.

[262] 336 U.S. 1 (1949) (SEC amicus curiae). *See, e.g., id.* at 6, 8: "The aim of the expanded controls over reorganization fees and expenses is clear.... A statute establishing such broad supervision... cannot be presumed to be niggardly in its grant of authority...."

For another manifestation of the spirit of *Brown* and *Leiman* during Period 2, see Anderson v. Abbott, 321 U.S. 349, 363 (1944) ("dealing... with a principle of liability which is concerned with realities not forms" in applying provisions of the National Banking Act).

[263] 350 U.S. 462 (1956) (SEC party respondent).

[264] 11 U.S.C. §§ 401 et seq. (1970).

[265] Including the court's submission of the reorganization plan to the SEC for an advisory report, *id* § 572.

the course of proceeding. Justice Frankfurter's dissent[266] argued that the district court had based its decision on an oversimplification of *SEC v. United States Realty & Improvement Co.*[267] in holding that Chapter X was proper simply because the debtor was a large corporation. Furthermore, he maintained, the congressional elimination of the statutory requirement that a Chapter XI arrangement be "fair and equitable" constituted "the clearest possible indication that Chapter XI should be given a more generous scope than even the narrowest reading of *United States Realty* might suggest."[268] Nevertheless, Justice Douglas, writing for the Court, upheld the district court. His opinion agreed that the *Realty* case did not create a strict rule which determined the type of proceeding simply on the basis of the size of the corporation involved. The essential discrimination was not to be "between the small company and the large company but between the needs to be served"[269] in the resolution of the particular case. Reasoning from this basis, Douglas avoided the "fair and equitable" difficulty raised by Justice Frankfurter, and concluded that "the paramount issue at present concerns what is 'feasible' "[270] according to the realities of the marketplace. Then, apparently ignoring Justice Frankfurter's other objection, Justice Douglas found that the lower court had concluded, within the proper range of discretion, that feasibility required proceeding according to Chapter X.[271]

---

[266] 350 U.S. at 468.
[267] 320 U.S. 434 (1940).
[268] 350 U.S. at 472.
[269] *Id.* at 466.
[270] *Id.* at 467-68.
[271] *Id.* at 468. For additional instances of a functional approach to corporate questions during this period, *see, e.g.,* Justice Douglas' dissent, joined by Justices Burton and Minton, in St. Joe Paper Co. v. Atlantic Coast Line R.R., 347 U.S. 298, 321, (1954), dealing with the ICC's power to impose a merger upon a railroad in bankruptcy reorganization. Professor Countryman terms the dissenters' position in *St. Joe Paper* "[c]ertainly ... the most

SEC v. Drexel Co.,[272] decided during the same period, illustrates Douglas' willingness to adopt a construction supportive of the SEC's administration of the regulatory statutes.[273] As part of its reorganization under the Public Utility Holding Company Act of 1935,[274] Bond & Share Company was to divest itself of a subsidiary known as Electric, which was itself involved in further reorganization. The Commission consolidated the proceedings on the two companies' coordinated plans, and entered one order. It approved the Bond & Share plan, and also approved the Electric plan, but explicitly reserved jurisdiction over certain fees and expenses in connection with Electric's "[p]lan ... [and] the transactions incident thereto."[275] By virtue of sections 10[276] and 12[277] of the Act it was clear that the Commission had power to scrutinize the fees in connection with Bond & Share's part of the plan, just as it was clear that it had such power under section 11[278] to scrutinize fees in connection with Electric's part. The sole question, which divided the Court, was whether the Commission had retained jurisdiction over the fees charged in connection with Bond & Share's half of the plan.

---

realistic, and fair interpretation of section 77's ... reference to the merger provisions of the Interstate Commerce Act." Countryman, *supra* note 248, at 823. *See also* Smith v. Sperling, 354 U.S. 91 (1957); Swanson V. Traer, 354 U.S. 114 (1957) (majority of Court in both cases, per Douglas, J., adopting the more realistic course in regard to diversity questions in shareholders' derivative suits); General Protective Comm. v. SEC. 346 U.S. 521 (1954) (unanimous court, per Douglas, J., finding no abuse of SEC discretion in submitting only part of reorganization plan for approval and enforcement by district court).

[272] 348 U.S. 341 (1955).
[273] General Protective Comm. v. SEC, 346 U.S. 521 (1954), also demonstrates Justice Douglas' concern for the administrative necessities of the agency. For evidence that the same concern prevailed in later years, see note 292 *infra* & cases cited therein.
[274] 15 U.S.C. § 79a et seq. (1970).
[275] 348 U.S. at 346.
[276] 15 U.S.C. § 79j (1970).
[277] *Id.* § 79 l.
[278] *Id.* § 79k.

Justice Douglas, writing for the majority, ruled that the Commission had retained jurisdiction over the fees charged Bond & Share because the Commission's proceedings were consolidated and because its order referred not to fees incurred in connection with Electric's plan, but to those incurred in connection with its transactions. "The latter," he argued, "obviously included the matters under § 10 and § 12, for they were the chief collateral ones before the Commission."[279] The difficulty with this reasoning is simply that it is not convincing, given the Commission's apparently separate treatment of the two corporations in its order. Douglas' two observations do not require his conclusion, but only a conclusion that the Commission *intended* to retain jurisdiction. Contrary to Justice Frankfurter's close and discriminating approach to the statute in dissent,[280] Justice Douglas referred to the most general legislative purposes:

> Congress was explicit in making [fees payable by a registered holding company] in connection with the transactions covered by § 10 and by § 12, subject to Commission approval. Congress had before it the detailed record of holding company activities and knew that many of them had a proclivity for predatory practices. The fees were not only large; they were often loaded on affiliated companies.... Congress decided to put an end to the worst of these practices and control the critical ones. When it came to the intricacies of holding company finance, Congress expressed the desire to have the amount of the fees paid brought to light and to have the Commission decide who pays them and what amounts are reasonable.[281]

---

[279] 348 U.S. at 346.
[280] *Id.* at 349. (The dissent was joined by Burton, J.).
[281] *Id.* at 348-49 (footnote omitted).

On this broad statutory base, he rested his conclusion: "We cannot be faithful to that statutory design without granting the Commission the jurisdiction asserted here."[282]

Douglas wrote *General Stores* and *Drexel Co.* at a time when his voting pattern in tax cases had become substantially anti-government.[283] Nevertheless, his attitude towards the statutes regulating corporations and their administration had not changed. Throughout the last decade Douglas has held to his original view of the acts' purposes, and his determination to give them support. Now, however, that view places him frequently in dissent.

In *Blau v. Lehman*,[284] decided in 1962, a stockholder of Tide Water Associated Oil Company sued on behalf of the corporation to recover short swing profits on sales of Tide Water stock. Pursuant to section 16(b) of the Securities Exchange Act of 1934,[285] the company could recover such profits realized by a director of the corporation.[286] In fact, Lehman Brothers, a partnership engaged in investment banking, had realized the profit, but one partner was a director of Tide Water. The facts showed that in its purchases and sales of Tide Water stock Lehman Brothers did not implement or have access to any inside knowledge which the director-partner might have had. Thus the issue was whether the partnership should be

---

[282] *Id.* at 349.
[283] *See* Appendix, Table 1, *infra*.
[284] 368 U.S. 403 (1962) (SEC participating as amicus curiae).
[285] 15 U.S.C. § 78p(b) (1970).
[286] The statute provides in part:
　　For the purpose of preventing the unfair use of information which may have been obtained by such beneficial owner, director, or officer by reason of his relationship to the issuer, any profit realized by him from any purchase and sale, or any sale and purchase, of any equity security of such issuer ... within any period of less than six months ... shall inure to and be recoverable by the issuer, irrespective of any intention on the part of such beneficial owner, director, or officer. . . .
　　Id.

found, as a matter of law, to come within the reach of section 16(b) and be required to forfeit its profits. The court, per Justice Black, held Lehman Brothers not liable chiefly because Congress had not overruled an earlier Second Circuit decision so holding.[287]

Justice Douglas, dissenting,[288] refused to rely on congressional silence to "give § 16(b) a strict and narrow construction."[289] Rather, he based his view that Lehman Brothers was within the broad reach of the statute on two considerations. First, finding "the root of the present problem [to be] the scope and degree of liability arising out of fiduciary relations,"[290] Douglas cited familiar general support in legislative history which emphasized a desire to curtail insider exploitation of information and position. Thus armed with a legislative purpose, he found, second, that the practical effect of the Court's result was to thwart that purpose by "substantially [eliminating] 'the Great Wall Street trading firms' from the operation of § 16(b)."[291] In his view, such an unrealistic position was untenable. *Blau v. Lehman* was decided, of course, during the period in which Douglas' tax opinions appear most consistently to have supported the taxpayer over the Government.

Two of Justice Douglas' opinions from the 1971 Term illustrate his continued commitment to statutory purpose and congressional design. *Superintendent of Insurance v. Bankers Life & Casualty Co.*[292] arose in connection with the following alleged scheme. One Begole obtained a

---

[287] Rattner v. Lehman, 193 F.2d 564 (2d Cir. 1952).
[288] 368 U.S. at 414.
[289] *Id.* at 419.
[290] *Id.* at 416.
[291] *Id.* at 414.
[292] 404 U.S. 6 (1971) (SEC amicus curiae). *See also, e.g.,* Caplin v. Marine Midland Grace Trust Co., 406 U.S. 416 (1972) (SEC, supporting petitioner, participating as "unnamed respondent," *id.* at 419 n.8) (holding that trustee in Chapter X Bankruptcy Act proceeding does not have standing to raise claims of misconduct by an indenture trustee; Douglas, J., joined by Brennan, White and Blackmun, JJ., dissenting, at 435, on the ground that the

$5,000,000 check from Irving Trust Company, although he had no funds on deposit at the time. He then used that check to buy all the stock of Manhattan Casualty Company from Bankers Life. Finally, Begole's cohort, the president of Manhattan, sold all of Manhattan's United States Treasury bonds in order to cover the original check from Irving Trust. "As a result, Begole owned all the stock of Manhattan, having used $5,000,000 of Manhattan's assets to purchase it."[293] Petitioner, a representative of Manhattan, sued under rule 10b-5,[294] alleging a fraud on Manhattan in connection with the sale of Manhattan's United States Treasury bonds, which were "securities" covered by the Act.[295] The critical issue in deciding

---

majority "decision reflects a misunderstanding of the important [functions] which a reorganization trustee . . . is supposed to perform"). Perhaps the clearest example of Justice Douglas' construction of a corporate regulation statute in response to the administrative needs of the SEC, also arising in this period, is SEC v. New England Elec. System, 384 U.S. 176 (1966). Justice Douglas, speaking for the majority, concluded, upon an examination of certain legislative history, that

> [T]he phrase [of the statute to be construed] is admittedly not crystal clear. But the Commission's construction seems to us to be well within the permissible range given to those who are charged with the task of giving an intricate statutory scheme practical sense and application.

Id. at 185, Justice Harlan's vigorous dissent rebutted Douglas' conclusion, *id.* at 185, making plain the practical difference between the two possible interpretations considered, and persuasively demonstrated the weakness of the majority's interpretation in light of the specifics of the legislative history.

[293] 404 U.S. at 8. Another layer of deception was laid on the scheme as well, but is irrelevant here.

[294] 17 C.F.R. § 240.10b-5 (1972):

> It shall be unlawful for any person, directly or indirectly . . .
> (1) To employ any device, scheme, or artifice to defraud,
> (2) . . . or
> (3) To engage in any act, practice, or course of business which operates or would operate as a fraud or deceit upon any person, in connection with the purchase or sale of any security.

[295] 15 U.S.C. § 78j(b) (1970):

> It shall be unlawful for any person. . .[t]o use or employ, in connection with the purchase or sale of any security registered on a national securities exchange or any security not so registered, any manipulative or deceptive device or contrivance in contravention of such rules and regulations as the Commission may prescribe as necessary or appropriate in the public interest or for the protection of investors.

whether the district court had properly dismissed the claim was whether Congress had designed section 10(b), which allows the SEC to prescribe rules "as necessary or appropriate in the public interest or for the protection of investors,"[296] to apply to this type of fraud.

The Court, in a unanimous opinion by Justice Douglas, agreed with the lower courts that "Congress by § 10(b) did not seek to regulate transactions which constitute no more than internal corporate mismanagement."[297] However, the statute was to be read "flexibly, not technically and restrictively" and since fraudulent practices "constantly vary . . . . broad discretionary powers"[298] were to be recognized in the agency charged with defining the limits of the statute's proscriptions. Thus, because Manhattan was injured "as a result of deceptive practices touching its sale of securities as an investor"[299] in them; even though the ultimate victims were Manhattan's creditors, the statute properly applied to the scheme in question and the trial court's dismissal of the action was in error.

The Court decided *Reliance Electric Co. v. Emerson Electric Co.*[300] narrowly, literally. Like *Blau v. Lehman*, it involved section 16(b) of the Securities Exchange Act of 1934;[301] *Reliance* dealt with the applicability of the forfeiture provisions to the short swing profits of a beneficial owner of ten percent of the outstanding stock of the corporation whose stock was traded. Emerson had purchased 13.2% of the stock of Dodge Manufacturing Company in June of 1967 in an attempt to take control of Dodge. When the attempt failed, Emerson sold out its shares in two sales which occurred in August and

---

[296] 404 U.S. at 10 n.6.
[297] *Id.* at 12.
[298] *Id.*
[299] *Id.*
[300] 404 U.S. 418 (1972).
[301] 15 U.S.C. § 78p(b) (1970).

September. The August sale reduced Emerson's holdings to 9.96% of the Dodge stock, and in September it sold the remainder. Emerson argued with respect to the second sale that it was not a ten-percent owner of the Dodge stock "both at the time of the purchase and sale, or the sale and purchase"[302] as required for application of the statute. The majority, finding no legislative history directly on the issue, concluded that the express language of the statute required a holding that Emerson's second sale was not within its terms.

Justice Douglas' dissent[303] noted both that the prophylactic purpose of the statute was to preclude "surething" speculation on the basis of insider knowledge, and that that purpose had been flexibly and broadly applied in the past, "even departing where necessary from the literal statutory language."[304] The dissent criticized the majority's interpretation as poorly fitted to achieve the policy of the statute. Furthermore, Douglas argued, "the literal language of the statute would not preclude an analysis in which the two transactions . . . [were] treated as part of a single 'sale.' "[305] Following this analysis, he said the statute should be construed as allowing "a rebuttable presumption that any such series of dispositive transactions will be deemed to be part of a single plan of disposition, and will be treated as a single 'sale' for the purposes of § 16(b)."[306]

---

[302] In so holding, the majority refused to accept an alternative construction (suggested by the SEC as amicus curiae) of the critical requirement that a beneficial owner be such both at the time of purchase and sale. The proffered reading construed the requirement as simply intended to provide an exception to the Act for a person upon whom ownership of the securities devolved involuntarily. 404 U.S. at 425-27.

[303] *Id.* at 427. The dissent was joined by Justices Brennan and White. Since Justices Powell and Rehnquist took no part, the decision was 4-3.

[304] *Id.* at 433, *quoting* Feder v. Martin Marietta Corp., 406 F.2d 260, 262 (2d Cir. 1969).

[305] 404 U.S. at 434.

[306] *Id.* at 438.

Justice Douglas' *Reliance* opinion is not striking for its dedication to an interpretation based on the statute viewed as a whole, for that approach is common to his opinions in this area. However, one is struck by the sharp contrast between Douglas' approach in *Reliance* and that in the tax case of *Knetsch v. United States,*[307] decided in 1960. Both are essentially cases in which a party thought that he had found a loophole in the statutory scheme, yet Douglas construed the tax statute according to its letter, and the securities act in spite of it. *Reliance* contrasts with Douglas' recent tax opinions in another respect as well. In both *Skelly Oil*[308] and *Generes,*[309] for example, he asserted that the Court should not take tax cases only to "iron out ambiguities" in the Code.[310] In *Reliance*, however, Douglas maintained that it was necessary to stretch the terms of the statute beyond the meaning they

---

[307] 364 U.S. 361 (1960). For discussion of *Knetsch*, see notes 136-43 *supra* & accompanying text. *Cf.* Shanahan, *Court Holds to the Letter of the Law,* N.Y. Times, Jan. 16, 1972, § 3 (Business & Finance), at 3, col. 5 (criticizing the *Reliance* decision as contrary to normal judicial decision-making). Shanahan said that the courts have held and should hold that if a transaction is of a type which Congress had sought to prohibit, then the statute prohibits it, even if the language reveals that Congress had not foreseen the particular transaction. She indicated that Justice Douglas' dissent rested on just that point and she concluded with the fearful speculation that if the majority's approach in *Reliance* were used in tax cases there might be little "Government revenues left to regulate business or anything else." *Id* at 11, col. 8. Shanahan was correct, albeit unaware that Justice Douglas' approach in tax cases is precisely like that of the Court's in *Reliance*. *See* United States v. Generes, 405 U.S. 93, 113 (1972) (Douglas, J., dissenting), discussed at text accompanying notes 206-11 *supra*.

[308] 394 U.S. 678 (1969). For discussion of *Skelly Oil*, see notes 197-205 *supra* & accompanying text.

[309] 405 U.S. 93 (1972). For discussion of *Generes*, see text accompanying notes 206-33 *supra*.

[310] *Id.* at 113, 114-15. Justice Douglas' articulated reason for protesting resort to the Court to solve tax code ambiguities is that the Treasury and the Joint Committee on Internal Revenue Taxation are "much abler than are we to forecast revenue needs and spot loopholes where abuses thrive." But this reasoning avails nothing in its application to any given case, since the legislative and administrative branches cannot eliminate all ambiguity, and they are rendered less capable when they are denied the parallel development and articulation of a consistent judicial extrapolation of the statutory scheme.

might require, to whatever meaning they would "allow"[311] in order to reach the result which he thought would effectuate congressional policy.

The corporate insider cases which we have discussed are, of course, too few in number to be conclusive.[312] They suggest strongly, however, as do the exhaustive analyses of Professor Countryman[313] and others,[314] that Justice Douglas' commitment to the grand design which Congress fashioned, and to the agency which implements it, did not undergo the erosion in this area of the law which we have detailed in the tax field.

Douglas nowhere explains his dissimilar treatment of these two areas of the law. It may be that during the 1930's, particularly as an SEC Member and Chairman, he developed a strong, well-defined sense of what the corporate regulation statutes meant and what they were enacted to do. Perhaps he retained that outlook because it had been reached through his substantial involvement in the creation and administration of the statutes. It may be that because Douglas lacked a similar background in tax law he allowed his commitment to the system which Congress had created in that field to disintegrate.[315]

---

[311] 404 U.S. at 431-34. A number of cases may be contrasted in the same way as *Generes* and *Reliance*. Tax opinions consistent with *Generes* are cited therein, 405 U.S. at 114-15. For other corporate regulation cases similar to *Reliance*, in which the opinion contrary to Justice Douglas' recommends resolution of the problem by congressional means, see, *e.g.,* Caplin v. Marine Midland Grace Trust Co., 406 U.S. 416, 434-35 (1972); Blau v. Lehman, 368 U.S. 403, 411-12 (1962). The flexible, functional approach noted in the insider regulation cases may be contrasted with the analysis in each of a number of Justice Douglas' later tax opinions.

[312] Tables were not prepared for this section because they were not thought necessary. The groundwork for analysis of Justice Douglas' opinions in this area has been amply laid elsewhere, see authorities cited *supra* note 248.

[313] *See* Countryman, *supra* note 248.

[314] *See* authorities cited, *supra* note 248.

[315] Interestingly, Justice Douglas' opinion in United States v. Randall, 401 U.S. 513 (1971), concerns the resolution of a conflict between the Bankruptcy Act and the Internal Revenue Code. The bankruptcy court (under Chapter XI of the Bankruptcy Act, 11 U.S.C. § 701 et seq. (1970)) had

Labor Law

The labor cases are too numerous for an exhaustive study in an article concerned primarily with tax cases. Our purpose here, then, is more restricted. First, we will draw some statistical comparisons between the seeming patterns of Justice Douglas' votes in the tax and labor cases. Second, we will illustrate by reference to a limited number of opinions an apparent inconsistency in Douglas' approach to the federal labor legislation, and a growing distrust of the National Labor Relations Board itself.

The statistics[316] for the labor law cases permit several

---

required the corporate debtor to maintain a separate bank account for the deposit of payroll taxes withheld from employees; withdrawals from that account could be used only to pay such taxes to the government. The debtor withheld the required taxes, but failed to deposit them as directed. After the debtor was adjudicated a bankrupt, the Government sought to have its tax claim paid prior to the costs and expenses of administration of the bankruptcy proceedings. The Government's position was based on INT. REV. CODE OF 1954, § 7501(a), which provided that withheld taxes constituted a trust in favor of the Government.

Justice Douglas wrote for a 5-4 majority, denying the Government's claim. In answer to the Government's contention based upon § 7501(a), he said simply that "the debtor-in-possession failed to segregate the taxes so withheld; hence there was no trust." 401 U.S. at 515. The Government's counterargument was that the misconduct of the debtor-in-possession, a court-appointed officer, should not defeat the trust. Furthermore, the Government argued, a holding for the Government would not unfairly harm the creditors since the taxes withheld were never an asset of the estate. That is, as the dissent pointed out, *id.* at 518 (Blackmun, J., dissenting), absent the withholding scheme the moneys involved would have been paid as gross income to the employees, and would not have been available for the creditors anyway.

Justice Douglas did not dispute that argument on its own terms. He concluded rather that the "Bankruptcy Act ... is an overriding statement of federal policy on this question of priorities." *Id.* at 515 (majority opinion). Although the Bankruptcy Act did not explicitly resolve the issue, Justice Douglas noted "a progressive legislative development that (1) marks a decline in the grant of a tax preference to the United States and (2) marks an ascending priority for costs and expenses of administration." *Id.* at 516. On that basis, he held against the Government.

[316]The sample for these statistics includes all cases decided under the National Labor Relations Act, 29 U.S.C. § 141 et seq. (1970), in which Justice Douglas participated, whether or not he wrote an opinion, and whether

important observations. First, unions have generally prevailed over employers in the opinions both of the Court (in 74% of the cases) and of Justice Douglas (in 79%). Second, the incidence of union preference by both the Court and Justice Douglas does not vary significantly from period to period, although in the last decade Douglas has sided with the union somewhat less often than before.

Additionally, both the Court (in 75% of the cases) and Justice Douglas (in 73%) usually have voted to uphold the Labor Board. When in dissent, however, Douglas has favored the Board in only 31% of the labor cases.

The Court has supported the Board in 75% or more of the cases in each period except Period 3. [317] In contrast to the Court's relative consistency, however, Douglas' percentages are quite uneven. He voted to uphold the Board in 90% of the first period labor cases, but in only 62% of the cases in the fourth period. This pattern is most noticeable in his dissents. In period one, 100% of Justice Douglas' dissents favored the Board; in period four, 17%. Significantly, the trend of Douglas' votes against the Board resembles the trend of his votes against the IRS in tax cases.

Some specific contrasts between the labor and tax cases are worth noting. Douglas' positions regarding the

---

or not the National Labor Relations Board was a party. Cases such as Retail Clerks Local 1625 v. Schermerhorn, 373 U.S. 746 (1963); Teamsters Union v. Oliver, 358 U.S. 283 (1959); and Guss v. Utah Labor Bd., 353 U.S. 1 (1957), dealing primarily with federal labor law preemption of or conflicts with the state labor regulation are not included. Also omitted is Travis v. United States, 364 U.S. 631 (1961), involving a venue issue in criminal prosecution for making false affidavits of Communist Party nonmembership. The statistics are based only on "relevant" cases; cases arising out of a conflict between two unions are not considered relevant to union or employer preference statistics.

[317] In Period 3 Justice Douglas wrote for the Court in 4 related cases holding against the Board: Typographical Union v. NLRB, 365 U.S. 705 (1961); NLRB v. News Syndicate Co., 365 U.S. 695 (1961); Teamsters Local 357 v. NLRB, 365 U.S. 667 (1961); Carpenters Local 60 v. NLRB, 365 U.S. 651 (1961). Were these 4 cases counted as 1, the percentage of relevant cases decided by the Court in favor of the Board during that period would be 65%.

Labor Board, as reflected in his dissents, vary (as in tax cases) over the periods, but since 1943 he has dissented considerably less frequently in labor. Additionally, he has registered far fewer dissents without opinion in labor cases, and far fewer dissents in which no other member of the Court joined him. Finally, throughout his tenure Justice Douglas has continued to write a fair share of labor opinions for the Court.

APPROACH TO THE STATUTE

Inconsistencies in Justice Douglas' approach to statutory construction are readily apparent in the labor cases although no particular trend emerges. In *Republic Steel Corp. v. NLRB*[318] the Court held that the Board's back pay order could not include restitution to government agencies for work relief paid to wrongfully discharged employees. Justices Douglas and Black dissented in a joint opinion,[319] combining a literal statutory construction with what they felt best effectuated the purpose of the Wagner Act. Since back pay served both a remunerative as well as a punitive function, the dissent saw no reason to lessen the erring employer's burden by deducting from the back pay order any amount earned through work relief. "The 'back pay' provision is clear and unambiguous. Hence, it is enough here for us to determine what Congress meant from what it said."[320]

When what Congress said did not suffice to determine what Congress meant, however, Douglas discounted the former. In *Packard Motor Car Co. v. NLRB*[321] the Court determined that the term "employee," defined in the Taft-Hartley Act[322] as "any employee," included fore-

---

[318] 311 U.S. 7 (1940).
[319] *Id.* at 13.
[320] *Id.* at 14-15.
[321] 330 U.S. 485 (1947).
[322] Labor Management Relations Act, ch. 372, § 2 (49 Stat. 450), *as amended*, 29 U.S.C. § 152(3) (1970).

Table VIII-1
Douglas' Votes in All Labor Cases

Period	Number Relevant Cases	Court pro Union	Douglas pro Union	Number Relevant Cases	Court pro Board	Douglas pro Board
1	20	14 (70%)	17 (85%)	19	14 (74%)	17 (90%)
2	59	42 (71%)	49 (83%)	58	45 (78%)	40 (69%)
3	16	15 (94%)	14 (88%)	23	13 (57%)	10 (43%)
4	33	24 (73%)	21 (64%)	36	30 (83%)	22 (62%)
Totals	128	95 (74%)	101 (79%)	137	103 (75%)	100 (73%)

Table VIII-2
Douglas' Dissents in Labor Cases

Period	Dissents pro Union	Dissents pro Employer	Dissents pro Board	Dissents con Board
1	3 (100%)	0	3 (100%)	0
2	12 (71%)	5	6 (35%)	11
3	0 (0%)	1	0 (0%)	3
4	4 (36%)	7	2 (17%)	10
Totals	19 (59%)	13	11 (31%)	24

men. In so construing the Act to protect the unionization of foremen, the majority refused to consider legislative history, since there was "no ambiguity in this Act to be clarified."[323] Justice Douglas, dissenting,[324]

---

[323] 330 U.S. at 492.
[324] *Id.* at 493.

Table VIII-3
Douglas' Votes in Labor Cases in which He Wrote an Opinion

Period	Number Relevant Cases	Court pro Union	Douglas pro Union	Number Relevant Cases	Court pro Board	Douglas pro Board
1	6	3 (50%)	4 (67%)	6	3 (50%)	4 (67%)
2	12	8 (67%)	8 (67%)	11	8 (73%)	4 (36%)
3	5	4 (80%)	4 (80%)	9	3 (33%)	2 (22%)
4	9	7 (78%)	5 (56%)	12	11 (92%)	6 (50%)
Totals	32	22	21	38	25	16

Table VIII-4
Type of Douglas' Opinions in Labor Cases

Period	Number Cases Douglas Participating	Number Douglas Wrote for Court	Number Douglas Dissents	Number Douglas Wrote Dissents	Number Douglas Silent Dissents	Number Douglas Solitary Dissents
1	20	3	3 (15%)	1	0	0
2	60	7	17 (28%)	6	1	1
3	23	5	3 (13%)	1	2	2
4	36	5	12 (33%)	7	1	3
Totals	139	20	35 (25%)	15	4	6

rejected the majority's literal method of interpretation which would, he said, mean that vice presidents and all other management except directors would be granted the Act's protection in their attempts to unionize. Rather, he argued that "[t]he term 'employee' must be considered in the context of the Act,"³²⁵ and that the court should consider "[t]he evil at which the Act was aimed,"³²⁶ legislative history, and related legislation. These considerations convinced Douglas that, in drafting the Act, Congress was not concerned with the bargaining problems of foremen, and in fact was "legislating *against* the activities of foremen, not on their behalf."³²⁷ Congress later amended the act to accord with Justice Douglas' reading. ³²⁸

Writing for the Court in *Textile Workers Union v. Lincoln Mills*,³²⁹ Douglas adhered to this underlying policy approach to statutory construction and upheld specific enforcement of an arbitration agreement under section 301(a) of the Labor Management Relations Act. ³³⁰ That section, which Justice Frankfurter's dissent called "plainly procedural"³³¹ provided that "[s]uits for violation of contracts between an employer and a labor organization representing employees in an industry affecting commerce ... may be brought in any district court of the United States having jurisdiction of the parties...." Justice Douglas rejected the literal view that the statute merely extended jurisdiction, and held that it provided a substantive federal remedy as well: "It seems, therefore, clear to us that Congress adopted a policy which placed sanctions behind agreements to arbitrate grievance disputes.... We would undercut the Act and defeat its policy if we read § 301 narrowly as only conferring jurisdiction over labor organizations."³³²

---

³²⁵*Id.* at 495 (Douglas, J., dissenting).
³²⁶*Id.* at 496.
³²⁷*Id.* at 499.
³²⁸ 29 U.S.C. 152(3) (1970).
³²⁹ 353 U.S. 448 (1957).
³³⁰ 29 U.S.C. § 185 (1970).
³³¹ 353 U.S. at 461 (Frankfurter, J., dissenting).
³³²*Id.* at 456 (majority opinion). *See also id.* at 457-58, considering "whether jurisdiction to compel arbitration of grievance disputes is withdrawn

But Douglas again shifted position in *NLRB v. Local 825, Operating Engineers*,[333] involving a union's strike against two co-contractors to pressure a third co-contractor to accept a certain plan of job assignments. The primary issue was whether section 8(b)(4)(B) of the National Labor Relations Act[334] proscribed the union's strike because its "object" was to force the two co-contractors to "cease doing business" with the third co-contractor. The majority concluded in the affirmative: "To hold that this flagrant secondary conduct with these most serious disruptive effects was not prohibited by § 8(b)(4)(B) would be largely to ignore the original congressional concern."[335] Justice Douglas approached the statute literally and, without discussing legislative intent, dissented.[336] Thus, he opened his opinion stating simply: "If we take the words of the Act, rather than what the courts have interpolated, and lay them alongside the facts of this cause, I do not see how we can fairly say that Local 825 engaged in an 'unfair labor practice' within the meaning of § 8(b)(4)(B)."[337]

That rather simplistic approach conflicts, in turn, with Douglas' later opinion for the Court in *NLRB v. Nash-Finch Co.*[338] In *Nash-Finch* Justice Douglas found *implied* authority to enable the Labor Board to obtain injunctive relief in a federal district court against state

---

by the Norris-LaGuardia Act, 47 Stat. 70, 29 U.S.C. § 101:" "Though a literal reading might bring the dispute within the terms of the Act ... we see no justification in policy for restricting § 301(a) to damage suits, leaving specific performance of a contract to arbitrate grievance disputes to the inapposite procedural requirements of the Act." (footnote omitted).

[333] 400 U.S. 297 (1971). See also Local 357, Teamsters v. NLRB, 365 U.S. 667, 674 (1961), discussed at notes 348-49 *infra* & accompanying text: "There being no *express* ban of hiring halls in any provisions of the Act, those who add one, whether it be the Board or the courts, engage in a legislative act." (emphasis added).
[334] 29 U.S.C. § 158(b)(4)(B) (1970).
[335] 400 U.S. at 305.
[336] *Id.* at 306.
[337] *Id.* (Douglas, J., dissenting).
[338] 404 U.S. 138 (1971).

action which trespassed on the exclusive federal labor jurisdiction and held that the Board, as a federal agency, was not bound by the anti-injunction statute.[339]

The contradictions in Douglas' approach to statutory construction are clear, although a more exhaustive study might reconcile some inconsistencies. Even more clearly established is a developing mistrust of the National Labor Relations Board.

ATTITUDE TOWARDS THE LABOR BOARD

In tracing the shift in Justice Douglas' attitude toward the NLRB, one finds that his early opinions reflect respect for the Board's discretion and autonomy. This respect is illustrated, for instance, in *Machinists' Lodge 35 v. NLRB.*[340] The Board had determined that an employer committed an unfair labor practice by assisting the efforts of an ultimately successful union, the Machinists, to compete with another union, the UAW, in an organizational drive. Douglas, writing for the Court, upheld the Board's factual findings of employer involvement, saying that, in a complex situation such as the one before it, "[t]he detection and appraisal of . . . imponderables are indeed one of the essential functions of an expert administrative agency."[341] The Board had additionally determined that the wrong should be righted by compelling the employer to bargain with the UAW. Broadly embracing the Board's independent power, Justice Douglas upheld the Board's remedy:

> Where as a result of unfair labor practices a union cannot be said to represent an uncoerced majority, the

---

[339] 28 U.S.C. § 2283 (1970): "A court of the United States may not grant an injunction to stay proceedings in a State court except as *expressly* authorized by Act of Congress, or where necessary in aid of its jurisdiction, or to protect or effectuate its judgments." (emphasis added).
[340] 311 U.S. 72 (1940).
[341] *Id.* at 79.

Board has the power to take appropriate steps to the end that the effect of those practices will be dissipated. That necessarily involves an exercise of discretion on the part of the Board—discretion involving an expert judgment as to ways and means of protecting the freedom of choice guaranteed to the employees by the Act. It is for the Board, not the courts, to determine how the effect of prior unfair labor practices may be expunged.[342]

Similarly, in *NLRB v. Express Publishing Co.*[343] Justice Douglas disagreed with the Court's modification of a Board order against an employer who had refused to bargain. The Board had issued an order restraining the employer from unfair labor practices which he had not been found to commit and which were unrelated to the unfair practice proven against him. The Court ruled, however, that the Board had no authority to restrain the employer from such unproven and unrelated activities. Douglas, in a separate opinion,[344] would have let the Board's discretion as to the appropriate remedy prevail, as the order was not "patently *ultra vires*"[345] the Board.

> I think it is important to remind that we do not sit as an administrative agency with discretion to adjust the remedies accorded by the Act to what we think are ... the exigencies of specific situations, with the duty to pass on the wisdom of administrative policies. Congress has invested the Board, not us, with discretion to choose and select the remedies necessary or appropriate for the evil at hand.
>
> . . . .
>
> Whether the remedy chosen by the Board was

---

[342] *Id.* at 82.
[343] 312 U.S. 426 (1941).
[344] *Id.* at 439.
[345] *Id.* at 440 (Douglas, J., dissenting).

reasonably necessary in this case is not for us to determine.[346]

In recent years Douglas' opinions have been considerably less deferential. This is most true of the cases chiefly concerned with the definition of, or remedy for, an unfair labor practice.[347] In *Teamsters Local 357 v. NLRB*,[348] for example, Justice Douglas, writing for the Court, held that the Board could not condemn a hiring hall agreement between a union and employer as illegal per se, but rather could strike down such an agreement only upon a finding of actual discrimination against nonunion employees: "Where, as here, Congress has aimed its sanctions only at specific discriminatory practices, the Board cannot go farther and establish a broader, more pervasive regulatory legislative scheme."[349]

This attitude is further developed in his dissent in *NLRB v. Strong*.[350] The Board had required an employer, who had committed an unfair labor practice by refusing to sign a collective bargaining agreement, to sign the agreement and to make retroactive payments of fringe benefits specified in the contract. The Court, considering only the authority to direct payment of the fringe benefits, upheld the Board. Justice Douglas' dissent noted first that while ordinary back pay awards were explicitly authorized by statute,[351] the award of fringe benefits in

---

[346]*Id.* at 441, 442 (Douglas, J., dissenting).

[347]*But see* H.K. Porter Co. v. NLRB, 397 U.S. 99, 110 (1970) (Douglas J., dissenting in favor of upholding NLRB power to impose contract term about which employer had refused to negotiate).

[348] 365 U.S. 667 (1961).

[349]*Id.* at 676. Justice Clark's argument in dissent, *id.* at 685, 691, echoed Justice Douglas' earlier positions. Justice Clark argued that the Board had permissibly relied on its experience in evaluating the discriminatory effects of the hiring hall practice, and that concerning "the gravity of such a situation the Board is the best arbiter and best equipped to find a solution." *Id.* at 691.

[350] 393 U.S. 357, 362 (1969).

[351] National Labor Relations Act (Taft-Hartley Act), § 10(c), 29 U.S.C. § 160(c) (1970).

this situation was not. Douglas believed that arbitration, not the Labor Board, was the appropriate institution for determining whether such fringe benefits were to be paid as a remedy for breach of a collective bargaining agreement, and he commented on the Board's encroachment into the area of contract enforcement. "The jurisdiction of any agency or branch of government has a built-in impetus for growth and expansion. Seldom does a department restrict its powers narrowly and assume a self-denying attitude. The tendency is to construe express powers broadly. The organism grows by subtle and little-noticed extensions of authority."[352]

While Douglas' opinion in *NLRB v. Nash-Finch Co.*[353] may suggest a tendency to accord the Board greater leeway in cases involving predominantly procedural questions, his dissent in *NLRB v. Wyman-Gordon Co.*[354] is strongly to the contrary. In *Wyman-Gordon* the Labor Board had ordered an employer to furnish a list of employee names and addresses in connection with a representation election. The Board based its order on a rule laid down in a previous decision, *Excelsior Underwear, Inc.*[355] That rule, however, had not been promulgated according to the rulemaking procedures specified in the Administrative Procedure Act.[356] While Justice Douglas and a plurality of the Court were in agreement that the Board should have gone through a proper rulemaking procedure, a different plurality of the Court nevertheless upheld the order. Douglas, in an opinion highly critical of the Board's disregard for proper procedure, dissented on the ground that only rulemaking could insure responsible administrative action.[357] He would, he said, "hold the

---

[352] 393 U.S. at 364.
[353] 404 U.S. 138 (1971). For the discussion of *Nash-Finch*, see text accompanying notes 338-39 *supra*.
[354] 394 U.S. 759, 775 (1969).
[355] 156 N.L.R.B. 1236 (1966).
[356] 5 U.S.C. § 1553 (1970).
[357] 394 U.S. at 775.

agencies governed by the rule-making procedure strictly to its requirements and not allow them to play fast and loose as the National Labor Relations Board apparently likes to do."[358]

Douglas' more recent opinions also reflect a somewhat restricted view of the Court's role in the labor cases. In his *Strong*[359] dissent, after commenting on the tendencies of agencies to expand their own power, Justice Douglas continued, "Courts are no exception; and part of their tendency to find easy extensions of their authority was seen in their early contest with administrative agencies."[360] This view is manifest as well in two other dissents since 1961 in which, echoing his view in tax cases,[361] Douglas expressed the opinion that the Court should not consider the cases because "the problem presented was in the keeping of the Court of Appeals"[362] and "the courts of appeals, and not this Court, are the watchdogs of the Board."[363]

These cases and statistics suggest, then, that neither union nor employer preference has been a dominant theme in Douglas' approach to labor cases, but that in recent periods he has been concerned with limiting the expanding power of the Board. These attitudes may be undergoing a shift, however, as the individual employee becomes a common litigant in labor cases. In the recent case of *NLRB v. Boeing Co.*[364] the Court affirmed the Board's

---

[358]*Id.* at 779.

[359]For the discussion of *Strong*, see text accompanying notes 350-52 *supra*.

[360]*Id.* at 364 (Douglas, J., dissenting).

[361]*See* text accompanying notes 205, 211 *supra*.

[362]Local 761, Elec. Workers v. NLRB, 366 U.S. 667, 682 (1961) (Douglas, J., dissenting). *See also* NLRB v. J. H. Rutter-Rex Mfg. Co., 396 U.S. 258, 266 (1969) (Douglas, J., dissenting, voting to dismiss certiorari as improvidently granted). Justice Douglas thought certiorari should not have been granted in *Electrical Workers* as well, and both opinions rely, in this respect, on Universal Camera Corp. v. NLRB, 340 U.S. 474 (1951).

[363]NLRB v. J.H. Rutter-Rex Mfg. Co., 396 U.S. 258, 268 (1969) (Douglas, J., dissenting).

[364]412 U.S. 67 (1973).

abdication of any power on its part to review the reasonableness of union-imposed fines, leaving review only to state courts. Justice Douglas dissented,[365] thereby voting against the Board's position, but in favor of expanding its power to protect a union member from the union itself: "The Labor Board, which knows the nuances of this problem better than any other tribunal, is the keeper of the conscience under the Act."[366] Additionally, in *NLRB v. Marine Workers*[367] and *NLRB v. Textile Workers, Local 1029*[368] where the Board had acted to protect the rights of the individual laborer against his union, Justice Douglas wrote for the Court affirming such action. Thus, one may speculate that his previously voiced disappointment with administrative action might give way to a sympathy for the agency consistent with the agency's protection of the individual, an attitude similar to that evident in Douglas' welfare opinions.

Welfare Law

The welfare cases are particularly relevant because in many ways they represent the other side of the tax system. No changing or evolutionary trend in Douglas' attitude toward statutory construction or the administrative agency is apparent in the welfare cases, perhaps because all but one of the Court's relevant[369] welfare cases date from

---

[365]*Id.* at 79.
[366]*Id.* at 83.
[367]391 U.S. 418, 428 (1968) (relying on Labor Management Reporting and Disclosure Act, § 101(a)(4), 29 U.S.C. § 411(a)(4) (1970) to hold that the Labor Board "might consider whether a particular [union] procedure [for processing grievances against the union] was 'reasonable' and entertain [a] complaint even though those procedures had not been 'exhausted' ").
[368]409 U.S. at 213 (1972) (unfair labor practice for union to fine employees who had been union members, but had resigned during a lawful strike and returned to work).
[369]The Court has decided 20 welfare cases (not including those dealing with collection of the social security tax). One of those cases, Social Security

1968, and perhaps also because the identity of the underdog has always been clear. While the sample is small, the statistics are striking. Justice Douglas has favored the welfare recipient in 17 out of the 19 relevant cases decided (89%).[370] In those cases the Court decided in favor of the recipient 11 times (58%). Thus, Justice Douglas has dissented in favor of the recipient in 6 cases (32%), and has never dissented against him.

This voting pattern in favor of the welfare recipient mirrors Douglas' preference for the taxpayers in tax cases arising during the last two periods.[371] Unlike his action in the later tax cases, however, Douglas has frequently written opinions in welfare cases. In 19 cases before the Court, he has written 4 majority opinions and 3 concurrences in addition to his 5 dissents. He has never dissented silently or alone in a welfare case.

The Social Security Act[372] is so imprecisely drawn that a judge without further guidance than the language of the statute may often find support for whatever

---

Bd. v. Nierotko, 327 U.S. 358 (1946) (involving determination of whether back pay award granted under NLRA is to be considered as wages for purposes of credit on old age and survivorship insurance under the Social Security Act), is only tangentially relevant to our discussion, and is not listed on Table IX. (Justice Douglas did vote in favor of the employee in *Nierotko*, however.) Also omitted from Table IX are per curiam orders vacating and remanding lower court opinions without passing on the merits: Richardson v. Wright, 405 U.S. 208 (1972) (Douglas J., dissenting in favor of the recipient on the merits); Wyman v. Rothstein, 398 U.S. 275 (1970) (Douglas, J., participating in Court's holding not in favor of the recipient).

[370] In Hopkins v. Cohen, 390 U.S. 530 (1968), one of the two cases in which Justice Douglas did not vote for the welfare recipient, he held for the recipient's lawyer in a dispute over attorney's fees. In the other case, New York State Dep't of Social Servs. v. Dublino, 413 U.S. 405 (1973), the Court held that the work incentive provisions of the Social Security Act did not preempt the work rules of the New York Social Welfare Law for persons participating in AFDC programs. Justices Marshall and Brennan dissented, 413 U.S. at 423.

[371] Justice Douglas' percentage of dissents in favor of taxpayers were: Period 1 (1939-1943), 0%; Period 2 (1944-1958), 33%; Period 3 (1959-1963), 67%; Period 4 (1964-1973), 48%.

[372] 42 U.S.C. § 301 et seq. (1970).

interpretation he favors. Douglas' approach has not diminished the difficulty this presents. In his interpretation of the Social Security Act, Justice Douglas has adhered to the canon that this Act, as remedial legislation, should be liberally construed,[373] and that the Court "should enforce [these rules] in the spirit in which they were written."[374] This has led him to discount statutory language to the extent he finds it inconsistent with or less demanding than what he believes to be the statute's general purpose.

While this attitude is most apparent in Douglas' dissents[375] in favor of the recipient, it is also evident in his majority opinion in *Hopkins v. Cohen*[376] favoring the recipient's attorney. The case involved the interpretation of a provision in the Social Security Act which allows an attorney representing a claimant in a court action for social security benefits to receive a fee "not in excess of 25 percent of the total of the past-due benefits to which the claimant is entitled. . . ."[377] In the case before the Court, the lawyer had recovered benefits for the claimant as a disabled person.[378] On the basis of that recovery the Bureau of Disability Insurance sent an allowance to the claimant's family, who were entitled to recover as relatives of an eligible disabled person,[379] as well. The claimant's family had not been parties to the claimant's suit in the

---

[373] *E.g.,* Jefferson v. Hackney, 406 U.S. 535, 554 n.3 (1972) (Douglas, J., dissenting): "Finally, by giving the Social Security Act a miserly interpretation, the Court disregards the canon that remedial legislation, such as the Social Security Act, is to be interpreted liberally to effectuate its purposes." (citation omitted).
[374] Richardson v. Perales, 402 U.S. 389, 414 (1971) (Douglas, J., dissenting).
[375] *E.g.,* Jefferson v. Hackney, 406 U.S. 535, 554 (1972); Richardson v. Perales, 402 U.S. 389, 414 (1971); Dandridge v. Williams, 397 U.S. 471, 504-505 (1970).
[376] 390 U.S. 530 (1968).
[377] Social Security Act § 206(b)(1), 42 U.S.C. § 406(b)(1) (1970).
[378] On the basis of *id.* § 223, 42 U.S.C. § 423 (1970).
[379] On the basis of *id.* § 202, 42 U.S.C. § 402 (1970).

Table IX
Douglas' Positions in Welfare Cases

Citation	Case Name	Douglas' Result Favored	Type of Opinion
363 U.S. 603	Flemming v. Nestor	Recipient	Wrote dissent
390 U.S. 530	Hopkins v. Cohen	Recipient's lawyer	Wrote for Court
392 U.S. 309	King v. Smith	Recipient	Wrote concurrence
394 U.S. 618	Shapior v. Thompson	Recipient	M
397 U.S.			
254	Goldberg v. Kelly	Recipient	M
397	Rosado v. Wyman	Recipient	Wrote concurrence
471	Dandridge v. Williams	Recipient	Wrote dissent
552	Lewis v. Martin	Recipient	Wrote for Court
400 U.S. 309	Wyman v. James	Recipient	Wrote dissent
402 U.S.			
121	Calif. Dep't Human Resources v. Java	Recipient	Wrote concurrence
389	Richardson v. Perales	Recipient	Wrote dissent
403 U.S. 365	Graham v. Richardson	Recipient	M
404 U.S.			
23	Engelman v. Amos	Recipient	M
78	Richardson v. Belcher	Recipient	Wrote dissent
282	Townsend v. Swank	Recipient	M
406 U.S.			
535	Jefferson v. Hackney	Recipient	Wrote dissent
598	Carleson v. Remillard	Recipient	Wrote for Court
409 U.S. 413	Philpott v. Essex County Welfare Bd.	Recipient	Wrote for Court
413 U.S. 405	New York State Dep't of Social Serv. v. Dublino	Agency	M

district court, however, and the claimant argued that the attorney was entitled to a fee computed on the basis of the claimant's recovery alone, and not on his family's award. Writing for the Court, Justice Douglas held that the attorney's fee was to be based on the entire family "package" of disability benefits recovered, and he rejected the alternative argument as "too technical a construction of the Act which we need not adopt."[380]

In *Dandridge v. Williams*,[381] Justice Douglas dissented[382] from the Court's determination that Maryland's family maximum grant regulation was neither inconsistent with the Social Security Act, nor violative of the equal protection clause of the fourteenth amendment. Douglas interpreted the language in section 402(a)(10) of the Act (having to do with the furnishing of aid to all eligible individuals), to mean that grant maximums were inconsistent with the Act's purpose and therefore impermissible. The majority relied in part upon the fact that Congress had acknowledged the existence of maximum grant limitations when it added section 402(a)(23)[383] to the Act to provide a cost of living increase to AFDC recipients:

> [The State shall] provide that by July 1, 1969, the amounts used by the State to determine the needs of individuals will have been adjusted to reflect fully changes in living costs since such amounts were established, and any maximums that the State imposes on the amount of aid paid to families will have been proportionately adjusted. . . .

Constrained to explain away Congress' obvious recognition of the existence of family grant maximums, Douglas was forced to read words out of the Act in order to effectuate

---
[380] 390 U.S. at 534.
[381] 397 U.S. 471 (1970).
[382] *Id.* at 490.
[383] 42 U.S.C. § 602(a)(23) (1970).

what he saw to be its purpose:

> Congress was, to be sure, acknowledging the existence of maximum grant regulations. But every congressional reference to an existing practice does not automatically imply approval of that practice. The task of statutory construction requires more. It requires courts to look to the context of that reference, and to the history of relevant legislation. In the present context, the reference to maximum grants was necessary to preserve the integrity of the cost-of-living adjustment required by the bill. No further significance can legitimately be read into that reference.[384]

No well-defined, consistent attitude towards the administrative agency comes through in Justice Douglas' welfare opinions. In some cases he attached considerable weight to administrative rulings or regulations. For example, in *King v. Smith*[385] the Court found that an Alabama regulation which denied AFDC[386] benefits to a child whose mother "cohabits," in or outside the home, with a man not required by law to support those children, was inconsistent with the federal statute,[387] and thus invalid. Justice Douglas, concurring,[388] reached the Court's result on constitutional grounds. He resorted to constitutional, rather than statutory, grounds for decision, he said, only because of "insurmountable" problems of statutory construction. The problem as he saw it was that "longstanding administrative construction" approved indistinguishable state AFDC plans, and that that ad-

---

[384] 397 U.S. at 504-05 (Douglas, J., dissenting).
[385] 392 U.S. 309 (1968).
[386] Aid to families with dependent children. *See* Social Security Act, §§ 401-10, 42 U.S.C. §§ 601-10 (1970).
[387] In that it adopted a definition of the term "parent" different from that the Court read into § 406(a) of the Social Security Act, 42 U.S.C. § 606(a) (1970), and thus resulted in a failure to provide benefits to eligible children, contrary to § 402(a)(9) of the Act, 42 U.S.C. § 602(a)(9).
[388] 392 U.S. at 334.

ministrative construction was "entitled to great weight."[389] In his dissent in *Dandridge v. Williams*, however, Douglas took an apparently different approach to the significance of the agency's failure to challenge a state plan:

> HEW seldom has formally challenged the compliance of a state welfare plan with the terms of the Social Security Act.... The mere absence of such a formal challenge, whatever may be said for its constituting an affirmative determination of the compliance of a state plan with the Social Security Act, is not such a determination as is entitled to decisive weight in the judicial determination [here].[390]

In *Lewis v. Martin*,[391] a subsequent case, Justice Douglas wrote for the Court in overruling the determination of a three-judge court that an HEW regulation[392] promulgated in response to *King v. Smith* was invalid. That regulation provided that only the resources of natural parents or those stepparents with a uniformly similar legal duty of support could be considered as available for the use of a child for purposes of determining AFDC eligibility. The regulation thus contradicted and superseded California provisions[393] requiring consideration of the resources of either a nonadoptive stepfather or a "man assuming the role of spouse" to the child's mother, whether or not those resources were actually available or legally required to be available for the support of the child. Douglas said: "Nothing in this record shows that this administrative judgment does not correspond to the facts.

---

[389] *Id.* at 334-35.
[390] 397 U.S. 471, 507-08 (1970).
[391] 397 U.S. 552 (1970).
[392] 33 Fed. Reg. 11290 (1968).
[393] CALIFORNIA STATE DEP'T OF SOCIAL WELFARE, PUBLIC SOCIAL SERVICES MANUAL §§ 42-531, 42-535, 44-113.-42, 44-133.5 (1967).

We give HEW the deference due the agency charged with the administration of the Act...."[394]

Douglas' deference turned to disdain, however, in a heated dissent in *Richardson v. Perales*.[395] In that case the Court sustained the denial of relief in a disability claim hearing where the only evidence against the claimant was hearsay: medical examiners' written reports, which were orally evaluated by a medical expert who had no connection with their preparation. Douglas argued that hearsay evidence could not meet the statutory requirement of "substantial evidence"[396] in support of the administrator's determination, and criticized "[t]he use by HEW of its stable of defense doctors without submitting them to cross-examination [as] the cutting of corners—a practice in which certainly the Government should not indulge."[397]

Perhaps more significant than the details of Douglas' approach to statutory interpretation and attitude toward the administrative agency in welfare opinions is the philosophy he articulated in some of those cases. The opinions reveal a grave mistrust of the power of government to invade and oppress the lives of individuals, and a profound concern that the government's power may be used to discriminate unfairly.[398] In his *Perales* dissent, for example, Justice Douglas took the occasion to protest:

> This case is miniscule in relation to the staggering problems of the Nation. But when a grave injustice is

---

[394] 397 U.S. at 559.
[395] 402 U.S. 389, 411 (1971).
[396] Social Security Act, § 205(g), 42 U.S.C. § 405(g) (1970).
[397] 402 U.S. at 414 (Douglas, J., dissenting). *See also id.* at 413: "The use [by HEW] of circuit-riding doctors who never see or examine claimants to defeat their claims should be beneath the dignity of a great nation."
[398] On the issue of discrimination in particular, see Jefferson v. Hackney, 406 U.S. 535, 557-58 (1972) (Douglas, J., dissenting); Richardson v. Belcher, 404 U.S. 78, 84-88 (1971) (Douglas, J., dissenting). *Cf.* Carleson v. Remillard, 406 U.S. 598, 604 (1972) (Douglas, J., writing for the Court); King v. Smith, 392 U.S. 309, 335 (1968) (Douglas, J., concurring).

wreaked on an individual by the presently powerful federal bureaucracy, it is a matter of concern to everyone, for these days the average man can say: 'There but for the grace of God go I.'[399]

These concerns are strongly pronounced in Justice Douglas' dissent in *Wyman v. James,*[400] a case in which the Court upheld home visits by case workers as valid conditions of receiving AFDC assistance. Douglas' dissent centered on a discussion of the "new property"[401] and the implications of government largesse. The basic question, as he saw it, was "whether the government by force of its largesse has the power to 'buy up' rights guaranteed by the Constitution."[402] His conclusion, of course, was negative. Douglas adamantly protested against the application of a dual standard of constitutional protections:

If the regime under which Barbara James lives were enterprise capitalism as, for example, if she ran a small factory geared into the Pentagon's procurement program, she certainly would have a right to deny inspectors access to her *home* unless they came with a warrant.[403]

For Justice Douglas this dual standard paralleled that being applied in the dissimilar policing of expenditures to differently situated recipients of government largesse:

Judge Skelly Wright has stated the problem succinctly: 'Welfare has long been considered the equivalent of charity and its recipients have been subjected to all kinds of dehumanizing experiences in the government's effort to police its welfare payments.

---

[399] 402 U.S. at 413.
[400] 400 U.S. 309, 326 (1971).
[401] *See* Reich, *The New Property*, 73 YALE L. J. 733 (1964).
[402] 400 U.S. at 328 (footnote omitted).
[403] *Id.* at 331.

In fact, over half a billion dollars are expended annually for administration and policing in connection with the Aid to Families with Dependent Children program. Why such large sums are necessary for administration and policing has never been adequately explained. No such sums are spent policing the government subsidies granted to farmers, airlines, steamship companies, and junk mail dealers, to name but a few. The truth is that in this subsidy area society has simply adopted a double standard, one for aid to business and the farmer and a different one for welfare.'[404]

Such discrimination, as Douglas argued, is improperly imported into the constitutional sphere. The opinion concludes with a comment on governmental power, the power of the "lumbering" bureaucracy, to intrude into individual lives. The concern with governmental oppression of the individual manifested in these cases will be discussed further in Part III.

---

[404] *Id.* at 332-33, *quoting* Wright, *Poverty, Minorities, and Respect for Law*, 1970 DUKE L. J. 425, 437-38.

III. An Attempt at Explanation

Our effort in this part is to seek an explanation for Justice Douglas' shifting approaches in tax cases to both the Internal Revenue Code and the Service. For this it seems helpful to begin with a summary of the important trends we have already noted.

Early in Douglas' tenure he wrote frequently for the Court in federal tax cases, and usually voted to support the Government's position. His opinions were marked by attention to detail and a search for legislative intent. Later years saw an increasing tendency to vote in favor of the taxpayer, a developing antipathy towards the IRS and a failure to explain his votes with reasoned opinions.

In the labor cases we noted that Justice Douglas' percentage of opinions in favor of unions over employers has remained fairly constant throughout his years on the Court and that neither preference for union nor for employer has been a dominant theme. While we could discern no consistent mode of statutory construction, in recent periods he appears to have become disenchanted with the administration of the Labor Board.

In the welfare cases Douglas has voted with remarkable consistency in favor of the recipient. Although he has not articulated any particular philosophy as to the role of the national administrative agency, he has deferred in cases in which regulations by that agency limited the discretion of local authorities to impose restrictions on welfare eligibility or to allocate funds less generously to welfare recipients; but he has been critical in other cases where the national administration has worked to the detriment of individual welfare recipients.

In the field of corporate insider regulation Justice Douglas' positions have remained consistent, giving breadth to the statutes in light of their most general purpose and scope to the areas of agency discretion. Douglas' approach in cases involving corporate insider regulation thus stands in striking contrast to the trends observed in relation to the other statutory areas we have reviewed, a contrast perhaps explainable by the strength of Douglas' early association with the SEC, *his* agency.

The cases in other fields suggest, then, that a growing dissatisfaction with administrative agencies generally, and their expanding exercise of power, may partially explain Douglas' behavior in tax cases. While the best evidence for this speculation lies in the cases themselves, the theory finds additional support in Justice Douglas' extrajudicial writings.

Dissatisfaction with Administrative Agencies

The problem of administrative government has been a central concern in Douglas' writings,[405] but the sym-

---

[405] *See, e.g.,* W. Douglas, POINTS OF REBELLION 78-88 (1969) [hereinafter cited as POINTS OF REBELLION]; W. Douglas, WE THE JUDGES 161-91, 236-43 (1956) [hereinafter cited as WE THE JUDGES]; DEMOCRACY AND FINANCE, *supra* note 251, at 243-70; Douglas, *Legal Institutions in America* in LEGAL INSTITUTIONS TODAY AND TOMORROW 274-78 (M. Paulsen ed., 1959) [hereinafter cited as *Legal Institutions in America*]; Douglas, *Law and the American Character,* 37 CAL. STATE B. J. 753, 759-64 (1962) [hereinafter cited as *Law and the American Character*].

pathies those writings reflect have changed profoundly. Douglas came to the Court in 1939 from the Chairmanship of the SEC. He came with the faith of a New Dealer and a respect and enthusiasm for the institution of the administrative agency.[406] "Administrative government is here to stay," he said in 1938, "It is democracy's way of dealing with the over complicated social and economic problems of today."[407] At that time Douglas faced the challenge of maintaining the dedication and high standards of professionals in administrative government,[408] and yet was confident of success.[409] He later wrote proudly of his days with the SEC:

> We had an able, earnest, and dedicated group of people administering these acts. We had youth and idealism on our side. We had caught some of the vision of Franklin D. Roosevelt and the manifest destiny he represented. We were not concerned with ideas of personal gain or preferment. None in those early days would have dreamed of leaving his government post to go to work for the people we regulated. If anyone had done it, he would have been ostracized.
>
> There doubtless is much sentiment in my recollections of what we did. But as I look back and see the long-term acceptance our work has enjoyed, and view the impressive scholarly record of Commission rulings and opinions that shine through such books as Loss, *Securities Regulation* (1951) I am proud of the men and women who came to Washington, D.C., for these pioneer undertakings. I think we did much to raise the level of performance of the administrative agency in a turbulent and exciting age.[410]

---

[406] *See* DEMOCRACY AND FINANCE, *supra* note 251, at 243-67.
[407] *Id.* 246.
[408] *Id.* 247.
[409] *Id.* 255.
[410] Douglas, *Foreword*, 28 GEO. WASH. L. REV. 1, 5 (1959).

But Douglas' perception of the administrative agencies did not remain fused with the original vision. His evolving skepticism and distrust paralleled the gradual demise of the New Deal and the influx of uncommitted petty bureaucrats into positions once filled by men and women with the Roosevelt ideal.[411] Thus, in a 1962 address, Justice Douglas spoke of the institution of the "administrative agency which some call 'professional' government but which over-all deserves no such accolade."[412] In particular he found at that time a "need to bring into harness the activities of agencies that today are freewheeling, that make momentous decisions within the bureaucracy, and that need not and do not give the public any opportunity to be heard."[413] Furthermore, he said, unreviewed administrative power was subject to corruption and political pressure.[414] Similarly, in his 1956 book, *We the Judges*, Douglas said, speaking of the administrative agency, "Reforms of its practices have been numerous. Judicial surveillance over it has been close. Yet, in spite of all the reforms and all the surveillance, abuses will continue when there is absent a high standard of the public service."[415] In a more recent work, *Points of Rebellion*, Douglas expressed a disillusionment with the present state of administrative agencies that is polar to his New Deal view. One of the great tasks before America, he pleaded, "is the problem of creating some control or surveillance over key administrative agencies,"[416] that powerful bureaucracy which had been captured by the Establishment it was intended to regulate. Significant to

---

[411] *Cf. Legal Institutions in America, supra* note 405, at 278.

[412] *Law and the American Character, supra* note 405, at 759.

[413] *Id.* 762-63.

[414] *Id.* 763. A 1951 address by Justice Douglas focused on the problem of corruption in government and throughout society. Douglas, *Honesty in Government*, 4 OKLA. L. REV. 279 (1951).

[415] WE THE JUDGES, *supra* note 405, at 190-91.

[416] POINTS OF REBELLION, *supra* note 405, at 64.

this view is the perceived ubiquity of agency power. As Justice Douglas wrote in *Wyman v. James*,

> The bureaucracy of modern government is not only slow, lumbering, and oppressive; it is omnipresent It touches everyone's life at numerous points. It pries more and more into private affairs, breaking down the barriers that individuals erect to give them some insulation from the intrigues and harassments of modern life.[417]

This perception, of course, is particularly relevant to the reach of the taxing authorities, first because the tax system produces one of the most frequent and direct government-citizen contact points, and second because, as Justice Douglas has said, "The income tax ... has also given centralization [of power in the national government] a powerful push."[418]

In a very strong sense his disillusionment and his mistrust of the exercise of governmental power appear to underlie Justice Douglas' solicitude for the taxpayer at bar (big or little). Repeatedly he expressed concern that administrative procedures afford insufficient protection to defenseless persons,[419] demanding that ambiguities in the statute should not be resolved by litigation,[420] and that the Government should "turn square corners" in dealing with the taxpayer.[421] His fear of misuse of agency power

---

[417] 400 U.S. 309, 335 (1971) (Douglas, J., dissenting).

[418] WE THE JUDGES, *supra* note 405, at 42-43.

[419] *See id.* 182, 190; *Legal Institutions in America, supra* note 405, at 276; *Law and the American Character, supra* note 405, at 762-63. *See also* NLRB v. Wyman-Gordon Co., 394 U.S. 755, 759 (1969) (Douglas, J., dissenting), discussed at text accompanying notes 354-58 *supra*. *Cf.* POINTS OF REBELLION, *supra* note 405, at 79-80.

[420] *See, e.g.,* United States v. Generes, 405 U. S. 93, 113 (1972) (Douglas, J., dissenting); United States v. Skelly Oil Co., 394 U. S. 678, 687 (1969) (Douglas, J., dissenting). For discussion of *Generes* and *Skelly Oil*, see notes 197-211 *supra* & accompanying text.

[421] Commissioner v. Lester, 366 U. S. 299, 306 (1961) (Douglas, J., concurring), discussed at text accompanying notes 165-69 *supra*.

surfaces in complaints that regulations are changing the meaning of the statute.[422] Concerned with protection of privacy, Douglas also warned in *Points of Rebellion* that:

> Big Brother in the form of an increasingly powerful governnent and in an increasingly powerful private sector will pile the records high with reasons why privacy should give way to national security, to law and order, to efficiency of operations, to scientific advancement, and the like. The cause of privacy will be won or lost essentially in legislative halls and in constitutional assemblies. If it is won, this pluralistic society of ours will experience a spiritual renewal. If it is lost we will have written our own prescription for mediocrity and conformity.[423]

The same theme lies behind his dissent in the fourth period case of *United States v. Powell*,[424] in which he urged that the IRS should be powerless to subpoena certain tax records without supervision by a district court. Other cases reflect, though less directly, a similar skepticism toward the exercise of governmental power.[425]

---

[422] *See, e.g.,* United States v. Correll, 389 U. S. 299, 307 (1967) (Douglas, J., dissenting); Commissioner v. Stidger, 386 U. S. 287, 297 (1967) (Douglas, J., dissenting). For discussion of *Correll* and *Stidger*, see notes 218-34 *supra* & accompanying text. *But cf.* United States v. Generes, 405 U. S. 93, 114 (1972) (Douglas, J., dissenting), discussed at text accompanying notes 206-11 *supra,* arguing that ambiguities in the Code should be clarified, inter alia, through the promulgation of regulations; United States v. Skelly Oil Co., 394 U. S. 678, 691 n.4 (1969) (Douglas, J., dissenting).

[423] POINTS OF REBELLION, *supra* note 405, at 29. *See also* Douglas, *Foreword: Project, The Computerization of Government Files: What Impact on the Individual?*, 15 U.C.L.A. L. REV. 1371, 1374 (1968). This attitude of course extends over into other fields as well. *See, e.g.,* Public Utilities Comm'n v. Pollack, 343 U.S. 451, 467 (1952) (Douglas, J., dissenting) (protesting Court's upholding of constitutionality of Commission's requirement that streetcars carry radio receivers fixed tuned to a particular station).

[424] 379 U. S. 48, 59 (1964), discussed at notes 213-17 *supra* & accompanying text.

[425] *Compare, e.g., Law and the American Character, supra* note 405, *with*

Thus, Justice Douglas' antipathy towards IRS is consistent with a general distrust of government and those who govern. In a 1951 address,[426] he warned of growing corruption at all levels of state and federal government. "How far its rot has extended no one knows. But it is time America made a close inquiry into these doings."[427] In the same year Justice Douglas dissented in *United States v. Wunderlich*,[428] protesting the Court's failure to review closely the decision of a government agent given authority for resolving disputes over a government dam contract:

> Law has reached its finest moments when it has freed man from the unlimited discretion of some ruler, some civil or military official, some bureaucrat. Where discretion is absolute, man has always suffered. At times it has been his property that has been invaded; at times, his privacy; at times, his liberty of movement; at times, his freedom of thought; at times, his life. Absolute discretion is a ruthless master. It is more destructive of freedom than any of man's other inventions.[429]

At least to some extent Douglas may see his role in tax cases as one of checking the expansion of government power and its concurrent abuse of discretion, in order to protect the rights of citizens,[430] even though he has never explained why the IRS in particular poses this threat.

Arrowsmith v. Commissioner, 344 U.S. 6, 9 (1952) (Douglas, J., dissenting), discussed at text accompanying notes 82-86 *supra*; Commissioner v. Harmon, 323 U.S. 44, 49 (1944) (Douglas, J., dissenting), discussed at notes 69-75 *supra* & accompanying text. *Cf.* Wyman v. James, 400 U.S. 309, 326 (1971) (Douglas, J., dissenting), discussed at notes 400-04 *supra* & accompanying text.

[426] W. Douglas, *Honesty in Government*, 4 OKLA. L. REV. 279 (1951).
[427] *Id.*
[428] 342 U.S. 98 (1951).
[429] *Id.* at 101 (Douglas, J., dissenting).
[430] *See* Wyman v. James, 400 U.S. 309, 335 (1971) (Douglas, J., dissenting).

Antipathy to the Internal Revenue Code

In *We the Judges*, Justice Douglas expounded the conventional wisdom as to judicial construction of statutes: "Some words of a statute may be words of art, having a definite meaning. Others may take their meaning from their setting in a statute and be defined only in light of the purpose of the legislature and the objective sought to be reached."[431] To the same effect, he wrote in 1959:

> A judge worthy of the tradition does not draw from the well of his prejudices in construing statutory words. . . . The problem is to stick with the legislative scheme and determine which construction is most consonant with it. . . .
>
> What may be the clear meaning of words to some creates ambiguities for others. The truth is that while we start with the words of the act, that is the beginning, not the end of the search. For words are inexact tools to say the least.
>
> . . . [T]he recent tendency in the federal system has been to ransack the entire legislative history for what light can be thrown on the problem of interpretation. More and more does the search for the meaning of words take one through the morass of legislative history, looking for help from any competent source.[432]

But these passages fail entirely to explain Douglas' own conduct in the later tax cases. In early cases, such as *Maguire v. Commissioner*[433] and *Clifford*,[434] he did seem to look for the purposes underlying the statutes. And in

---

[431] WE THE JUDGES, *supra* note 405, at 179.

[432] *Legal Institutions in America, supra* note 405, at 289-90.

[433] 313 U.S. 1, 5 (1941), discussed at text accompanying notes 25-28 *supra*.

[434] For discussion of *Clifford*, see notes 29-35 *supra* & accompanying text.

some cases this was entirely consistent with taking precise statutory language at face value.[435] But in recent cases, such as *Correll*,[436] he looked rather simplistically to the words of the statute alone, refusing to probe for legislative purpose. Similarly, in the early case of *United States v. Stewart*,[437] Justice Douglas considered exhaustively the legislative history of the statutory language, while in the fourth period *Davis*[438] case, in which the majority's analysis rested on legislative history contrasting the 1939 and 1954 versions of the Code, Douglas relied on the authority of 1939 Code cases, ignoring the pressing thrusts of legislative history. Douglas has not adhered to the doctrines of statutory construction suggested in his own writing, and his votes in tax cases in the recent periods seem more closely tied to his own preferences than to a reasoned elaboration of congressional design.

The thread connecting most of his later tax decisions, especially those of the 1960's, may be a contempt for the Internal Revenue Code and the burdens which he believes it unfairly imposes on those not able to lobby successfully for their special preference. In Justice Douglas' 1961 review of Louis Eisenstein's provocative book, *The Ideologies of Taxation*,[439] he lauded the author's effort to expose some of the tax system's inequities. According to Douglas: "Our tax system was not designed by noble men

---

[435] *See, e.g.,* Virginian Hotel Corp. v. Helvering, 319 U.S. 523 (1943), discussed at text accompanying notes 58-64 *supra*; Scaife Co. v. Commissioner, 314 U.S. 459 (1941), discussed at notes 19-24 *supra* & accompanying text; J.E. Riley Inv. Co. v. Commissioner, 311 U.S. 55 (1940), discussed at notes 14-18 *supra* & accompanying text. *Cf.* Republic Steel Corp. v. NLRB, 311 U.S. 7 (1940), discussed at notes 318-20 *supra*.

[436] For discussion of *Correll*, see text accompanying notes 227-34 *supra*.

[437] 311 U.S. 60 (1940), discussed at text accompanying notes 47-57 *supra*.

[438] For discussion of *Davis*, see notes 236-41 *supra* & accompanying text.

[439] L. Eisenstein, THE IDEOLOGIES OF TAXATION (1961),*reviewed*, Douglas, N.Y. Herald Tribune, Sept. 24, 1961. § 6 (Books), at 13, col. 1.

only to be subverted by base people. It represents a series of victories by special interest groups, each motivated by selfish ends."[440] Douglas touched approvingly on several of the Eisenstein exposures, dwelling particularly on the various "incentives" for business and investment. "Should not artists, poets, and authors need incentives as well as businessmen?"[441] He spoke to the fallacy behind the wildcat driller rationale for percentage depletion, since it no longer takes the major oil companies nine holes to strike oil in one. And he opted for reform "unless one thinks that repeal of percentage depletion would make us, as a people, appear ungrateful for all the oil companies have done for us."[442] In the area of capital gains, Justice Douglas was outraged by the subtle classifications of income-producing activity:

> Inventors are taxed on the basis of capital gains, while authors are taxed on the basis of ordinary income. Who but an author would think the two were birds of a feather? It also seems obvious that profits on the sale of pigs unbred are plainly ordinary income unlike profits on the sale of pigs bred, which are taxed as capital gains. Pigs and turkeys are alike, are they not? Pigs and chickens are unlike? The ways of equity are mysterious; but plainly all are equal "whom the law has elected to equalize" as Edmund Cahn once said.[443]

The review concluded in a spirit of radical reform, as Douglas united his conscience with Eisenstein's. Taxation, he said, "is the heart of the political process. The few have mainly succeeded in being protected from the many. The task ahead is largely making sure that the many are protected from the few."[444] Specific references to

---
[440] *Id.*
[441] *Id.*
[442] *Id.*
[443] *Id.*
[444] *Id.*

Eisenstein surface in two of Justice Douglas' dissenting opinions, *Stidger*[445] and *Skelly Oil,*[446] and the spirit of the Eisenstein review echoes in still other opinions[447] and writings. In *Points of Rebellion*, for example, Douglas criticized the unequal treatment resulting from the capital gains preference, and he contrasted the tax system with the welfare system:

> I believe it was Charles Adams who described our upside down welfare state as 'socialism for the rich, free enterprise for the poor.' The great welfare scandal of the age concerns the dole we give rich people. Percentage depletion for oil interests is, of course, the most notorious. But there are others. Any tax deduction is in reality a 'tax expenditure,' for it means that on the average the Treasury pays 52 percent of the deduction. When we get deeply into the subject we learn that the cost of public housing for the poorest twenty percent of the people is picayune compared to federal subsidy of the housing costs of the wealthiest twenty percent. Thus for 1962, Alvin Schoor in *Explorations in Social Policy*, computed that, while we spent 870 million dollars on housing for the poor, the tax deductions for the top twenty percent amounted to 1.7 billion dollars.[448]

It is not surprising, then, that in cases involving capital gains and depletion—two areas singled out for particular criticism in these extrajudicial writings—Justice Douglas has generally voted against the taxpayer.[449]

---

[445] 386 U.S. 287, 298 n.2 (1967). For discussion of *Stidger*, see notes 218-26 *supra* & accompanying text.

[446] 394 U.S. 678, 687 (1969). For discussion of *Skelly Oil*, see notes 197-205 *supra* & accompanying text.

[447] *See, e.g.,* Rudolph v. United States, 370 U.S. 269, 278 (1962) (Douglas, J., dissenting), discussed at notes 170-86 *supra* & accompanying text.

[448] POINTS OF REBELLION, *supra* note 405, at 68-69.

[449] *See* notes 243, 246 *supra* & accompanying text.

Exposure of the Code's inequities through a popular book like Eisenstein's may be one step toward reforming the tax system, but Douglas' reaction to the Tax Code has not been limited to extrajudicial disapproval of the statute's intentional preferences, or to rejection of taxpayer claims for capital gains or depletion allowance benefits. He may feel that Government victories against taxpayers, even big and rich taxpayers, help preserve an undeserving and evil structure. Or so one can speculate when confronted with his enigmatic behavior. His attitude toward the Code seems to have led to a refusal, as a Justice, to support the tax system created by Congress. Thus he asserted in *Skelly Oil* [450] and *Generes* [451] that the Court should avoid tax cases virtually altogether, leaving the burden on the lower courts and Congress. Douglas' own failure to reason on the merits of cases before the Court, and indeed his tendency to dissent without any opinion at all seem to reflect the same attitude of eschewal. [452] Significantly, both in the cases in which he wrote dissents suggesting the Court should not review and in those cases where he dissented without opinion, Justice Douglas' result would favor the taxpayer. [453]

Furthermore, Douglas has attempted to blunt the effect of the Code's intended preferences by an expansive interpretation of deductions and exclusions. Often when he has written, as in *Stidger*, [454] he has seemed to justify

---

[450] For discussion of *Skelly Oil*, see notes 197-205 *supra* & accompanying text.

[451] For discussion of *Generes*, see text accompanying notes 206-11 *supra*.

[452] In *Generes* Justice Douglas said that he would have voted to dismiss the writ of certiorari as improvidently granted, were he not constrained by the necessary implication of the "rule of four." 405 U.S. at 115-16 (Douglas, J., dissenting).

[453] *See* text accompanying notes 133-34, 138 *supra*.

[454] *See, e.g.,* 386 U.S. at 298 (Douglas, J., dissenting):
While equity is seldom an ingredient of the tax laws, while they are indeed inherently discriminatory in many ways, reflecting perquisites obtained by pressure groups, we need not increase their harshness by

AN EXPLANATION

his vote for the taxpayer on a premise, not inferable from the facts of the case, that only a victory for the litigant taxpayer could equalize that taxpayer and others with the pressure groups which have obtained a congressionally mandated preference.[455]

A populist philosophy such as that expressed in *Points of Rebellion* might have led another judge to the injudicious support of all revenue protecting efforts of the Government, at least when the cases involve rich corporate taxpayers. Yet taxpayers like the Skelly Oil Company are the beneficiaries of Justice Douglas' tax votes despite his cry for support of the public against the special interest groups. The result of Douglas' position in *Skelly Oil* would have been to expand the special dispensations allowed to oil companies to which he so strongly objected in his alliance with Eisenstein. Indeed, since usually only the taxpayer with a substantial amount at stake wends his way through litigation up to the Supreme Court, most of Douglas' dissents work to the immediate benefit of the affluent. If Justice Douglas' bent for the welfare recipient is a manifestation of his social philosophy, that philosophy gives way in his handling of tax cases.

---

giving simple words unusual or strained meanings—unless of course Congress has plainly made an arbitrary choice.
For discussion of *Stidger*, see notes 218-26 *supra* & accompanying text.

[455]*Cf.* United States v. Gilmore, 372 U.S. 39, 52 (1963) (Douglas, J., dissenting); United States v. Kaiser, 363 U.S. 299, 326 (1960) (Douglas, J., concurring); Commissioner v. Duberstein, 363 U.S. 278, 293 (1960) (Douglas, J., dissenting), in which Justice Douglas supported a "broader" interpretation of tax benefits. For discussion of these cases, see text accompanying notes 149-64 *supra*. *Cf.* Rudolph v. United States, 370 U.S. 269, 282 (1962) (Douglas, J., dissenting), discussed at notes 170-86 *supra* & accompanying text.

IV. Conclusion

We have seized on filmy threads, reaching far afield from taxation, in our effort to understand Justice Douglas' puzzling record in tax cases. At best, our theories explaining his behavior are speculative, made the more difficult because Douglas has so often refused to reason or explain as he recorded his vote. But wholly apart from his motive, it is the result and the significance of his disturbing performance as a Justice in the tax court of last resort that requires appraisal.

In his rather caustic review of Justice Douglas' *The Anatomy of Liberty*[456] and *Freedom of the Mind*,[457] the political scientist Yosal Rogat observed: "[I]t is clear that Douglas rejects the austerity and detachment traditionally imposed upon a judge. Indeed, he has come to think of himself as no mere judge, but a moralist, a political visionary, a universal philosopher."[458] Rogat, while dealing chiefly with Douglas' extrajudicial writings, noted the same attitude in Justice Douglas' judicial opinions:

---

[456] (1963).
[457] (1964).
[458] Rogat, Book Review, N.Y. Rev. Books, Oct. 22, 1964, at 5.

"He seems to think that Supreme Court Justices should answer legal questions by *directly* applying their beliefs about the overall needs of the country, or even about the world."[459] Further criticizing his expository writing, Rogat accused Douglas of adopting a simplistic view of both the universe and the Constitution.

> [H]e reduces the most complex political and legal difficulties to a few abstract moral principles, and the sharpest antagonisms to a flabby and homogeneous togetherness....
>
> ... [A] case does not present a tangle of competing principles, but a single transcendent principle—for instance, free speech or religious freedom—which need only be identified for the solution to be plain. In this way, he avoids the task, so basic to legal analysis, of reconciling competing principles. Instead, he substitutes simple labels and lines: 'the abuse of speech can be punished but the right itself cannot be.' Unfortunately, few cases are so simple.[460]

As Rogat demonstrated, Douglas' expression of every concept in universal terms leads inevitably to contradictions.[461] Similar conflicts, reflecting Douglas'

---

[459] *Id.* 6. *See also id.* n.*.
[460] *Id.* 5-6.
[461] *Compare, e.g.,* Poulos v. New Hampshire, 345 U.S. 395, 425 (1953) (Douglas, J., dissenting) ("[E]ven a reasonable regulation of the right to free speech is not compatible with the First Amendment.") *with* Dennis v. United States, 341 U.S. 494, 585 (1951) (Douglas, J., dissenting) ("There comes a time when even speech loses its constitutional immunity."). *But cf.* Casper, *The Liberal Faith: Some Observations on the Legal Philosophy of Mr. Justice William O. Douglas,* 22 FED. B.J. 179, 180 (1962) (attempting to reconcile the statements). *Compare* Zorach v. Clauson, 343 U.S. 306, 313 (1952) (Douglas, J.) ("We are a religious people whose institutions presuppose a Supreme Being.") *with* United States v. Ballard, 322 U.S. 78, 87 (1944) (Douglas, J.) ("Man's relation to his God was made no concern of the state.") *But cf.* Louisell, *The Man and the Mountain: Douglas on Religious Freedom,* 73 YALE L.J. 975, 982 (1964) (suggesting that another sentence in the same paragraph of the *Ballard* quotation foreshadowed the *Zorach* quotation.

changing attitude toward the taxpayer, are manifest in his tax decisions. For example, holding in favor of the government in *Clifford*[462] Justice Douglas proclaimed for the Court in 1940 that: "Technical considerations, niceties of the law of trusts or conveyances, or the legal paraphernalia which inventive genius may construct as a refuse from surtaxes should not obscure the basic issue."[463] Thus he read the statutory term "income" to have a sweep that ultimately required legislation to contain.[464] But in 1960, in *Knetsch*,[465] Justice Douglas refused to accept the Court's holding that because the uneconomic "loan" transaction in question was entered only for the purpose of avoiding taxes, the taxpayer should not escape taxation:

> Tax avoidance is a dominating motive behind scores of transactions. It is plainly present here. . . . The remedy is legislative. Evils or abuses can be particularized by Congress. . . . Since these transactions were real and legitimate in the insurance world and were consummated within the limits allowed by insurance policies, I would recognize them tax-wise.[466]

More significant than merely highlighting contradictions among cases, however, Douglas' undiscriminating approach obscures conflicting factors within a given case, so that he fails to come to grips with their details and significance, and rarely clarifies the actual

---

[462] For discussion of *Clifford*, see notes 29-35 *supra* & accompanying text.
[463] 309 U.S. at 334.
[464] *See* INT. REV. CODE OF 1954, §§ 673-75. *But cf.* B. BITTKER & L. STONE, FEDERAL INCOME, ESTATE AND GIFT TAXATION 390 (4th ed. 1972).
[465] For discussion of *Knetsch*, see notes 136-48 *supra* & accompanying text.
[466] 364 U.S. at 371 (Douglas, J., dissenting).

determinants of his votes.[467] Thus Justice Douglas did not recognize the conflict presented by *Clifford* when he wrote his *Knetsch* dissent. Similarly, in *Generes*[468] Justice Douglas dissented:

> I protest now what I have repeatedly protested, and that is the use of this Court to iron out ambiguities in the Regulations or in the Act, where the responsible remedy is either a recasting of the Regulations by Treasury or presentation of the problem to the Joint Committee on Internal Revenue Taxation which is a standing committee of the Congress that regularly rewrites the Act and is much abler than are we to forecast revenue needs and spot loopholes where abuses thrive.[469]

Yet while he referred in *Generes* to similar views he had expressed in his opinions in *Skelly Oil,*[470] *Lester*[471] and *Knetsch*, he ignored the active and farreaching role he had forged for the Court in *Clifford*. And he ignored, too, that his dissents were but dissents, thus remaining unforgiving and unreformed, unwilling to accept the Court's rejection of his now more limited view of the Court's role, long after that rejection had been made clear.[472] Similar failures to

---

[467] We must take issue with the evaluation by Rodell, *Justice Douglas: An Anniversary Fragment for a Friend*, 26 U. CHI. L. REV. 2, 4 (1958), referring specifically to Justice Douglas' opinions in such areas as tax, labor, patents and economics: "And the quality of his opinions, backed by his technical expertise and inspired by his concern for FDR's 'common man,' has been uniformly high."

[468] For discussion of *Generes*, see text accompanying notes 206-11 *supra*.

[469] 405 U.S. at 114-15 (Douglas, J., dissenting) (footnote omitted).

[470] For discussion of *Skelly Oil*, see notes 197-205 *supra* & accompanying text.

[471] For discussion of *Lester*, see text accompanying notes 165-69 *supra*.

[472] In this connection it is interesting to note Justice Douglas' treatment of United States v. Lewis, 340 U.S. 590 (1951), in Arrowsmith v. Commissioner, 344 U.S. 6, 9 (1952) (Douglas, J., dissenting), discussed at text accompanying notes 82-84 *supra*, and his treatment of Poe v. Seaborn, 282

attend to the detail required by respectable legal process punctuate Douglas' tax opinions throughout the last two periods. The prime example of course is the *Rudolph* dissent,[473] in which Justice Douglas cited a regulation limited to the withholding tax for the proposition that the award of an expense free trip to a salesmen's convention was exempted from the income tax altogether. And certainly the suggestion is simply unacceptable that the expense of the wives' attendance should be deductible because their presence was necessary in order to prevent the convention from degenerating into a stag party. Only an overwhelming orientation to result seems to explain such an opinion.[474] Professor Rogat's comments on Justice Douglas' expository writing seem applicable here as well:

> [H]ow can such a man, trained in the law, with its scruples and its insistence on detail, become so careless? The answer lies, apparently, in indifference to the texture of legal analysis, which arises from an exclusively political conception of the judicial role.[475]

U.S. 101 (1930), in Commissioner v. Harmon, 323 U.S. 44, 49 (1944) (Douglas, J., dissenting), discussed at notes 69-75 *supra* & accompanying text. *Compare* Lesnick, *Preemption Reconsidered: The Apparent Reaffirmation of Garmon*, 72 COLUM. L. REV. 469, 484 (1972), in which Professor Lesnick emphasizes Justice Harlan's commitment to the law laid down in an earlier decision of the Court although he had dissented in the earlier case.

[473] For discussion of *Rudolph*, see notes 170-86 *supra* & accompanying text.

[474] If one wonders whether to pin the blame on an inartful research job by Justice Douglas' law clerk, it is interesting to note the comments of William Cohen, Justice Douglas' law clerk in an earlier period, in his article *Justice Douglas: A Law Clerk's View*, 26 U. CHI. L. REV. 6, 7 (1958):

> Nor is there a cavalier disregard for detail. Particularly, each statement of fact must be checked carefully against the record in the case. Discussion of background state law must be scrupulously accurate. His law clerk soon learns that the one failing that can never be excused is the imprecise and inaccurate utilization of legal material.

[475] Rogat, *supra* note 458, at 6. He noted additionally that,

> [t]o a lesser extent, the same kind of carelessness characterizes Douglas'

In *Commissioner v. Estate of Noel*,[476] the Court, in a short, direct and clear-cut opinion, reversed the court of appeals and held that the proceeds of a flight insurance policy were includable, as life insurance proceeds, in a decedent's gross estate for estate tax purposes.[477] There were two possible bases for taxpayer victory in *Noel*. One, adopted by the court of appeals, but convincingly rejected in the Supreme Court's opinion, distinguished the decedent's accident insurance from "life insurance" includable according to the statute. The other, rejected by the Tax Court[478] and the court of appeals[479] as well as the Supreme Court, would have required a finding that the decedent had retained no incidents of ownership in the insurance policy. Justice Douglas alone dissented, and dissented without explanation, without a word. He may have thought the reasons for his dissent were obvious. They are not to us. Such a response to the case and judgment fails to square with Justice Douglas' duties to the Court, to the parties before him, and to all who look for understanding to Supreme Court opinions, whether majority, concurring or dissenting. And certainly the carelessness of his opinions when he does write casts great doubt on whether a reasoned basis in law underlies his silent dissents.

In a 1949 speech, Douglas addressed the importance of explained decisions, and compared the Supreme Court of 1886 with that of 1941: "[W]hatever the view on the merits all will agree, I think, that the recent Court was more faithful to the democratic tradition. It wrote in

---

work on the court. True, many of his decisions have been courageous and admirable. But at issue is the texture of legal reasoning; not the similarities in *what* Douglas and Mr. Justice Black decide, but the difference in *how* they decide.

Id. n.*.

[476] 380 U.S. 678 (1965).
[477] *See* INT. REV. CODE OF 1954, § 2042(z).
[478] 39 T.C. 466 (1962).
[479] 332 F.2d 950 (3d Cir. 1964).

words that all could understand why it did what it did. That is vital to the integrity of the judicial process." [480] Although in that passage he was discussing majority opinions of the Court, Douglas recognized that the same standards must be met by dissenting opinions as well. In a 1948 speech defending the dissenting opinion, Justice Douglas embraced the view of Chief Justice Hughes:

> A dissent in a court of last resort is an appeal to the brooding spirit of the law, to the intelligence of a future day, when a later decision may possibly correct the error into which the dissenting judge believes the court to have been betrayed. [481]

Eight years later in *We the Judges* Douglas described the Court as "one of the great cohesive forces in America" and lauded the "respect and reverence" the people of this nation have for the Court "born of decades of experience." [482] Although he is a person who appreciates the importance of reasoned opinions, as a Justice he has been repeatedly unwilling to write a reasoned basis for his judicial vote in tax cases. Such a Justice does not enforce the cohesion nor can he long attract the respect to the Court which he says he values so highly. [483]

---

[480] Douglas, *Stare Decisis*, 49 COLUM. L. REV. 735, 739 (1949).
[481] Douglas, *The Dissenting Opinion*, 8 LAWYERS GUILD REV. 467, 469 (1948).
[482] WE THE JUDGES, *supra* note 405, at 82.
[483] Nor have Justice Douglas' dissents lived up to the role of the dissent outlined by Chief Justice Vinson in 1949, who added three more limited points to Chief Justice Hughes' dictum:
  The dissenting opinion itself is of value in many different respects. For example, an opinion circulated to the Court as a dissent sometimes has so much in logic, reason, and authority to support it that it becomes the opinion of the Court....
  In the second place, the dissent gives assurance to counsel and to the public that the decision was reached only after much discussion, thought, and research—that it received full and complete consideration before being handed down.

The conception of the judiciary which Douglas expresses in *We the Judges* is an undisputably noble one:

> It can and should, in the critical crises that affect the reputations and fortunes of men, be alert to create if necessary, new safeguards for the liberty of the citizen. The judiciary sits in a quiet and dignified place, one that is far removed from the tumult and passion of crowds.[484]

But Justice Douglas does not seem to have detached himself from that tumult and passion. If impatience with the long, tortuous road to total legislative reform of the tax code and an inequity-free statute lies behind Douglas' action in tax cases, that is unfortunate indeed. One need not favor a negative income tax system to understand that in many respects welfare is but one side of the federal pulley, with tax on the other. Respect for the Court's decisions in welfare cases, like the money for the welfare recipients, depends on the Court's willingness to enforce the tax statute as it is, in accordance with congressional purpose, with the Court seeking it out diligently and honestly. We have not the luxury of time or resources to apply the tax statute to none until it applies to all, even if this were our preference.

Taxation is too important, the Court's role too fundamental, and Justice Douglas too capable for him to continue refusing to judge in tax cases. We trust that in his remaining years on the Court this Justice, whose tenure exceeds all others' and whose vision of a free America in a system of law has often provided hope and guidance, will judge tax cases as he has stated judges should judge, and that he will reason and will share his reasoning with us.

In the third place, a dissent may have far-reaching influence in bringing to public attention the ramifications of the Court's opinion and by sounding a warning note against further extension of legal doctrine, or the dissenter's conviction that existing doctrine has been unduly limited.
Work of the Federal Courts, 69 U.S. v, (1949).

[484] WE THE JUDGES, *supra* note 405, at 443.

Afterword

Our study did not include cases decided after the Term that ended in June, 1973. In May and June, 1974, however, the Court decided four tax cases, three of them for the government. Justice Douglas wrote the opinion for the Court in the one decided (unanimously) for the taxpayer, *Snow v. Commissioner*,[485] only the second tax opinion he has written for the Court since 1958.[486] He was with the unanimous Court that held for the government in *Commissioner v. National Alfalfa Dehydrating Co.*[487] In *Central Tablet Manufacturing Co. v. United States*,[488] he joined with Justices Brennan and Powell in a dissenting opinion written by Justice White in favor of the taxpayer. In the final tax decision of the Term ended July, 1974, handed down after the publication of our study in the University of Pennsylvania Law Review, Justice Douglas, dissenting alone, wrote an opinion for the taxpayer in a case involving depreciation of public utility assets, *Com-*

---

[485] 416 U.S. 500 (1974).
[486] See note 134 *supra*, and accompanying text.
[487] 417 U.S. 134 (1974).
[488] 417 U.S. 673 (1974).

missioner v. Idaho Power Co.[489] In that opinion he stated his *suspicion* that if the factual bases of the parties' positions had been reversed, the principle on which the Commissioner relied would have yielded to his eagerness to maximize revenues. He then added that the statement of his suspicion was "not to impugn the integrity of IRS. It is only an illustration of the capricious character of how law is construed to get from the taxpayer the greatest possible return that is permissible under the law."[490]

---

[489] 418 U.S. 1 (1974). See note 210 *supra*.
[490] Id. at 21.

Appendix

TABLE I
TAX CASES DECIDED BY SUPREME COURT, 1939-1973

Volume U.S. Reports	Number of Cases	Won by Taxpayer	Douglas for Taxpayer
Period 1 (1939-1943)			
307	1	0	0
308	9	3	3
309	9	2	2
310	4	1	1
311	12	4	3
312	11	2	1
313	9	0	0
314	4	1	1
315	9	2	2
316	7	3	1
317	5	½	0
318	7	4	2
319	4	0	0
Totals	91	22½ (25%)	16 (18%)
Period 2, First Part (1943-1952)			
320	7	2	3
321	6	1	3
322	2	0	0
323	7	4	6
324	11	3	4
325	5	1	3
326	10	3	3
327	4	1	1 (of 3)
328	1	1	0
329	1	0	0
330	1	1	1
331	4	0	2
332	2	0	2
333	2	0	1
334	0	0	0
335	3	0	1
336	4	0	1
337	2	0	0 (of 1)
338	6	1	0 (of 0)
339	2	2	1 (of 1)
340	3	1	2
341	0	0	0
342	0	0	0
343	3	1	0 (of 2)
Totals	86	22 (26%)	34 (of 76) (45%)

TABLE I *(Continued)*

Volume U.S. Reports	Number of Cases	Won by Taxpayer	Douglas for Taxpayer
Period 2, Second Part (1952-1959)			
344	2	1	1
345	4	0	3
346	1	0	1
347	0	0	0
348	4	0	3
349	2	1	1
350	5	2	2
351	1	0	0
352	3	0	0
353	3	1	2
354	2	1	2
355	0	0	0
356	5	2	2
357	4	2	2
358	2	0	1
359	2	0	0
Totals	40	10 (25%)	20 (50%)
Totals for combined period 2	126	32 (25%)	54 (of 116) (47%)
Period 3 (1959-1964)			
360	1	0	1
361	2	1	2
362	1	0	0
363	4	1	2 (of 3)
364	6	0	5
365	1	0	1
366	2	2	2
367	2	0	1
368	1	0	0
369	2	1	2
370	2	0	1
371	1	0	0
372	3	0	3
373	2	0	1
374	1	0	1
375	3	1	1 (of 2)
376	1	0	1
Totals	35	6 (17%)	24 (of 33) (73%)

APPENDIX

TABLE I *(Continued)*

Volume U.S. Reports	Number of Cases	Won by Taxpayer	Douglas for Taxpayer
Period 4 (1964-1973)			
377	0	0	0
378	0	0	0
379	0	0	0
380	3	2	3
381	4	0	0
382	0	0	0
383	4	3	3
384	1	0	0
385	0	0	0
386	1	0	1
387	2	1	2
388	0	0	0
389	1	0	1
390	1	0	0
391	1	0	0
392	0	0	0
393	1	0	½
394	2	0	2
395	1	0	1
396	0	0	0
397	3	0	1
398	1	1	1
399	0	0	0
400	1	0	0
401	0	0	0
402	0	0	0
403	2	0	1
404	0	0	0
405	3	1	2
406	0	0	0
407	0	0	0
408	1	1	1
409	0	0	0
410	2	0	1
411	1	1	1
412	1	0	1
413	1	0	0
Totals	38	10 (26%)	22½ (59%)
Totals for 1939-1973	290	70½ (24%)	116½ (of 278) (41%)

Table II
Cases in Which Douglas Differed with the Court

Period	Number of Cases in which Douglas Participated	Number Douglas in Minority	Percentage in Minority	Number Douglas Alone	Percentage Alone
		All cases			
1	91	6½	7%	0	0%
2 (First Part)	76	19	25%	6	8%
2 (Second Part)	40	14	35%	5	12%
3	33	18	54%	9	27%
4	38	18½	35%	6	16%
Totals	278	71	26%	26	9%
		Won by Taxpayer			
1	22½	6½	29%	0	0%
2 (First Part)	19	2	10%	1	5%
2 (Second Part)	10	2	20%	1	10%
3	6	0	0%	0	0%
4	10	0	0%	0	0%
Totals	67½	10½	16%	2	3%
		Won by Government			
1	68½	0	0%	0	0%
2 (First Part)	57	17	30%	5	9%
2 Second Part)	30	12	40%	4	13%
3	27	18	67%	9	33%
4	28	13½	48%	6	21%
Totals	210½	60½	29%	24	11%

TABLE III
How Douglas Made his Dissenting Views Known

Period	Number of Cases in which Douglas Participated	Number Douglas in Minority	Number Wrote Dissent[1]	Number Dissent Without Opinion	Percentage Dissent Without Opinion
		All cases			
1	91	6½	1	1	1%
2 (First Part)	76	19	5	7	9%
2 (Second Part)	40	14	3	8	20%
3	33	18	8	7	21%
4	38	13½	10	2	5%
Totals	278	71	27	25	9%
		Won by Taxpayer			
1	22½	6½	1	1	4%
2 (First Part)	19	2	0	2	10%
2 (Second Part)	10	2	0	2	20%
3	6	0	0	0	0%
4	10	0	0	0	0%
Totals	67½	10½	1	5	7%
		Won by Government			
1	68½	0	0	0	0%
2 (First Part)	57	17	5	5	9%
2 Second Part)	30	12	3	6	20%
3	27	18	8	7	26%
4	28	13½	10	2	7%
Totals	210½	60½	26	20	10%

[1] Where Justice Douglas is listed as having written no opinion, but is not listed as dissenting without opinion, he joined the opinion of another justice.

TABLE IV
SOLITARY DISSENTS IN TAX CASES

United States Reports		Case	Justice	Losing Party[2]
Vol.	Page			
307	277	Woodrough	Butler	T
309	149	Fitch	McReynolds	T
310	69	Fuller	Reed	G
310	381	Sunshine Anthracite	McReynolds	T
311	60	Stewart	Roberts	T
311	504	Hammel	Roberts	T
318	176	Smith	Roberts	T
318	184	Robinette	Roberts	T
324	177	Smith	Roberts	T
324	303	Wemyss	Roberts	T
324	542	Wheeler	Roberts	T
325	293	Angelus Milling	Douglas	T
326	465	Flowers	Rutledge	T
326	480	Estate of Holmes	Douglas	T
326	521	Talbot Mills	Rutledge	T
326	599	Kirby Petroleum	Douglas	G
327	404	Wilcox	Burton	G
332	524	Liberty Glass	Douglas	T
332	535	Noble	Douglas	T
337	733	Culbertson	Jackson	T
339	583	Brown Shoe	Black	G
339	619	Korell	Black	G
340	590	Lewis	Douglas	T
343	711	Robertson	Jackson	T
345	278	Healy	Douglas	T
348	426	Glenshaw Glass	Douglas	T
350	308	Southwest Exploration	Douglas	T
352	82	Putnam	Harlan	T
353	180	Automobile Club of Michigan	Harlan	T (1 issue)
353	380	Libson Shops	Douglas	T
354	271	Korpan	Douglas	T
354	351	Calamaro	Burton	G
357	63	Flora	Whittaker	T
360	446	Hansen	Douglas	T
363	278	Duberstein	Douglas	T
364	122	Hertz	Douglas	T
364	131	Gillette Motor Transport	Douglas	T
365	753	Bulova Watch	Douglas	T
369	499	Bilder	Douglas	T
373	193	Whipple	Douglas	T
374	65	Braunstein	Douglas	T
375	59	Zacks	Black	T
376	503	Jackson	Douglas	T
380	678	Estate of Noel	Douglas	T
383	569	Malat	Black	T
394	741	Bingler	Douglas	T
395	316	Estate of Grace	Douglas	T
400	4	Maryland Savings	Harlan	T*
403	345	Lincoln Savings	Douglas	T
405	93	Generes	Douglas	T
410	441	Bayse	Douglas	T
413	838	Fausner	Blackmun	T*

[2] T denotes taxpayer; G denotes government. * signifies that the dissenter would set the case for full argument.

TABLE IV (Continued)

Justice	Totals Solitary Dissents	Losing Party
Douglas	26	(25T, 1G)
Roberts	7	(all T)
Black	4	(2T, 2G)
Harlan	3	(all T)
Burton	2	(both G)
Jackson	2	(both T)
McReynolds	2	(both T)
Rutledge	2	(both T)
Butler	1	(for T)
Reed	1	(for G)
Whittaker	1	(for T)
Blackmun	1	(for T)

TABLE V
DISSENTS WITHOUT OPINION IN TAX CASES[3]

United States Reports		Case	Justice	Losing Party
Vol.	*Page*			
309	149	Fitch	McReynolds	T
310	80	Leonard	Hughes Roberts McReynolds	T
311	83	Neuberger	Roberts Douglas Black	T
324	308	Merrill	Roberts	T
325	293	Angelus Milling	Douglas	T
326	425	Hercules Gasoline	Burton	T
326	480	Estate of Holmes	Douglas	T
326	599	Kirby Petroleum	Douglas	G
328	25	Burton-Sutton Oil	Douglas Black	G
332	524	Liberty Glass Co.	Douglas	T
332	535	Noble	Douglas	T
333	496	South Texas Lumber Co.	Douglas Burton	T
343	118	Lykes	Black	T
343	711	Robertson	Jackson	T
344	167	Alison	Douglas Burton	G
345	278	Healy	Douglas	T
346	335	Lober	Douglas Jackson	T
348	254	Koppers Co.	Douglas Reed	T
348	426	Glenshaw Glass	Douglas	T
350	55	Anderson, Clayton & Co.	Douglas Burton	G
350	308	Southwest Exploration Co.	Douglas	T
353	382	Libson Shops	Douglas	T
360	446	Hansen	Douglas	T
364	131	Gillette Motor Transport Co.	Douglas	T
365	753	Bulova Watch Co.	Douglas	T
372	53	Patrick	Douglas Black	T
373	193	Whipple	Douglas	T
374	65	Braunstein	Douglas	T
376	503	Jackson	Douglas	T
380	678	Estate of Noel	Douglas	T
383	569	Malat	Black	G
410	441	Bayse	Douglas	T

[3] The list of cases includes those in which the following language was used: "Mr. Justice Douglas dissents," "Mr. Justice McReynolds thinks that the judgment below should be affirmed." It does not include cases with such language as "Mr. Justice Black agrees with the Court of Claims and would affirm its judgment," or "Mr. Justice Roberts would affirm for the reasons given in the opinion below." Nor does it include cases in which a precedent is cited or a reason for the dissent is given in a short sentence or paragraph.

TABLE V (Continued)

Justice	Totals Silent Dissents	Losing Party
Douglas	25	(20T, 5G)
Black	5	(2T, 3G)
Burton	4	(2T, 2G)
Roberts	3	(2T, 1G)
Jackson	2	(2T)
McReynolds	2	(2T)
Hughes	1	(T)
Reed	1	(T)

Justice[a]	Silent Dissents Alone	Losing Party
Douglas	18	(17T, 1G)
Black	2	(1T, 1G)

[a] Justices Burton, Jackson, McReynolds, and Roberts each dissented once silently and alone for the taxpayer.

TABLE VI
CASES SUBDIVIDED BY TYPE[5]

A. *Substantive Income Tax Issues*

1. Income and Realization

Taxable Event				Attributing Trust's Income to Grantor			
Bruun	309	U	G	Wood	309	U	T
Davis	370	U	G	Clifford	309	G	G
				Stuart	317	T	G
Definition							
Bruun	309	U	G	*Attributing Income of Family Partnership to Father*			
Anderson	310	U	G				
Stewart	311	G	G	Tower	327	G	G
Sprouse	318	T	T	Lusthaus	327	G	G
Griffiths	318	T	G	Culbertson	337	G	G
Wilcox	327	T	T				
Brown Shoe	339	T	T	*Exemption from Tax Laws*			
Rutkin	343	G	T	Scottish Am.	323	U	G
Robertson	343	G	G	Maximov	373	U	G
Gen. Am. Inv.	348	U	G				
Glenshaw	348	G	T	*Alimony Included in Husband's Income*			
Anderson-Clayton	350	T	G				
Haynes	353	T	T	Fitch	309	G	G
James	366	T	T	Leonard	310	G	G
Johnson	394	G	T	Fuller	310	T	T
Mitchell	403	U	G	Pearce	315	G	G[6]
				Lester	366	U	T[7]
Anticipatory Assignment							
Horst	311	G	G	*Section 102 Gifts*			
Eubank	311	G	G	Am. Dental	318	T	T
Joliet	315	U	G	Jacobson	336	G	T
Harmon	323	G	T	LoBue	351	U	G
Sunnen	333	G	G	Duberstein	363	G	T
Bayse	410	G	T	Stanton	363	G	T
				Kaiser	363	T	T

2. Deductions from Gross Income

Section 162				Depreciation			
Dupont	308	G	G	Lazarus	308	U	T
Higgins	312	U	G	Va. Hotel	319	G	G
Pyne	313	U	G	Detroit Ed.	319	U	G
City Bank	313	U	G	Brown Shoe	339	T	T
Textile Mills	314	U	G	Hertz	364	G	T
Spreckles	315	U	G	Massey	364	G	T
Interstate Transit	319	G	G	Waterman S.S.	381	U	G
Heininger	320	U	T	Fribourg	383	T	T
Flowers	326	G	G	Chi. B.Q.R.	412	G	T
Burton-Sutton Oil	328	T	G				

[5] Each entry in this table consists of an abbreviated case name, the volume of United States Reports in which the case may be found, the party for whom the Court decided (except that U denotes a unanimous decision for the party listed to the right), and the party for whom Justice Douglas voted. Table VII provides the complete citation to each case.

[6] The wife, who was the taxpayer, lost.

[7] The husband was permitted to deduct.

APPENDIX

Section 162 (Cont.) — TABLE VI (Continued)

Name	Page			Name	Page		
Lykes	343	G	G	*Obsolescence*			
T.T. Rentals	356	U	G	Real Title Co.	309	U	G
Sullivan	356	U	T				
Hoover	356	U	G	*Depletion*			
Peurifoy	358	G	T	Wilshire Oil	308	U	G
Cammarano	358	U	G	Douglas	322	G	G
Rudolph	370	G	T	Kirby Petroleum	326	T	G
Patrick	372	G	T	S.W. Exploration	350	G	T
Gilmore	372	G	T	Parsons	359	U	G
Tellier	383	U	T	Cannelton	364	U	G
Stidger	386	G	T	Monolith	371	U	G
Correll	389	G	T	Paragon Jewel	380	G	G
Lincoln	403	G	T	Skelly Oil	394	G	T
Fausner	413	G	G				
				Amortization of Bond Premiums			
Interest				Hanover	369	U	T
Dupont	308	G	G				
Equitable	321	U	G	*Insurance Co. Reserves*			
Knetsch	364	G	T	Ore. Mut. Life	311	U	T
Miss. Chem.	405	U	G				
				Net Operating Loss			
Taxes				Olympic Radio	349	G	G
Supplee	316	U	G	Lewyt	349	T	T
Dixie Pine	320	U	G	Libson Shops	353	G	T
Wis. Gas	322	G	G				
				Section 212			
Losses				McDonald	323	G	T
Smith	308	G	G	Bingham	325	U	T
Price	309	U	G	Woodward	397	U	G
Boehm	326	U	G	Hilton Hotel	397	U	G
Bad Debts				*Section 213*			
Putnam	352	G	G	Bilder	369	G	T
Whipple	373	G	T				
Generes	405	G	T				

3. Accounting, Year of Income or Deduction, Claim of Right

Name	Page			Name	Page		
Enright	312	U	G	Lewis	340	G	T
Dixie Pine	320	U	G	Alison	344	T	G
Security Flour	321	G	T	Arrowsmith	344	G	T
Putnam	394	U	T	Healy	345	G	T
Wilcox	327	T	T	Auto. Club Mich.	353	G	G
Elec. Storage Batt.	329	G	G	Hansen	360	G	T
S. Tex. Lumber	333	G	T	Consol. Edison	366	U	T
				AAA	367	G	T
				Schlude	372	G	T
				Catto	384	U	G

4. Capital Gains and Losses

Name	Page			Name	Page		
Capital Asset				*Sale or Exchange*			
Hort	313	U	G	McClain	311	U	G
Kisselback	317	U	G	Hammel	311	U	G
Corn Prods.	350	U	G	Flaccus	313	U	G
P. G. Lake	356	U	G	Brown	380	G	G
Gillette Motor	364	G	T				
Midland-Ross	381	U	G	*Collapsible Corporations &*			
Dixon	381	U	G	*Corporate Distributions*			
Malat	383	T	T	Braunstein	374	G	T
				Gordon	391	U	G
				Davis	397	G	T

TABLE VI (Continued)

Basis				Holding Period			
Maguire	313	G	G	Gambrill	313	G	T[a]
Reynolds	313	G	G				
Crane	331	G	T				

5. Constitutionality of Income, Estate or Gift Tax as Applied

Griffiths	318	T	G
Rompel	326	U	G
Weiner	326	U	G
Atlas Life Ins.	381	U	G
Md. Sav.	400	G	G

6. Corporations

Nonrecognition				*Identity of Taxpayer*			
Section 351				*Individual or Corporation*			
Cement Inv.	316	U	T	Griffiths	308	U	G
				Moline Properties	319	U	G
Reorganization				*Parent or Subsidiary*			
LeTulle	308	U	G	Interstate Transit	319	G	G
Ala. Asphaltic	315	U	T	Nat'l Carbide	336	U	G
Palm Springs	315	U	T	United Gas Pipe			
Bondholders	315	U	G	Line	386	G	T
S.W. Consol.	315	U	G	First Security	405	T	T
Bedford	325	U	G				
Munter	331	U	G	*Undistributed Profits in General*			
Bazley	331	G	T	Hercules Gasoline	326	G	G
Phipps	336	G	G	Ogilvie Hardware	330	T	T
Libson Shops	353	G	T				
Turnbow	368	U	G	*Dividends Paid Credit*			
Nash	398	T	T	Credit Alliance	316	T	G
				Sabine Transp.	318	T	G
Dividends Rec. Credit							
Am. Chicle	316	U	G	*Indebtedness Credit*			
				N.W. Steel	311	U	G
Excess Profits Tax				Ohio Leather	317	G	G
Olympic Radio	349	U	G				
G.D. Searle	367	U	G	*Accumulated Earnings Tax*			
				Donruss Co	393	G	T

7. Partnerships

Neuberger	311	T	G

B. Estate Tax

1. Gross Estate

Transfer to Take							
Effect at Death				*Transfer in Contemplation of Death*			
Hallock	309	G	G	Trust Co. of Ga.	326	U	T
LeGierse	312	G	G	City Bank	323	U	T
Goldstone	325	G	T				
Holmes	326	G	T				
Spiegel	335	G	G				
Church	335	G	G				

[a] This characterization applies to the Court's holding only on this issue.

APPENDIX 153

Table VI (Continued)

Asset or Income in Gross Estate				Decedent's Power of Appointment			
				General			
Maass	312	T	G	Morgan	309	U	G
Lober	346	G	T	Safe Deposit	316	G	G
Fidelity Phila.	356	T	T	Rogers	320	G	G
Noel	380	G	T				
				Special			
				O'Malley	383	G	G
				Grace	395	G	T
				Byrum	408	T	T
				Jointly Held Property			
				Chandler	410	U	G

2. Deductions

Expenses				*Charitable Deduction*			
Stapf	375	U	G	Northern Trust	311	U	G
				Merchants Nat'l Bank	320	G	T
Marital Deduction				Union Planters			
Meyer	364	G	T	Banks	335	G	T
Jackson	376	G	T	Sternberger	348	G	T
N.E. Penna Bank	387	T	T				

3. Valuation

Cartwright	411	T	T

C. Gift Tax

1. Existence and Amount of Gift

Sanford	308	U	G
Humphreys	308	U	T
Rasquin	312	U	G
Ryerson (1)	312	U	G
Smith	318	G	G
Robinette	318	G	G
Harris	340	T	T

2. Annual Exclusion

Hutchings	312	U	T
Pelzer	312	U	G
Ryerson (2)	312	U	G
Disston	325	U	G

D. Selective Excises

Sunshine	310	G	G	Fitch	323	U	G
Winchester	315	U	G	Wis. Elec. Power	336	U	G
Merion	315	U	G	Sanchez	340	U	G
Wash. Balt. &				Kahriger	345	G	T
Annap. Realty	316	U	G	Calamaro	354	T	T
Colgate				Korpan	354	G	T
Palmolive	320	U	G	Cory	363	G	G
Goodrich	321	U	G				
Seattle First Nat'l	321	U	T				

TABLE VI (Continued)

E. Regulations: Validity

Haggar Co.	308	U	T	Wash. Balt. &			
Wilshire Oil	308	U	G	Annap. Realty	316	U	G
F.H.E. Oil	308	U	G	Credit Alliance	316	T	G
Janney	311	U	T	Mother Lode Co.	317	U	G
Taft	311	U	T	Douglas	322	G	G
Textile Mills	314	U	G	Cammarano	358	U	G
				Hertz	364	G	T
				Massey	364	G	T
				Cartwright	411	T	T

F. Procedure and Enforcement
1. Refund

Timeliness of Claim

				Sufficiency of Claim			
Kreider	313	U	G	Angelus Milling	325	G	T
Kales	314	U	T				
Rosenman	323	U	T	*Interest on Overpayment*			
Liberty Glass	332	G	T	Bulova Watch	365	G	T
Noble	332	G	T	*Payment of Deficiency*			
Elec. Storage				*as Condition on Bringing Suit*			
Batt.	329	G	G	Flora	357	G	G
				Flora	362	G	G

2. Res Judicata

Is T Barred?

				Is G Barred?			
Kales	314	U	T	Nunnally	316	G	T
				Sunnen	333	G	G
				Int'l Bldg.	345	U	G

3. Definitions

"First Return" as Including Amendments

				"Willfully"			
Haggar Co.	308	U	T	Spies	317	U	T
Riley	311	U	G	Marchetti	390	T	T
Scaife Co.	314	U	G	Mathis	391	T	T
				Donaldson	400	U	G
				Couch	409	G	T
				Bishop	412	G	T

4. Assessment: Statute of Limitations

Germantown Trust	309	U	T	Price	361	G	T
Lane-Wells Co.	321	U	G	Powell	379	G	T
Colony Inc.	357	T	T	Ryan	379	G	T
				Habig	390	U	G

5. Review of Tax Court (not inclusive)

Chi. Stockyards	318	U	G	Claridge	323	U	T
Gooch Milling	320	U	G	Boehm	326	G	G
Dobson	320	U	T	Talbot Mills	326	G	G
Dixie Pine	320	U	G	John Kelley Co.	326	T	T
Equitable	321	U	G	Crane	331	G	T

Table VI (Continued)

6. Application of Due Process Developments in Tax Evasion Cases

Powell	379	G	T	Sansone	380	G	T
Ryan	379	G	T	Grosso	390	T	T
Jaben	381	G	T				

7. Lien (Existence, not Priority)

Stern	357	T	T	Sims	359	U	G
Bess	357	U	G	Meyer	375	T	T

8. Court of Claims: Jurisdiction

Wilson & Co.	311	U	G

9. Effect of State Law Characterization

Bosch	387	G	T

10. Joint Return

Taft	311	U	T	Janney	311	U	T

11. Interest on Deficiency

Koppers Co.	348	G	T

12. Finality of Decision

Simpson & Co.	321	G	T

13. Penalty

Acker	361	T	T

Table VII
A Summary of Douglas' Votes in All Tax Cases, 1939-1973[9]

307 U.S.

277	O'Malley v. Woodrough	G 7-1	M

308 U.S.

39	Estate of Sanford v. Comm'r	G 8-0	
54	Rasquin v. Humphreys	T 8-0	
90	Helvering v. Wilshire Oil Co.	G 7-0	Wrote for Court
104	F.H.E. Oil Co. v. Comm'r†	G 7-0	Wrote for Court
252	Helvering v. F. & R. Lazarus & Co.	T 7-0	
355	Griffiths v. Comm'r	G 8-0	
389	Haggar Co. v. Comm'r	T 8-0	
415	LeTulle v. Scofield	G 8-0	
473	Higgins v. Smith	G 6-2	M
488	Deputy v. DuPont	G 6-2	Wrote for Court

309 U.S.

13	Real Estate Land Title & Trust Co. v. U.S.	G 6-0	Wrote for Court
78	Morgan v. Comm'r	G 8-0	
106	Helvering v. Hallock	G 6-2	M
149	Helvering v. Fitch	G 7-1	Wrote for Court
304	Germantown Trust Co. v. Comm'r	T 9-0	
331	Helvering v. Clifford	G 7-2	Wrote for Court
344	Helvering v. Wood	T 9-0	Wrote for Court
409	Helvering v. Price	G 8-0	
461	Helvering v. Bruun	G 8-0	

310 U.S.

69	Helvering v. Fuller	T 8-1	Wrote for Court
80	Helvering v. Leonard	G 6-3	Wrote for Court
381	Sunshine Anthracite Coal Co. v. Adkins	G 8-1	Wrote for Court
404	Anderson v. Helvering	G 9-0	

311 U.S.

46	Helvering v. Northwest Rolling Steel Mills, Inc.	G 9-0	
54	Crane-Johnson Co. v. Helvering†	G 9-0	
55	J.E. Riley Inv. Co. v. Comm'r	G 9-0	Wrote for Court
60	U.S. v. Stewart	G 8-1	Wrote for Court
83	Neuberger v. Comm'r	T 6-3	Dissent without opinion
104	Wilson & Co. v. U.S.	G 9-0	
112	Helvering v. Horst	G 6-3	M
122	Helvering v. Eubank	G 6-3	M

[9] Cases in this table include income, estate, gift and excise tax cases but not cases involving social security taxes. M denotes a case in which Justice Douglas voted with the majority, D denotes a case in which Justice Douglas joined in dissent. * signifies a one paragraph dissent in which Justice Douglas joined with one or more other Justices, and for which authorship is unclear. These opinions are counted as though Justice Douglas had joined the opinion of another Justice. † denotes an extremely short opinion in which the Court disposed of a case on all fours with a companion case in which it wrote a full opinion. Such cases are omitted from Tables I, II, III, IV, V & VI. ‡ denotes a case dealing primarily with criminal law and procedure. Such cases are omitted from Tables I, II, III, IV & V.

Table VII *(Continued)*

189	Helvering v. Janney	T 8-0	
195	Taft v. Helvering	T 8-0	
267	Helvering v. Oregon Mut. Life	T 9-0	
272	Helvering v. Pan-American Life†	T 9-0	
504	Helvering v. Hammel	G 8-1	M
513	Electro-Chemical Engraving Co. v. Comm'r†	G 8-1	M
527	McClain v. Comm'r	G 9-0	

312 U.S.

212	Higgins v. Comm'r	G 8-0	
254	Guggenheim v. Rasquin	G 8-0	Wrote for Court
259	Powers v. Comm'r	G 8-0	Wrote for Court
260	U.S. v. Ryerson	G 8-0	Wrote for Court
393	Helvering v. Hutchings	T 8-0	
399	U.S. v. Pelzer	G 8-0	
405	Ryerson v. U.S.	G 8-0	
443	Maass v. Higgins	T 7-2	D*
531	Helvering v. LeGierse	G 6-2	M
543	Estate of Keller v. Comm'r	G 6-2	M
636	Helvering v. Estate of Enright	G 8-0	
646	Pfaff v. Comm'r†	G 8-0	

313 U.S.

1	Maguire v. Comm'r	G 6-2	Wrote for Court
11	Helvering v. Gambrill	G 6-2	Wrote for Court
15	Helvering v. Campbell	G 6-2	Wrote for Court
28	Hort v. Comm'r	G 8-0	
121	City Bank Farmers Trust Co. v. Helvering	G 8-0	
127	U.S. v. Pyne	G 8-0	
247	Helvering v. Flaccus Leather Co.	G 8-0	
428	Helvering v. Reynolds	G 6-2	Wrote for Court
441	Cary v. Comm'r†	G 6-2	Wrote for Court
443	U.S. v. A.S. Kreider Co.	G 8-0	

314 U.S.

186	U.S. v. Kales	T 8-0	
326	Textile Mills Corp. v. Comm'r	G 8-0	Wrote for Court
459	Scaife Co. v. Comm'r	G 9-0	Wrote for Court
463	Helvering v. Lerner Stores	G 9-0	Wrote for Court

315 U.S.

32	White v. Winchester Club	G 8-0	
42	Merion Cricket Club v. U.S.	G 8-0	
44	U.S. v. Joliet & Chicago R.R.	G 8-0	Wrote for Court
179	Helvering v. Alabama Asphaltic L. Co.	T 8-0	Wrote for Court
185	Palm Springs Holding Corp. v. Comm'r	T 8-0	Wrote for Court
189	Bondholders Comm. v. Comm'r	G 8-0	Wrote for Court
194	Helvering v. Southwest Consol. Corp.	G 8-0	Wrote for Court
543	Pearce v. Comm'r	G 7-2	Wrote for Court
626	Spreckels v. Comm'r	G 8-0	

Table VII (Continued)

316 U.S.			
56	Helvering v. Safe Deposit & Trust Co.	G 5-4	M
69	Magruder v. Walsh., Balt. & Annap. Realty	G 9-0	
107	Helvering v. Credit Alliance Corp.	T 5-3	D*
258	U.S. v. Nunnaly Investment Co.	T 5-3	D*
394	Magruder v. Supplee	G 9-0	
450	American Chicle Co. v. U.S.	G 9-0	
527	Helvering v. Cement Investors, Inc.	T 9-0	Wrote for Court

317 U.S.			
102	Helvering v. Ohio Leather Co.	G 8-0	
154	Helvering v. Stuart[10]		
222	Mother Lode Co. v. Comm'r	G 8-0	
399	Kisselbach v. Comm'r	G 8-0	
476	Harrison v. Northern Trust Co.	G 8-0	
492	Spies v. U.S.‡	T 8-0	

318 U.S.			
176	Smith v. Shaughnessy	G 7-1	M
184	Robinette v. Helvering	G 7-1	M
306	Helvering v. Sabine Transp. Co.	T 5-3	D
322	Helvering v. American Dental Co.	T 6-2	M
371	Helvering v. Griffiths	T 5-3	Wrote dissent
604	Helvering v. Sprouse	T 5-3	M
693	Helvering v. Chicago Stockyards Co.	G 9-0	

319 U.S.			
98	Detroit Edison Co. v. Comm'r	G 8-0	
436	Moline Properties Inc. v. Comm'r	G 9-0	
523	Virginian Hotel Corp. v. Comm'r	G 5-4	Wrote for Court
590	Interstate Transit Lines v. Comm'r	G 6-3	M

320 U.S.			
256	Merchant's Nat'l Bank v. Comm'r	G 7-2	Wrote dissent
410	Estate of Rogers v. Comm'r	G 5-2	M
418	Comm'r v. Gooch Milling Co.	G 9-0	
422	Colgate-Palm-Peet Co. v. U.S.	G 7-0	
467	Comm'r v. Heininger	T 9-0	
489	Dobson v. Comm'r	T 9-0	
516	Dixie Pine Products Co. v. Comm'r	G 9-0	

[10] Government and taxpayer each won one issue. Justice Douglas joined Justice Stone's dissent, holding for the Government on both.

APPENDIX

TABLE VII *(Continued)*

321 U.S.			
126	B.F. Goodrich Co. v. U.S.	G 9-0	
219	Comm'r v. Lane-Wells Co.	G 9-0	
225	R. Simpson & Co. v. Comm'r	G 6-3	Wrote dissent
281	Security Flour Mills Co. v. Comm'r	G 7-2	Wrote dissent
560	Equitable Life Assurance Soc'y v. Comm'r	G 9-0	Wrote for Court
583	U.S. v. Seattle-First Nat'l Bank	T 9-0	
322 U.S.			
275	Douglas v. Comm'r	G 6-2	M
526	Wisconsin Gas & Elec. Co. v. U.S.	G 8-0	M
323 U.S.			
44	Comm'r v. Harmon	G 7-2	Wrote dissent
57	McDonald v. Comm'r	G 5-4	D
119	Comm'r v. Scottish Amer. Investment Co.	T 9-0	
141	Claridge Apts. Co. v. Comm'r	T 9-0	
582	F.W. Fitch Co. v. U.S.	G 9-0	
594	City Bank Farmers Trust Co. v. McGowan	T 9-0	
658	Rosenman v. U.S.	T 9-0	
324 U.S.			
1	Choate v. Comm'r	T 9-0	Wrote for Court
18	Fondren v. Comm'r	G 9-0	
108	Fidelity-Philadelphia v. Rothensies	G 9-0	Wrote concurrence
113	Comm'r v. Estate of Field	G 9-0	Wrote concurrence
164	Webre-Steib Co. v. Comm'r	T 7-2	M
177	Comm'r v. Smith	G-8-1	M
303	Comm'r v. Wemyss	G 8-1	M
308	Merrill v. Fahs	G 5-4	D
331	Comm'r v. Court Holding Co	G 9-0	
393	Estate of Putnam v. Comm'r	T 9-0	
542	Comm'r v. Wheeler	G 8-1	M
325 U.S.			
283	Comm'r v. Estate of Bedford	G 9-0	
293	Angelus Milling Co. v. Comm'r	G 8-1	Dissent without opinion
365	Trust of Bingham v. Comm'r	T 9-0	
442	Comm'r v. Disston	G 9-0	
687	Goldstone v. U.S.	G 7-2	D
326 U.S.			
287	Boehm v. Comm'r	G 8-0	
340	Fernandez v. Wiener	G 8-0	Wrote concurrence
367	U.S. v. Rompel	G 8-0	Wrote concurrence
425	Hercules Gasoline Co. v. Comm'r	G 5-3	M
465	Comm'r v. Flowers	G 7-1	M
480	Comm'r v. Estate of Holmes	G 7-1	Dissent without opinion
521	Talbot Mills v. Comm'r	G 7-1	M
	John Kelley Co. v. Comm'r	T 6-2	M

Table VII *(Continued)*

599	Kirby Petroleum Co. v. Comm'r	T 7-1	Dissent without opinion
630	Allen v. Trust Co.	T 8-0	Wrote for Court

327 U.S.

280	Comm'r v. Tower	G 6-2	M
293	Lusthaus v. Comm'r	G 6-2	M
404	Comm'r v. Wilcox	T 7-1	M
512	Comm'r v. Fisher	G 6-0	Douglas took no part

328 U.S.

25	Burton-Sutton Oil Co. v. Comm'r	T 5-3	Dissent without opinion

329 U.S.

296	Rothensies v. Elec. Storage Batt.	G 6-3	M

330 U.S.

709	U.S. v. Ogilvie Hardware Co.	T 7-2	M

331 U.S.

1	Crane v. Comm'r	G 6-3	D
210	Comm'r v. Munter	G 9-0	
694	McWilliams v. Comm'r	G 8-0	
737	Bazley v. Comm'r	G 7-2	D

332 U.S.

524	Jones v. Liberty Glass Co.	G 8-1	Dissent without opinion
535	Kavanagh v. Noble	G 8-1	Dissent without opinion

333 U.S.

496	Comm'r v. South Texas Lumber Co.	G 7-2	Dissent without opinion
591	Comm'r v. Sunnen	G 7-2	M

334 U.S.

no cases

335 U.S.

595	Henslee v. Union Planters Nat'l Bank & Trust Co.	G 6-3	D
632	Comm'r v. Estate of Church	G 6-3	M
701	Estate of Spiegel v. Comm'r	G 6-3	M

336 U.S.

28	Comm'r v. Jacobson	G 7-2	D
176	Wisconsin Elec. Power Co. v. U.S.	G 9-0	
410	Comm'r v. Phipps	G 9-0	Concurrence without opinion
422	National Carbide Corp. v. Comm'r	G 9-0	

337 U.S.

369	Comm'r v. Wodehouse	G 5-3	Took no part
733	Comm'r v. Culbertson	G 8-1	M

APPENDIX 161

TABLE VII *(Continued)*

338 U.S.			
258	Comm'r v. Connelly	G 7-0	Douglas took no part
411	Wilmette Park Dist. v. Campbell	G 7-0	Douglas took no part
442	Reo Motors, Inc. v. Comm'r	G 8-0	Douglas took no part
451	U.S. v. Cumberland Pub. Serv. Co.	T 8-0	Douglas took no part
561	Manning v. Seeley Tube & Box Co.	G 8-0	Douglas took no part
692	U.S. v. Benedict	G 5-3	Douglas took no part
339 U.S.			
583	Brown Shoe Co. v. Comm'r	T 8-1	M
619	Comm'r v. Korell	T 6-1	Douglas took no part
340 U.S.			
42	U.S. v. Sanchez	G 9-0	
106	Harris v. Comm'r	T 5-4	Wrote for Court
590	U.S. v. Lewis	G 8-1	Wrote dissent
341-342 U.S.			
no cases			
343 U.S.			
90	Lilly v. Comm'r	T 8-0	Douglas took no part
118	Lykes v. U.S.	G 6-3	M
130	Rutkin v. U.S.‡	G 5-4	D
711	Robertson v. U.S.	G 7-1	Wrote for Court
344 U.S.			
6	Arrowsmith v. Comm'r	G 6-3	Wrote dissent
167	Alison v. U.S.	T 7-2	Dissent without opinion
345 U.S.			
22	U.S. v. Kahriger	G 6-3	D
278	Healy v. Comm'r	G 8-1	Dissent without opinion
502	U.S. v. Int'l Bldg. Co.	G 9-0	Wrote for Court
544	Watson v. Comm'r	G 6-3	D
346 U.S.			
335	Lober v. U.S.	G 7-2	Dissent without opinion
347 U.S.			
no cases			
348 U.S.			
187	Comm'r v. Estate of Sternberger	G 7-2	D
254	U.S. v. Koppers Co.	G 7-2	Dissent without opinion
426	Comm'r v. Glenshaw Glass Co.	G 7-1	Dissent without opinion
434	General Am. Investors Co. v. Comm'r	G 8-0	Concurrence without opinion
349 U.S.			
232	U.S. v. Olympic Radio & Television, Inc.	G 8-0	Wrote for Court
237	Lewyt Corp. v. Comm'r	T 5-3	Wrote for Court

TABLE VII *(Continued)*

350 U.S.				
46	Corn Products v. Comm'r	G 8-0	
55	U.S. v. Anderson, Clayton & Co.	T 7-2	Dissent without opinion
308	Comm'r v. Southwest Exploration Co.	G 7-1	Dissent without opinion
383	U.S. v. Leslie Salt Co.	T 9-0	
456	Millinery Center Building Corp. v. Comm'r	G 9-0	
351 U.S.			
243	Comm'r v. LoBue	G 9-0	
352 U.S.			
82	Putnam v. Comm'r	G 8-1	M
306	U.S. v. Allen Bradley Co.	G 9-0	
313	Nat'l Lead Co. v. Comm'r	G 9-0	
353 U.S.			
81	Haynes v. U.S.	T 6-2	M
180	Auto. Club v. Comm'r	G 5-3	M
382	Libson Shops Inc. v. Koehler	G 7-1	Dissent without opinion
354 U.S.			
271	U.S. v. Korpan	G 8-1	Wrote short dissent
351	U.S. v. Calamaro	T 7-1	M
355 U.S.			
no cases			
356 U.S.			
27	Comm'r v. Sullivan	T 9-0	Wrote for Court
30	Tank Truck Rentals v. Comm'r	G 9-0	
38	Hoover Motor Express Co. v. Comm'r	G 9-0	
260	Comm'r v. P.G. Lake	G 9-0	Wrote for Court
274	Fidelity-Phila. Trust Co. v. Smith	T 6-3	M
357 U.S.			
28	Colony, Inc. v. Comm'r	T 7-2	M
39	Comm'r v. Stern	T 6-3	M
51	U.S. v. Bess	G 9-0	
63	Flora v. U.S.	G 8-1	M
358 U.S.			
59	Peurifoy v. Comm'r	G 6-3	Wrote dissent
498	Cammarano v. U.S.	G 9-0	Wrote concurrence
359 U.S.			
108	Sims v. U.S.	G 9-0	
215	Parsons v. Smith	G 9-0	
360 U.S.			
446	Comm'r v. Hansen	G 7-1	Dissent without opinion

Table VII *(Continued)*

361 U.S.			
87	Comm'r v. Acker	T 6-3	M
304	U.S. v. Price	G 7-2	Wrote short dissent
362 U.S.			
145	Flora v. U.S.	G 5-4	M
363 U.S.			
194	U.S. v. Mfr.'s Nat'l Bank	G 8-0	Did not participate
278	Comm'r v. Duberstein	G 8-1	Wrote short dissent
299	U.S. v. Kaiser	T 6-3	Wrote concurrence
709	Cory Corp. v. Sauber	G 5-4	M
364 U.S.			
76	U.S. v. Cannelton Sewer Pipe Co.	G 9-0	
92	Massey Motors v. U.S.	G 5-4	D
122	Hertz Corp. v. U.S.	G 8-1	Wrote short dissent
130	Comm'r v. Gillette Motor Transp. Co.	G 8-1	Dissent without opinion
361	Knetsch v. U.S.	G 6-3	Wrote dissent
410	Meyer v. U.S.	G 6-3	Wrote dissent
365 U.S.			
753	Bulova Watch Co. v. U.S.	G 8-1	Dissent without opinion
366 U.S.			
213	James v. U.S.†	T 7-2	Joined partial concurrence[11]
299	Comm'r v. Lester	T 9-0	Wrote concurrence
380	U.S. v. ConEd Co.	T 9-0	
367 U.S.			
303	Jarecki v. G.D. Searle & Co.	G 9-0	
687	Am. Auto. Ass'n v. U.S.	G 5-4	D
368 U.S.			
337	Turnbow v. Comm'r	G 9-0	
369 U.S.			
499	Comm'r v. Bilder	G 6-1	Wrote short dissent
672	Hanover Bank v. Comm'r	T 7-0	
370 U.S.			
65	U.S. v. Davis	G 7-0	
269	Rudolph v. U.S.	G 5-2	Wrote dissent
371 U.S.			
537	Riddell v. Monolith Portland Cement Co.	G 8-0	

[11] Justice Douglas joined Justice Black's opinion, concurring in part and dissenting in part.

TABLE VII (Continued)

372 U.S.				
39	U.S. v. Gilmore	G 7-2	Wrote short dissent	
53	U.S. v. Patrick	G 7-2	Dissent without opinion	
128	Schlude v. Comm'r	G 5-4	D	
373 U.S.				
49	Maximov v. U.S.	G 9-0		
193	Whipple v. Comm'r	G 8-1	Dissent without opinion	
374 U.S.				
65	Braunstein v. Comm'r	G 8-1	Dissent without opinion	
375 U.S.				
59	U.S. v. Zacks	G 7-1	Douglas took no part	
118	U.S. v. Stapf	G 9-0		
233	Meyer v. U.S.	T 6-3	M	
376 U.S.				
503	Jackson v. U.S.	G 8-1	Dissent without opinion	
377-378				
no cases				
379 U.S.				
48	U.S. v. Powell‡	G 6-3	Wrote dissent	
61	Ryan v. U.S.‡	G 8-1	Dissent in above opinion	
380 U.S.				
343	Sansone v. U.S.‡	G 7-2	D	
563	Comm'r v. Brown	T 6-3	M	
624	Paragon Jewel Coal Co. v. Comm'r	T 7-2	M	
678	Comm'r v. Noel	G 8-1	Dissent without opinion	
381 U.S.				
54	U.S. v. Midland-Ross Corp.	G 9-0		
68	Dixon v. U.S.	G 9-0		
214	Jaben v. U.S.‡	G 6-3	D	
233	U.S. v. Atlas Life Ins. Co.	G 9-0		
252	Waterman S.S. Corp. v. U.S.	G 9-0		
382 U.S.				
no cases				
383 U.S.				
272	Fribourg Navigation Co. v. Comm'r	T 6-3	M	
569	Malat v. Riddell	T 7-1	M	
627	U.S. v. O'Malley	G 7-2	M	
687	Comm'r v. Tellier	T 9-0		
384 U.S.				
102	U.S. v. Catto	G 9-0		

APPENDIX

Table VII (Continued)

385 U.S.			
no cases			
386 U.S.			
287	Comm'r v. Stidger	G 6-3	Wrote dissent
387 U.S.			
213	Northeastern Pa. Nat'l Bank & Trust Co. v. U.S.	T 6-3	M
456	Comm'r v. Estate of Bosch	G 6-3	Wrote dissent
388 U.S.			
no cases			
389 U.S.			
299	U.S. v. Correll	G 5-3	Wrote short dissent
390 U.S.			
39	Marchetti v. U.S.‡	T 7-1	M
62	Grosso v. U.S.‡	T 7-1	M
222	U.S. v. Habig	G 8-0	
391 U.S.			
1	Mathis v. U.S.‡	T 5-3	M
83	Comm'r v. Gordon	G 8-0	
392 U.S.			
no cases			
393 U.S.			
297	U.S. v. Donruss Co.	G 6-3	Joined partial concurrence[12]
394 U.S.			
678	U.S. v. Skelly Oil Co.	G 6-3	Wrote dissent
741	Bingler v. Johnson	G 8-1	Wrote short dissent
395 U.S.			
316	U.S. v. Estate of Grace	G 6-1	Wrote dissent
396 U.S.			
no cases			
397 U.S.			
301	U.S. v. Davis	G 5-3	Wrote dissent
572	Woodward v. Comm'r	G 8-0	
580	U.S. v. Hilton Hotels Corp.	G 8-0	
398 U.S.			
1	Nash v. U.S.	T 6-2	Wrote for Court
399 U.S.			
no cases			

[12] Justice Douglas joined Justice Harlan's opinion, concurring in part and dissenting in part.

TABLE VII *(Continued)*

400 U.S.			
4	U.S. v. Md. Savings-Share Ins. Corp.	G 8-1	M
517	Donaldson v. U.S.‡	G 9-0	Wrote concurrence
401-402 U.S.			
no cases			
403 U.S.			
190	U.S. v. Mitchell	G 9-0	
345	Comm'r v. Lincoln Sav. & Loan Ass'n	G 8-1	Wrote dissent
405 U.S.			
93	U.S. v. Generes	G 6-1	Wrote dissent
298	U.S. v. Miss. Chem. Corp.	G 8-0	
394	Comm'r v. First Security Bank	T 6-3	M
408 U.S.			
125	U.S. v. Byrum	T 6-3	M
409 U.S.			
322	Couch v. U.S.‡	G 7-2	Wrote dissent
410 U.S.			
441	U.S. v. Basye	G 8-1	Dissent without opinion
257	U.S. v. Chandler	G 9-0	
411 U.S.			
546	Cartwright v. U.S.	T 6-3	M
412 U.S.			
346	U.S. v. Bishop‡	G 8-1	Wrote dissent
401	U.S. v. Chicago, B. & Q.R.	G 6-2	Wrote dissent
413 U.S.			
838	Fausner v. Comm'r	G 8-1	M

APPENDIX

Table VIII[13]
Douglas' Positions in Labor Cases

Cite	Case Name	Court Vote	Party	NLRB	Douglas' Position Type Opinion
309 U.S.					
206	NLRB v. Waterman S.S. Corp.	8-0	Union	pro	M
261	Amalgamated Util. Workers v. Consol. Edison Co.	8-0	Employer		M
350	Nat'l Licorice Co. v. NLRB	8-0	Union	pro	Separate opinion[14]
310 U.S.					
318	NLRB v. Bradford Dyeing Ass'n	8-0	Union	pro	M
311 U.S.					
7	Republic Steel Corp. v. NLRB	6-2	Union	pro	Wrote dissent
72	Int'l Ass'n of Machinists v. NLRB	9-0	Union	pro	Wrote for Court
514	H.J. Heinz Co. v. NLRB	8-0	Union	pro	M
584	NLRB v. Link-Belt Co.	8-0	Employer	con	Wrote for Court
312 U.S.					
426	NLRB v. Express Publishing Co.	8-0	Union	pro	Separate opinion[15]
313 U.S.					
23	NLRB v. White Swan Co.	8-0	Employer	con	Wrote for Court
146	Pittsburgh Plate Glass Co. v. NLRB	5-3	Union	pro	M
177	Phelps Dodge Corp. v. NLRB	7-0	Union	pro	Joined concurrence
212	Continental Oil Co. v. NLRB	7-0	Union	pro	Indicated concurrence in accord with *Phelps Dodge*
314 U.S.					
469	NLRB v. Virginia Elec. & Power Co.	7-0	Union	pro	M
315 U.S.					
100	Southport Petroleum Corp. v. NLRB	6-2	Union	pro	M
685	NLRB v. Elec. Vacuum Cleaner Co.	8-1	Union	pro	M[16]

[13] M denotes a case in which Justice Douglas voted with the majority; D denotes a case in which Justice Douglas joined in dissent. * signifies a one paragraph dissent in which Justice Douglas joined with one or more other Justices, and for which authorship is unclear. Such opinions are counted as though Justice Douglas had joined the opinion of another Justice.

[14] Justice Douglas' concurrence went further than the Court in support of the NLRB's position.

[15] Justice Douglas' concurrence went further than the Court in support of the NLRB's position.

[16] The majority's decision favored one union over the employer and rival unions.

TABLE VIII (Continued)

U.S. Cite	Case	Vote	Side	Direction	Type
316 U.S.					
31	S. S.S. Co. v. NLRB	5-4	Union	pro	D
317 U.S.					
no cases					
318 U.S.					
9	NLRB v. Ind. & Mich. Elec. Co.	5-3	Union	pro	D
319 U.S.					
50	NLRB v. S. Bell Tel. & Tel. Co.	8-0	Union	pro	M
533	Va. Elec. & Power Co. v. NLRB	6-3	Union	pro	M
320 U.S.					
no cases					
321 U.S.					
332	J.I. Case Co. v. NLRB	8-1	Union	pro	M
678	Medo Photo Supply Corp. v. NLRB	7-2	Union	pro	M
702	Franks Bros. Co. v. NLRB	8-0	Union	pro	M
322 U.S.					
111	NLRB v. Hearst Publications, Inc.	8-1	Union	pro	M
643	Polish Nat'l Alliance v. NLRB	8-0	Union	pro	Joined concurrence
323 U.S.					
248	Wallace Corp. v. NLRB	5-4	Union	pro	M
324 U.S.					
9	Regal Knitwear Co. v. NLRB	9-0	Union	pro	M
793	Republic Aviation Corp. v. NLRB	8-1	Union	pro	M
325 U.S.					
335	Int'l Union of Mine Workers v. Eagle-Picher Mining & Smelting Co.	5-4	Union	pro	D
697	Inland Empire Council, Lumber Workers v. Millis	8-1a	Union	pro	M[17]
326 U.S.					
376	May Dep't Stores Co. v. NLRB	5-3	Union	pro	M
327 U.S.					
385	NLRB v. Cheney Lumber Co.	8-0	Union	pro	M

[17] The majority's decision favored a certified union over a rival.

Table VIII (Continued)

328 U.S.						
no cases						
329 U.S.						
324	NLRB v. A.J. Tower Co.	8-1	Union	pro	M	
330 U.S.						
219	NLRB v. Donnelly Garment Co.	9-0	Union	pro	M	
485	Packard Motor Car Co. v. NLRB	5-4	Employer	con	Wrote dissent	
331 U.S.						
398	NLRB v. E.C. Atkins & Co.	6-3	Union	pro	M	
416	NLRB v. Jones & Laughlin Steel Corp.	5-4	Union	pro	M	
332-335 U.S.						
no cases						
336 U.S.						
226	NLRB v. Stowe Spinning Co.	6-3	Union	pro	M	
337 U.S.						
217	NLRB v. Crompton-Highland Mills, Inc.	6-3	Union	pro	D*	
656	NLRB v. Pittsburgh S.S. Co.	8-0	Union	pro	M	
338 U.S.						
355	Colgate-Palmolive-Peet Co. v. NLRB	6-2			Took no part	
339 U.S.						
563	NLRB v. Mexia Textile Mills, Inc.	7-2	Union	pro	M	
577	NLRB v. Pool Mfg. Co.	7-2	Union	pro	M	
340 U.S.						
361	NLRB v. Gullett Gin Co.	8-0	Union	pro	M	
474	Universal Camera Corp. v. NLRB	7-2	Union	pro	D*	
498	NLRB v. Pittsburgh S.S. Co.	9-0	Employer	con	M	
341 U.S.						
322	NLRB v. Highland Park Mfg. Co.	6-2	Union	pro	Wrote dissent	
665	NLRB v. Int'l Rice Milling Co.	9-0	Union	pro	M	
675	NLRB v. Denver Bldg. Trades Council	6-3	Union	con	Wrote dissent	
694	Int'l Bhd. of Elec. Workers v. NLRB	6-3	Union	con	D*	
707	Local 74, Carpenters v. NLRB	6-3	Union	con	D*	

Table VIII (Continued)

U.S. Cite	Page	Case	Vote	Party	Pro/Con	Notes
342 U.S.						
	237	Longshoremen's Union v. Juneau Spruce Corp.	9-0	Employer		Wrote for Court
343 U.S.						
	395	NLRB v. Am. Nat'l Ins. Co.	6-3	Union	pro	Joined dissent
344 U.S.						
	344	NLRB v. Seven-Up Bottling Co.	6-3	Employer	con	Wrote dissent
	375	NLRB v. Dant	9-0	Union	pro	M
345 U.S.						
	71	NLRB v. Rockaway News Supply Co.	6-3	Union	pro	D
	100	Am. Newspaper Publishers Ass'n v. NLRB	6-3	Employer	con	Wrote dissent
	117	NLRB v. Gamble Enterprises, Inc.	6-3	Union	pro	M
346 U.S.						
	464	NLRB v. Local 1229	5-3	Union	con	D
	482	Howell Chevrolet Co. v. NLRB	7-1	Employer	con	Dissent without opinion
347 U.S.						
	17	Radio Officer's Union v. NLRB	7-2	Employer	con	D
	501	Capital Serv. Inc. v. NLRB	7-1	Union	pro	Wrote for Court
348 U.S.						
	96	Brooks v. NLRB	8-0	Union	pro	M
349 U.S.						
no cases						
350 U.S.						
	107	NLRB v. Warren Co.	9-0	Union	pro	M
	264	NLRB v. Coca-Cola Bottling Co.	7-1	Union	pro	M
	270	Mastro Plastics Corp. v. NLRB	6-3	Union	pro	M
351 U.S.						
	105	NLRB v. Babcock & Wilcox Co.	8-0	Employer	con	M
	149	NLRB v. Truitt Mfg. Co.	6-3	Union	pro	M
352 U.S.						
	145	Leedom v. Mine Workers	9-0	Union	con	Wrote for Court
	153	Meat Cutters v. NLRB	9-0	Union	con	Wrote for Court
	282	NLRB v. Lion Oil Co.	6-2	Union	pro	M

APPENDIX

TABLE VIII (Continued)

U.S. Cite	Page	Case	Vote	Favored	Pro/Con	Opinion
353 U.S.	87	NLRB v. Truck Drivers Union	8-0	Employer	pro	M
	313	Office Employees Union v. NLRB	5-4	Union	con	M
	448	Textile Workers v. Lincoln Mills	7-1	Union		Wrote for Court
354 U.S.	no cases					
355 U.S.	453	NLRB v. Mine Workers Union	9-0	Employer	con	M
356 U.S.	342	NLRB v. Borg-Warner Corp.	6-3	Union	pro	M
357 U.S.	1	NLRB v. Duval Jewelry	9-0	Union	pro	Wrote for Court
	10	Lewis v. NLRB	9-0[18]		pro	Wrote for Court
	93	Carpenter's Union v. NLRB	6-3	Union	con	Wrote short dissent
	357	NLRB v. United Steelworkers	6-3	Union	con	D
358 U.S.	184	Leedom v. Kyne	7-2	Union	con	M
359 U.S.	no cases					
360 U.S.	203	NLRB v. Cabot Carbon Co.	9-0	Union	pro	M
	301	NLRB v. Fant Milling Co.	9-0	Union	pro	M
361 U.S.	398	NLRB v. Deena Artware Inc.	8-0	Union	pro	Wrote for Court
	477	NLRB v. Ins. Agent's Int'l Union	9-0	Union	con	M
362 U.S.	274	NLRB v. Drivers Local Union	9-0	Union	con	M
	411	Machinists Local 1424 v. NLRB	7-2[19]		con	M
363 U.S.	no cases					
364 U.S.	573	NLRB v. Radio Eng'rs	9-0[20]		con	M

[18] The Court's result apparently went against both union and employer.
[19] The NLRB brought this action against both the employer and the union.
[20] The case involved a dispute between two unions.

Table VIII (Continued)

365 U.S.						
651	Carpenters Local 60 v. NLRB	7-1	Union	con	Wrote for Court	
667	Teamsters Local 357 v. NLRB	6-2	Union	con	Wrote for Court	
695	NLRB v. News Syndicate Co.	6-2[21]		con	Wrote for Court	
705	Typographical Union v. NLRB	6-2	Union	con	Wrote for Court	
366 U.S.						
667	Elec. Workers v. NLRB	9-0	Employer	pro	Wrote concurrence	
731	Garment Workers v. NLRB	7-2[22]		con	Wrote dissent	
367 U.S.						
no cases						
368 U.S.						
318	NLRB v. Ochoa Fertilizer Corp.	8-1		con	Dissent without opinion[23]	
369 U.S.						
736	NLRB v. Katz	7-0	Union	pro	M	
370 U.S.						
9	NLRB v. Wash. Aluminum Co.	7-0	Union	pro	M	
371 U.S.						
no cases						
372 U.S.						
10	McCulloch v. Sociedad Nacional	8-0		con	Wrote single concurrence for both cases.[24]	
24	Incres Steamship Co. v. Int'l Maritime Workers	8-0		con		
373 U.S.						
221	NLRB v. Erie Resistor Corp.	9-0	Union	pro	M	
734	NLRB v. Gen. Motors Corp.	8-0	Union	pro	M	
374 U.S.						
no cases						
375 U.S.						
405	NLRB v. Parts Co.	9-0	Union	pro	M	

[21] The Court's position favored both union and employer.
[22] Douglas' opinion favored both employer and minority union.
[23] The Court held the Board's order against the unions and the employer valid as originally entered.
[24] The Court's result favored a foreign union over a domestic one.

Selected Bibliography

ABOUT DOUGLAS

Books

Countryman, V. DOUGLAS OF THE SUPREME COURT—A SELECTION OF HIS OPINIONS. New York: Doubleday, 1959.
Reviewed:
73 HARV. L. REV. 1040 (1960).
_____. THE JUDICIAL RECORD OF JUSTICE WILLIAM O. DOUGLAS. Cambridge: Harvard University Press. 1974.

Articles

Ares, C.; Countryman, V.; Dorsen, N.; Emerson, T. I., *Symposium: Mr. Justice Douglas' Contributions to the Law*, 74 COLUM. L. REV. 353 (1974).
  Emerson, T. I., "The First Amendment," p. 353.
  Dorsen, N., "Equal Protection of the Laws," p. 357.
  Ares, C., "Constitutional Criminal Law," p. 362.
  Countryman, V., "Business Regulation," p. 366.
Black, H. L.; Fortas, A.; Jennings, R. W.; Louisell, D. W., *Symposium*, 73 YALE L. J. 915 (1964).
  Black, H. L., "William Orville Douglas," p. 915.
  Fortas, A., "Mr. Justice Douglas," p. 917.
  Jennings, R. W., "Mr. Justice Douglas: His Influence on Corporate and Securities Regulation," p. 920.
  Louisell, D. W., "The Man and the Mountain: Douglas on Religious Freedom," p. 975.
Burger, W. E.; David, S.; Sovern, M. I.; Warren, E., *Symposium: In Honor of Mr. Justice William O. Douglas*, 74 COLUM. L. REV. 341 (1974).
  Warren, E., p. 342.   Sovern, M. I., p. 345.
  Burger, W. E., p. 344.   Davis, S., p. 347.

Casper, G., *The Liberal Faith: Some Observations on the Legal Philosophy of Mr. Justice William O. Douglas*, 22 FED. B. J. 179 (1962).

Cohen, W., and Rodell, F., *Symposium*, 26 U. CHI. L. REV. 2 (1958).
  Rodell, F., "Justice Douglas: An Anniversary Fragment for a Friend," p. 2.
  Cohen, W., "Justice Douglas: A Law Clerk's View," p. 6.

Cohen, W.; Countryman, V.; Karst, K. L.; Rodell, F.; Van Alstyne, W. W.; Warren, E., *Symposium: Mr. Justice Douglas: Three Decades of Service*, 16 U.C.L.A. L. REV. 699 (1969).
  Warren, E., "Introduction," p. 699.
  Cohen, W., "Introduction," p. 701.
  Rodell, F., "As Justice Douglas Completes His First Thirty Years on the Court: Herewith a Random Anniversary Sample, Complete With Casual Commentary, of Diverse Scraps, Shreds, and Shards Gleaned from a Forty-Year Friendship," p. 704.
  Karst, K. L., "Invidious Discrimination: Justice Douglas and the Return of the 'Natural-Law-Due-Process Formula,' " p. 716.
  Van Alstyne, W. W., "The Constitutional Rights of Public Employees: A Comment on the Inappropriate Use of an Old Analogy," p. 751.
  Countryman, V., "Justice Douglas: Expositor of the Bankruptcy Law," p. 773.

Cohn, H. S., *Mr. Justice Douglas and Federal Taxation*, 45 CONN. B. J. 218 (1971).

Countryman, V., *Justice Douglas and the Law of Business Regulation*, 91 BANKING L. J. 312 (1974).
  Editor's Headnotes: Dunne, G. T., "Justice Douglas and the Law of Banking," p. 307.

Countryman, V.; Linde, H.; Manning, L. F.; Ming, W. R., Jr.; Warren, E.; Williams, J. S., *Symposium*, 39 WASH. L. REV. 1 (1964).
  Warren, E., "Introduction—A Tribute to Justice Douglas," p. 1.
  Linde, H., "Justice Douglas on Freedom in the Welfare State," p. 4.
  Manning, L. F., "The Douglas Concept of God in Government," p. 47.

APPENDIX

TABLE VIII (Continued)

376 U.S.					
473	Boire v. Greyhound Corp.	8-1	Employer con	Dissent without opinion
492	United Steelworkers v. NLRB	8-0	Union pro	Concurrence without opinion

377 U.S.					
46	NLRB v. Servette, Inc.	9-0	Union	pro	M
58	NLRB v. Local 760, Fruit Packers	6-2			Douglas took no part

378 U.S.
no cases

379 U.S.					
21	NLRB v. Burnup & Sims, Inc.	8-1	Union	pro	Wrote for Court
203	Fibreboard Paper Prods. Corp. v. NLRB	8-0	Union	pro	Joined concurrence

380 U.S.					
263	Textile Workers Union v. Darlington Mfg. Co.	7-0	Union	pro	M
278	NLRB v. Brown	8-1	Employer	con	M
300	Am. Ship Bldg. Co. v. NLRB	9-0	Employer	con	M
438	NLRB v. Metropolitan Life Ins. Co.	8-1	Employer	con	Wrote short dissent

381-384 U.S.
no cases

385 U.S.					
421	NLRB v. C & C Plywood Corp.	9-0	Union	pro	M
432	NLRB v. Acme Indus. Co.	9-0	Union	pro	M

386 U.S.					
612	Nat'l Woodwork Mfrs. Ass'n v. NLRB	5-4	Employer	con	D
664	Insulation Contractors Ass'n v. NLRB	5-4	Employer	con	D

387 U.S.
no cases

388 U.S.					
26	NLRB v. Great Dane Trailers, Inc.	7-2	Union	pro	M
175	NLRB v. Allis-Chalmers Mfg. Co.	5-4	Employer	con	D

389 U.S.					
375	NLRB v. Fleetwood Trailer Co.	8-0	Union	pro	M

Table VIII (Continued)

390 U.S.					
254	NLRB v. United Ins. Co. of Am.	7-0	Union	pro	M
391 U.S.					
418	NLRB v. Marine Workers Union	8-1	Employee[25]	pro	Wrote for Court
392 U.S.					
no cases					
393 U.S.					
357	NLRB v. Strong	8-1	Employer	con	Wrote dissent
394 U.S.					
423	Scofield v. NLRB	7-1	Union	pro	M
759	NLRB v. Wyman-Gordon Co.	7-2	Employer	con	Wrote dissent
395 U.S.					
575	NLRB v. Gissel Packing Co.	8-0	Union	pro	M
396 U.S.					
258	NLRB v. J.H. Rutter-Rex Mfg. Co.	5-3	Employer	con	Wrote dissent
397 U.S.					
99	H.K. Porter Co. v. NLRB	4-2	Union	pro	Wrote dissent
398 U.S.					
25	NLRB v. Raytheon Co.	9-0	Union	pro	M
399 U.S.					
no cases					
400 U.S.					
297	NLRB v. Local 825, Operating Eng'rs	7-2	Union	con	Wrote dissent
401 U.S.					
137	Magnesium Casting Co. v. NLRB	9-0	Union	pro	Wrote for Court
402 U.S.					
600	NLRB v. Natural Gas Util.	8-1	Employer	con	M
403 U.S.					
no cases					
404 U.S.					
116	NLRB v. Plasterers, Local 79	9-0	Employer	pro	M
138	NLRB v. Nash-Finch Co.	7-2	Union	pro	Wrote for Court
157	Alkali Workers, Local 1 v. Pittsburgh Plate Glass Co.	6-1	Union	con	Dissent without opinion

[25] The cases involved an employee-union dispute.

APPENDIX

TABLE VIII (Continued)

405 U.S.						
117	NLRB v. Scrivener	9-0	Union	pro	M	
406 U.S.						
272	NLRB v. Burns Int'l Security Serv.	9-0 5-4	Employer Union	con pro	M M	
407 U.S.						
539	Central Hardware Co. v. NLRB	6-3	Union	pro	D	
408 U.S.						
no cases						
409 U.S.						
48	NLRB v. Int'l Van Lines	9-0	Union	pro	M	
213	NLRB v. Textile Workers, Local 1029	8-1	Employee	pro	Wrote for Court	
410-411 U.S.						
no cases						
412 U.S.						
67	NLRB v. Boeing Co.	6-3	Employee	con	Wrote dissent	
84	Booster Lodge 405, Machinists	9-0	Employer	pro	M	

Countryman, V., "The Constitution and Job Discrimination," p. 74.
Williams, J. S., "Critique of 'The Constitution and Job Discrimination,'" p. 96.
Ming, W. R., Jr., "Critique on 'The Constitution and Job Discrimination,'" p. 104.
Epstein, L. D., *Economic Predilections of Justice Douglas*, 1949 WIS. L. REV. 531 (1949).
Epstein, L. D., *Justice Douglas and Civil Liberties*, 1951 WIS. L. REV. 125 (1951).
Hopkirk, J. W., *William O. Douglas—His Work in Policing Bankruptcy Proceedings*, 18 VAND. L. REV. 663 (1965).
Irish, M. D., *Mr. Justice Douglas and Judicial Restraint*, 6 U. FLA. L. REV. 537 (1953).
Karst, K. L., and Van Alstyne, W. W., *Sit-Ins and State Action— Mr. Justice Douglas Concurring*, 14 STAN. L. REV. 762 (1962).
Linde, H. A., *Constitutional Rights in the Public Sector: Justice Douglas on Liberty in the Welfare State*, 40 WASH. L. REV.10 (1965).
Powe, L. A., Jr., *Evolution to Absolutism: Justice Douglas and the First Amendment*, 74 COLUM. L. REV. 371 (1974).
Thomas, H. S., *Justice William O. Douglas and the Concept of a Fair Trial*, 18 VAND. L. REV. 701 (1965).
Way, H. F., *Study of Judicial Attitudes: The Case of Mr. Justice Douglas*, 24 WEST. POL. Q. 12 (March, 1971).
Justice For Douglas?, 237 ECONOMIST 34 (26 December, 1970).

Dissertations

Hopkirk, J. W., "William O. Douglas—Individualist: a Study in the Development and Application of a Judge's Attitudes." (Ph.D. 1958, Princeton) 588 pp.
James, D. B., "Judicial Philosophy and Accession to the Court: The Case of Justices Jackson and Douglas," (Ph.D. 1966, Columbia) 222 pp.
Meek, R. L., "Justices Douglas and Black: Political Liberalism and Judicial Activism." (Ph.D. 1964, University of Oregon) 389 pp.
Oddo, G. L., "Justice Douglas and the Roosevelt Court." (Ph.D. 1952, Georgetown) 334 pp.

Pollock, P. K., "Judicial Libertarianism and Judicial Responsibilities: The Case of Justice William O. Douglas." (Ph.D. 1968, Cornell) 270 pp.
Resnick, S., "Black and Douglas: Variations in Dissent." (Ph.D. 1970, New School for Social Research) 505 pp.

BY DOUGLAS*

Books

GO EAST, YOUNG MAN: THE EARLY YEARS. New York: Random House, 1974.
Reviewed
Botein. 84 YALE L. J. 151 (1974).
Hentoff, N. N. Y. TIMES BK. R. p. 1 (14 April, 1974).
Lehman-Haupt, C. N. Y. TIMES p. 33 (22 April, 1974).
Simon, J. F. 74 COLUM. L. REV. 541 (1974).
THREE HUNDRED YEAR WAR—A CHRONICLE OF ECOLOGICAL DISASTER. New York: Random House, 1972.
Reviewed:
Nygaard, A. 97 LIBRARY J. 2633 (August, 1972).
Reed, K. R. 14 ARIZ. L. REV. 877 (1972).
127 AMERICA 267 (7 October, 1972).
40 KIRKUS 898 (1 August, 1972).
N. Y. TIMES BK. R. p. 38 (8 October, 1972).
202 PUB. WKLY. 48 (4 September, 1972).
HOLOCAUST OR HEMISPHERIC COOPERATION: CROSS CURRENTS IN LATIN AMERICA. New York: Random House, 1971.
Reviewed:
Page, J. A. N. Y. TIMES BK. R. p. 48 (28 November, 1971).
Silvert, K. H. 4 N.Y.U. J. INT. L. & POL. 519 (1971).
Snow, L. F. 96 LIBRARY J. 3766 (15 November, 1971).
Williams, B. D. 31 BEST SELL. 340 (1 November, 1971).
68 BOOKLIST 390 (1 January, 1972).
9 CHOICE 280 (April, 1972).
55 SAT. REV. 61 (22 January, 1972).

*In reverse chronological order under each subheading

INTERNATIONAL DISSENT: SIX STEPS TOWARD WORLD PEACE.
New York: Random House, 1971.
Reviewed:
Bingham, A. M. 54 SAT. REV. 30 (8 May, 1971).
Holtman, E. 96 LIBRARY J. 1988 (1 June, 1971).
Lopatkiewicz, S. M. 12 HARV. INT. L. J. 609 (1971).
8 CHOICE 1087 (October, 1971).
POINTS OF REBELLION. New York: Random House, 1970.
Reviewed:
Apple, J. G. 59 KY. L. J. 573 (1970-71).
Clark, T. C. 83 HARV. L. REV. 1931 (1970).
Davidow, R. P. 45 ST. JOHN'S L. REV. 179 (1970).
Eckstein, P. F. 46 NOTRE DAME LAW. 643 (1971).
Grossman, G. S. 95 LIBRARY J. 1388 (1 April, 1970).
Grossman, G. S. 1970 UTAH L. REV. 302 (1970).
Hayakawa, S. I. 50 B. U. L. REV. 493 (1970).
Herman, D. H. 46 WASH. L. REV. 195 (1970).
Hiller, J. A. 4 VAL. U. L. REV. 421 (1970).
Klink, V. R. 19 DEPAUL L. REV. 428 (1969).
Koplowitz, E. A. 5 LINCOLN L. REV. 80 (1969).
Lans, A. 40 AM. SCHOLAR 188 (Winter 1970-71).
Leahy, J. E. 37 BROOKLYN L. REV. 258 (1970).
Levy, N., Jr. 2 CONN. L. REV. 707 (1970).
Manning, L. F. 39 FORDHAM L. REV. 161 (1970).
Raphael, S. M. 21 BROOKLYN BAR 209 (1970).
Sedler, R. A. 59 KY. L. J. 578 (1970-71).
Stephenson, D. G., Jr. 119 U. PA. L. REV. 536 (1971).
Tietz, C. F. 43 TEMPLE L. Q. 418 (1970).
Yoder, E. M. BOOK WORLD 6 (29 March, 1970).
Zinn, H. 50 B. U. L. REV. 490 (1970).
7 CHOICE 940 (September, 1970).
16 HOW. L. J. 181 (1970).
TOWARDS A GLOBAL FEDERALISM. New York: New York University Press, 1968.
Reviewed:
Deutsch, E. P. 1969 U. ILL. L. F. 281 (1969).
Goodrich, L. M. 384 ANN. AM. ACAD. 135 (July, 1969).
Hay, P. 4 J. L. & ECON. DEVELOP. 386 (1969).
Holtman, E. 93 LIBRARY J. 4148 (1 September, 1968).
6 CHOICE 277 (April, 1969).

36 KIRKUS 1083 (15 September, 1968).
194 PUB. WKLY. 57 (30 September, 1968).
FAREWELL TO TEXAS: A VANISHING WILDERNESS. New York: McGraw-Hill, 1967.
Reviewed:
Bogre, T. M. 92 LIBRARY J. 1841 (1 May, 1967).
Bush, M. 73 AM. FORESTS 37 (September, 1967).
Dugger, R. BOOK WEEK 3 (16 July, 1967).
Gunter, P. A. 31 LIV. WILD. 48 (Spring/Summer 1967).
Hass, V. P. 4 BKS. TODAY 5 (9 July, 1967).
Kampelman, M. M. 41 NATL. PARKS 20 (December, 1967).
Richardson, D. CHRISTIAN SCIENCE MONITOR p. 7 (27 July, 1967).
Smith, W. W. 59 SOC. STUDIES 175 (April, 1968).
18 AM. BK. COLLEC. 28 (April, 1968).
63 BOOKLIST 1180 (15 July, 1967).
5 CHOICE 77 (March, 1968).
35 KIRKUS 308 (1 March, 1967).
89 TIME 122 (9 June, 1967).

BIBLE AND THE SCHOOLS, THE. Boston: Little, Brown, 1966.
Reviewed:
Berlin, G. A. 37 HARV. EDU. REV. 174 (Winter 1967).
Bernhard, H. A. 3 L. IN TRANS. Q. 206 (1966).
Johnson, S. 91 LIBRARY J. 114 (1 January, 1966).
Kurland, P. B. 3 BKS. TODAY 9 (30 January, 1966).
Richardson, D. CHRISTIAN SCIENCE MONITOR p. 9 (26 March, 1966).
62 BOOKLIST 639 (1 March, 1966).
83 CHRISTIAN CENTURY 118 (26 January, 1961).
33 KIRKUS 1211 (1 December, 1965).
49 SAT. REV. 92 (17 September, 1966).

WILDERNESS BILL OF RIGHTS, A. Boston: Little, Brown, 1965.
Reviewed:
Beck, R. E. 7 NAT. RESOURCES J. 456 (1967).
Bush, M. 71 AM. FORESTS 38 (October, 1965).
Fleischer, L. 190 PUB. WKLY. 104 (26 December, 1966).
Harrison, G. BOOK WEEK 10 (19 September, 1965).
Johnson, C. S. 90 LIBRARY J. 4788 (1 September, 1965).
Oehser, P. H. 29 LIV. WILD. 29 (Winter 1965/66).

Sorenson, M. CHRISTIAN SCIENCE MONITOR p. 9 (21 September, 1965).
Steffek, E. F. 44 HORTICULTURE 54 (February, 1966).
    Tarlock, A. D. 19 STAN. L. REV. 895 (1967).
    Udall, S. L. 75 NATUR. HIST. 6 (February, 1966).
    Weatherford, G. D. 45 ORE. L. REV. 341 (1966).
    62 BOOKLIST 184 (15 October, 1965).
    2 CHOICE 763 (January, 1966).
    33 KIRKUS 664 (1 September, 1965).
    1 PKS. & REC. 59 (January, 1966).
    1 SCI. BKS. 189 (March, 1966).
FREEDOM OF THE MIND. Garden City: Doubleday, 1964.
Reviewed:
    Henderson, R. W. 89 LIBRARY J. 644 (1 February, 1964).
    Rogat, Y. 3 N. Y. REV. OF BOOKS 5 (22 October, 1964).
ANATOMY OF LIBERTY, THE. New York: Trident Press, 1963.
Reviewed:
    Baldwin, R. 47 SAT. REV. 79 (4 January, 1964).
    Henderson, R. W. 88 LIBRARY J. 4782 (15 December, 1963).
    Rogat, Y. 3 N. Y. REV. OF BOOKS 5 (22 October, 1964).
    27 BEST SELLERS 43 (15 April, 1967).
    40 VA. Q. R. 1xxx (Spring, 1964).
MR. LINCOLN AND THE NEGROES. New York: Atheneum, 1963.
Reviewed:
    Baldi, J. J. 23 BEST SELLERS 205 (15 September, 1963).
    Clancy, T. H. 109 AMERICA 461 (19 October, 1963).
    Furnas, J. C. N. Y. TIMES BOOK R. p. 42 (29 September, 1963).
    LaFarge, J. 46 SAT. REV. 42 (14 December, 1963).
    Lancour, H. 88 LIBRARY J. 3075 (1 September, 1963).
    Littler, R. 16 STAN. L. REV. 782 (1964).
    Lowe, M. J. 30 BROOKLYN L. REV. 395 (1964).
    McConnell, R. C. 50 JNL. NEGRO HIST. 65 (January, 1965).
    Woodward, C. V. 1 BOOK WEEK 4 (22 September, 1963).
    88 LIBRARY J. 4099 (15 October, 1963).
DEMOCRACY'S MANIFESTO. Garden City: Doubleday, 1962.
LIVING BILL OF RIGHTS, A. Garden City: Doubleday, 1961.
Reviewed:
    Cahn, E. N. Y. HERALD TRIBUNE LIVELY ARTS p. 30 (12 February, 1961).

Harris, S. J. 44 SAT. REV. 52 (13 May, 1961).
Henderson, R. W. 86 LIBRARY J. 583 (1 February, 1961).
Isaak, G. E. 37 N.D. L. REV. 306 (1961).
Kiley, R. J. CHICAGO SUNDAY TRIBUNE p. 6 (5 March, 1961).
Lefkowitz, L. J. 30 FORDHAM L. REV. 209 (1961).
Morris, R. 193 CATH. WORLD 264 (July, 1961).
Oakes, J. B. N. Y. TIMES BK. R. p. 7 (12 February, 1961).
57 BOOKLIST 438 (15 March, 1961).
20 BOOKMARK 164 (April, 1961).
78 CHRISTIAN CENTURY 797 (28 June, 1961).
28 KIRKUS 1022 (1 December, 1960).
36 NOTRE DAME LAW. 455 (1961).
SPRINGFIELD REPUBLICAN p. 50 (12 February, 1961).

MUIR OF THE MOUNTAINS. Boston: Houghton Mifflin, 1961.
Reviewed:
Fitch, V. K. 86 LIBRARY J. 2362 (15 June, 1961).
Holden, R. N. Y. TIMES BK. R. pt. 2, p. 12 (14 May, 1961).
Libby, M. S. N. Y. HERALD TRIBUNE BOOKS p. 13 (27 August, 1961).
57 BOOKLIST 702 (15 July, 1961).
CHRISTIAN SCIENCE MONITOR p. 8B (11 May, 1961).
29 KIRKUS 264 (15 March, 1961).
44 SAT. REV. 21 (24 June, 1961).
57 WIS. LIB. BUL. 252 (July, 1961).

MY WILDERNESS: THE PACIFIC WEST. Garden City: Doubleday, 1960.
Reviewed:
Borland, H. N. Y. TIMES BK. R. p. 46 (20 November, 1960).
Foell, E. W. CHRISTIAN SCIENCE MONITOR p. 16 (17 November, 1960).
Gressley, G. M. 85 LIBRARY J. 3670 (15 October, 1960).
Hogan, W. SAN FRANCISCO CHRONICLE p. 31 (2 November, 1960).
Holbrook, S. CHICAGO SUNDAY TRIBUNE p. 6 (27 November, 1960).
Zahniser, H. N. Y. HERALD TRIBUNE BK. R. p. 3 (6 November, 1960).
57 BOOKLIST 200 (1 December, 1960).
20 BOOKMARK 42 (November, 1960).

28 Kirkus 663 (1 August, 1960).
193 Pub. Wkly. 131 (3 June, 1968).

Rule of Law in World Affairs, The. Santa Barbara: Center for the Study of Democratic Institutions, 1961.

America Challenged. Princeton: Princeton University Press, 1960.

Reviewed:

Bernt, H. H. 85 Library J. 2186 (1 June, 1960).

Cohn, E. N. Y. Herald Tribune Bk. R. p. 5 (12 June, 1960).

Davis, S. R. Christian Science Monitor p. 7 (7 September, 1960).

Harris, S. J. 43 Sat. Rev. 21 (2 July, 1960).

Kramer, E. F. 77 Christian Century 950 (17 August, 1960).

56 Booklist 566 (15 May, 1960).

39 Current Hist. 43 (July, 1960).

39 Foreign Affairs 147 (October, 1960).

28 Kirkus 255 (15 March, 1960).

My Wilderness: East to Katahdin. Garden City: Doubleday, 1960.

Reviewed:

Bagg, D. B. Springfield Republican p. 14C (19 November, 1961).

Borland, H. N. Y. Times Bk. R. p. 7 (5 November, 1961).

Cowle, J. Chicago Sunday Tribune p. 3 (22 October, 1961).

Ganett, L. N. Y. Herald Tribune Books p. 3 (22 October, 1961).

Henderson, R. W. 86 Library J. 3488 (15 October, 1961).

Hogan, W. San Francisco Chronicle p. 33 (24 October, 1961).

58 Booklist 216 (1 December, 1961).

21 Bookmark 95 (January, 1962).

79 Christian Century 87 (17 January, 1962).

29 Kirkus 863 (15 September, 1961).

37 New Yorker 245 (11 November, 1961).

193 Pub. Wkly. 131 (3 June, 1968).

Douglas of the Supreme Court. Edited by V. Countryman. Garden City: Doubleday, 1959.

EXPLORING THE HIMALAYA. New York: Random House, 1958.
Reviewed:
  Armstrong, E. CHICAGO SUNDAY TRIBUNE pt. 2, p. 34 (2 November, 1958).
  Berkvit, R. N. Y. TIMES p. 40 (15 February, 1959).
  Jackson, C. 202 ATLANTIC 100 (December, 1958).
  McFake, M. 83 LIBRARY J. 3006 (15 October, 1958).
  Taylor, M. CHRISTIAN SCIENCE MONITOR p. 15 (26 November, 1958).
  35 HORN BK. 138 (April, 1959).
  26 KIRKUS 510 (15 July, 1958).
RIGHT OF THE PEOPLE, THE. Garden City: Doubleday, 1958.
Reviewed:
  Anderson, W. R. 46 KY. L. 648 (1958).
  Brunn, R. R. CHRISTIAN SCIENCE MONITOR p. 5 (16 January, 1958).
  Butler, A. 12 SW. L. J. 402 (1958).
  Cahn, E. N. Y. TIMES p. 3 (19 January, 1958).
  Denonn, L. E. 44 A. B. A. J. 675 (1958).
  Dykstra, D. J. 6 UTAH L. REV. 148 (1958).
  Edwards, W. H. N. Y. HERALD TRIBUNE BK. R. p. 7 (26 January, 1958).
  Henderson, R. W. 83 LIBRARY J. 498 (1 February, 1958).
  Hogan, W. SAN FRANCISCO CHRONICLE p. 23 (15 January, 1958).
  Horsky, C. A. 44 VA. L. REV. 521 (1958).
  Howe, M. D. 71 HARV. L. REV. 1377 (1958).
  Keohane, R. 23 SOCIAL EDUC. 42 (January, 1959).
  King, W. L. CHICAGO SUNDAY TRIBUNE p. 2 (26 January, 1958).
  Kunstler, W. M. 41 SAT. REV. 4 (18 January, 1958).
  Kurland, P. B. 47 YALE R. 596 (June, 1958).
  Manning, L. F. 27 FORDHAM L. REV. 141 (1958).
  Matson, M. H. 19 U. PITT. L. REV. 834 (1958).
  Mosburg, L. G. Jr., 11 OKLA. L. REV. 368 (1958).
  Murphy, J. W. 3 VILL. L. REV. 591 (1958).
  Rice, W. G. 18 LAW. GUILD REV. 169 (1959).
  Satter, M. J. 39 CHI. B. REC. 436 (1958).
  Sobolik, D. M. 34 N.D. L. REV. 274 (1958).
  Traynor, R. J. 46 CALIF. L. REV. 301 (1958).

54 BOOKLIST 296 (1 February, 1958).
17 BOOKMARK 112 (February, 1958).
25 KIRKUS 856 (15 November, 1957).
SPRINGFIELD REPUBLICAN p. 18C (23 February, 1958).
3 STUDENT LAW J. 32 (1958).

WEST OF THE INDUS. Garden City: Doubleday, 1958.
Reviewed:
Arnold, S. SAN FRANCISCO CHRONICLE Sec. 3-3 (11 December, 1958).
Demery, P. 83 LIBRARY J. 3140 (1 November, 1958).
Godsell, G. CHRISTIAN SCIENCE MONITOR p. 15 (26 November, 1958).
McCutcheon, J. T. CHICAGO SUNDAY TRIBUNE p. 2 (23 November, 1958).
Ozbekkan, H. N. Y. TIMES p. 6 (9 November, 1958).
Schmidt, D. A. 41 SAT. REV. 18 (22 November, 1958).
Steele, A. T. N. Y. HERALD TRIBUNE BK. R. p. 1 (9 November, 1958).
55 BOOKLIST 111; 181 (1 November, 1958; 1 December, 1958).
18 BOOKMARK 62 (December, 1958).
26 KIRKUS 701 (1 September, 1958).
SPRINGFIELD REPUBLICAN p. 60 (14 December, 1958).
54 WIS. LIB. BUL. 515 (November, 1958).

RUSSIAN JOURNEY. Garden City: Doubleday, 1956.
Reviewed:
Bernt, H. H. 81 LIBRARY J. 903 (15 April, 1956).
Fainsod, M. 46 YALE R. 136 (Autumn 1956).
Harrison, J. G. CHRISTIAN SCIENCE MONITOR p. 7 (7 June, 1956).
Higgins, M. N. Y. HERALD TRIBUNE BK. R. p. 4 (24 June, 1956).
Hogan, W. SAN FRANCISCO CHRONICLE p. 21 (12 June, 1956).
Moore, W. CHICAGO SUNDAY TRIBUNE p. 6 (24 June, 1956).
Salisbury, H. E. N. Y. TIMES p. 3 (10 June, 1956).
Scoggin, M. C. 32 HORN BK. 372 (October, 1956).
Stevens, L. C. 39 SAT. REV. 12 (9 June, 1956).
52 BOOKLIST 373; 53:18 (15 May, 1956; 1 September, 1956).

15 BOOKMARK 31 (November, 1956).
183 CATH. WORLD 399 (August, 1956).
24 KIRKUS 259 (1 April, 1956).
32 NEW YORKER 90 (23 June 1956).
SPRINGFIELD REPUBLICAN p. 10C (17 June, 1956).
67 TIME 110 (11 June, 1956).
52 WIS. LIB. BUL. 212 (September, 1956).
WE THE JUDGES: STUDIES IN AMERICAN AND INDIAN CONSTITUTIONAL LAW FROM MARSHALL TO MUKHERJEA, Garden City: Doubleday, 1956.
Reviewed:
Bernt, H. 81 LIBRARY J. 77 (1 January, 1956).
Cahn, E. N. Y. TIMES p. 7 (22 January, 1956).
Clark, C. E. 35 TEX. L. REV. 470 (1957).
Fahy, C. 32 NOTRE DAME LAW. 353 (1957).
Freund, P. A. 42 IA. L. REV. 141 (1956).
Garcia-Mora, M. R. 34 U. DET. L. J. 203 (1956).
Gertz, E. 7 DECALOGUE 16 (1956).
Gledhill, A. 51 NW. U. L. REV. 506 (1956).
Havighurst, H. C. CHICAGO SUNDAY TIMES p. 3 (19 February, 1956).
Heinley, R. C. 32 N.D. L. REV. 168 (1956).
McCloskey, R. G. 70 HARV. L. REV. 189 (1956).
Merrill, M. H. 9 OKLA. L. REV. 357 (1956).
Overfelt, S. E. 24 U. KAN. CITY L. REV. 164 (1955/56).
Rackow, F. 8 WESTERN RES. L. REV. 234 (1957).
Ramaswamy, M. 8 STAN. L. REV. 756 (1956).
Rodell, F. 39 SAT. REV. 16 (14 February, 1956).
Sivasubramanian, L. R. 23 U. CHI. L. REV. 563 (1956).
Stumberg, G. W. 50 L. LIB. J. 60 (1957).
Weissman, D. L. 182 NATION 141 (18 February, 1956).
52 BOOKLIST 286 (15 March, 1956).
34 FOREIGN AFFAIRS 675 (1956).
N. Y. HERALD TRIBUNE BK. R. p. 11 (26 February, 1956).
12 U. S. QUARTERLY BK. R. 204 (June, 1956).
ALMANAC OF LIBERTY, AN. Garden City: Doubleday, 1954).
Reviewed:
Breaky, J. R., Jr. 18 U. DET. L. J. 347 (1955).
Denonn, L. E. 41 A.B.A. J. 254 (1955).
Duncan, J. P. 8 OKLA. L. REV. 258 (1955).

Frank, J. P. 55 COLUM. L. REV. 936 (1955).
Netterville, J. S. 28 SO. CALIF. L. REV. 107 (1954).
Rodell, F. 64 YALE L. J. 1099 (1955).
Rogers, W. D. 40 IA. L. REV. 674 (1955).
Stumpf, S. E. 30 N.Y.U. L. REV. 1459 (1955).
Vogel, Jon N. 31 N.D. L. REV. 209 (1955).

NORTH FROM MALAYA. Garden City, N.Y., Doubleday, 1953.
Reviewed:
Durdin, T. N. Y. TIMES p. 3 (31 May, 1953).
Hass, V. P. CHICAGO SUNDAY TRIBUNE p. 5 (7 June, 1953).
Jackson, J. H. SAN FRANCISCO CHRONICLE p. 19 (27 May, 1953).
Johnson, G. W. 128 NEW REPUBLIC 18 (15 June, 1953).
Lattimore, O. 177 NATION 34 (11 July, 1953).
McSorley, J. 178 CATH. WORLD 237 (December, 1953).
Michener, J. A. N. Y. HERALD TRIBUNE BK. R. p. 1 (31 May, 1953).
Payne, R. 36 SAT. REV. 14 (27 June, 1953).
Roth, H. L. 78 LIBRARY J. 914 (15 May, 1953).
Walker, G. CHRISTIAN SCIENCE MONITOR p. 11 (28 May, 1953).
49 BOOKLIST 355 (1 September, 1953).
12 BOOKMARK 204 (June, 1953).
25 CURRENT HIST. 320 (November, 1953).
29 HORN BK. 373 (October, 1953).
21 KIRKUS 240 (1 April, 1953).
29 NEW YORKER 151 (6 June, 1953).
SPRINGFIELD REPUBLICAN p. 9C (14 June, 1953).
9 U. S. QUARTERLY BK. R. 273 (September, 1953).
49 WIS. LIB. BUL. 171 (July, 1953).

BEYOND THE HIGH HIMALAYAS. Garden City: Doubleday, 1952).
Reviewed:
Haas, V. P. CHICAGO SUNDAY TRIBUNE p. 3 (7 September, 1952).
Krader, L. 66 HARV. L. REV. 382 (1952).
MacEoin, G. 57 COMMONWEAL 124 (7 November, 1952).
Muehl, J. F. 35 SAT. REV. 14 (20 September, 1952).
Peel, R. CHRISTIAN SCIENCE MONITOR p. 11 (25 September, 1952).

Ripley, D. 42 YALE R. 305 (1953).
Roth, H. L. 77 LIBRARY J. 1301 (1952).
Sawatzky, G. 1 KAN. L. REV. 381 (1953).
Scoggin, M. C. 28 HORN BK. 426 (December, 1952).
Steel, A. T. N. Y. HERALD TRIBUNE BK. R. p. 3 (21 September, 1952).
Straight, M. 127 NEW REPUBLIC 19 (29 September, 1952).
Trumbull, R. N. Y. TIMES p. 3 (21 September, 1952).
49 BOOKLIST 46 (1 October, 1952).
12 BOOKMARK 5 (October, 1952).
69 CHRISTIAN CENTURY 1530 (1952).
20 KIRKUS 391 (1 July, 1952).
77 LIBRARY J. 2189 (1952).
28 NEW YORKER 126 (20 September, 1952).
SAN FRANCISCO CHRONICLE p. 25 (2 November, 1952).
SPRINGFIELD REPUBLICAN p. 11C (12 October, 1952).
48 WIS. LIB. BUL. 213 (September, 1952).

STRANGE LANDS AND FRIENDLY PEOPLE. New York: Harper, 1951.
Reviewed:
Casgrain, J. D. 174 CATH. WORLD 318 (January, 1952).
Coon, C. S. 173 NATION 476 (1 December, 1951).
Fischer, L. N. Y. TIMES p. 1 (4 November, 1951).
Harrison, J. G. CHRISTIAN SCIENCE MONITOR p. 11 (1 November, 1951).
Henderson, R. W. 76 LIBRARY J. 1801 (1951).
Jackson, J. H. SAN FRANCISCO CHRONICLE p. 22 (2 November, 1951).
Jackson, J. H. CHICAGO SUNDAY TRIBUNE p. 12 (18 November, 1951).
Reynolds, Q. N. Y. HERALD TRIBUNE BK. R. p. 1 (4 November, 1951).
Sevareid, E. 34 SAT. REV. OF LIT. 17 (10 November, 1951).
48 BOOKLIST 57; 83 (15 October, 1951; 1 November, 1951).
11 BOOKMARK 56 (December, 1951).
CLEVELAND OPEN SHELF p. 27 (November, 1951).
55 COMMONWEAL 133 (16 November, 1951).
19 KIRKUS 506 (1 September, 1951).
27 NEW YORKER 173 (8 December, 1951).
SPRINGFIELD REPUBLICAN p. 30A (2 December, 1951).
47 WIS. LIB. BUL. 251 (November, 1951).

OF MEN AND MOUNTAINS. New York: Harper, 1950.
Reviewed:
Hass, V. P. CHICAGO SUNDAY TRIBUNE p. 4 (23 April, 1950).
Henderson, R. W. 75 LIBRARY J. 776 (1950).
Hutchens, J. K. N. Y. HERALD TRIBUNE BK. R. p. 1 (9 April, 1950).
Jackson, J. H. SAN FRANCISCO CHRONICLE p. 20 (12 April, 1950).
Morse, W. F. CHICAGO SUN p. 7 (21 April, 1950).
Neuberger, R. L. 86 SURVEY 334 (1950).
Sanderson, I. T. 33 SAT. REV. OF LIT. 53 (15 April, 1950).
Sawyer, R. CHRISTIAN SCIENCE MONITOR p. 5 (15 April, 1950).
Stewart, G. R. N. Y. TIMES p. 3 (9 April, 1950).
46 BOOKLIST 273 (1950).
9 BOOKMARK 208 (1950).
19 CURRENT HIST. 106 (1950).
18 KIRKUS 89 (1 February, 1950).
26 NEW YORKER 122 (20 May, 1950).
SPRINGFIELD REPUBLICAN p. 10C (14 May, 1950).
55 TIME 114 (17 April, 1950).
46 WIS. LIB. BUL. 19 (May, 1950).
BEING AN AMERICAN. New York: J. Day Co., 1948.
Reviewed:
Bresler, H. J. N. Y. TIMES p. 3 (15 August, 1948).
Burns, J. J. 34 A.B.A. J. 815 (1948).
Byse, C. 97 U. PA. L. REV. 452 (1949).
Donnelly, R. C. 34 VA. L. REV. 864 (1948).
Jackson, J. H. SAN FRANCISCO CHRONICLE p. 14 (17 August, 1948).
Janeway, E. 31 SAT. REV. OF LIT. 15 (21 August, 1948).
Johnson, G. W. N. Y. HERALD TRIBUNE WKLY. BK. R. p. 5 (15 August, 1948).
Landis, E. S. 34 CORNELL L. Q. 285 (1948).
Maurer, R. A. 37 GEO. L. J. 284 (1949).
Rodell, F. 10 U. PITT. L. REV. 605 (1949).
Sawyer, R. CHRISTIAN SCIENCE MONITOR p. 14 (14 August, 1948).
Schleicher, C. P. 28 ORE. L. REV. 88 (1948).

Schlesinger, A., Jr. 34 IA. L. REV. 729 (1949).
Taylor, H. S. 73 LIBRARY J. 1084 (1948).
White, W. H. 17 FORDHAM L. REV. 317 (1948).
45 BOOKLIST 29 (15 September, 1948).
CHICAGO SUN p. 8x (15 August, 1948).
48 COMMONWEAL 458 (1948).
16 KIRKUS 300 (1948).
SPRINGFIELD REPUBLICAN p. 7B (12 September, 1948).
44 WIS. LIB. BUL. 163 (October, 1948).
DEMOCRACY AND FINANCE. New Haven: Yale University Press, 1940.
Reviewed:
Abel, A. S. 26 WASH. U. L. Q. 289 (1941).
Ballantine, A. A. 39 MICH. L. REV. 951 (1941).
Dean, A. H. 50 YALE L. J. 725 (1941).
Eaton, C. S. 8 U. CHI. L. REV. 195 (1941).
Frank, J. 54 HARV. L. REV. 905 (1941).
Hoagland, H. E. 213 ANN. AM. ACAD. 220 (1941).
Janeway, E. 152 NATION 48 (11 January, 1941).
Jordan, H. P. 359 LIVING AGE 388 (1940).
Katz, W. G. 27 A.B.A. J. 118 (1941).
Larson, A. 16 TENN. L. REV. 890 (1941).
MacChesney, B. 36 ILL. L. REV. 247 (1941).
Sawyer, R. A. 65 LIBRARY J. 807 (1940).
Washington, G. T. 30 YALE R. 398 (1941).

Articles, Essays, Lectures, and Tributes

"The Meaning of Due Process: Harlan Fiske Stone Centennial Lecture," 10 COLUM. J. L. & SOC. PROB. 1 (1973).
"Grand Design of the Constitution," 7 GONZAGA L. REV. 239 (1972).
"Justice Brennan as a Jurist," 4 RUTGERS CAMDEN L. J. 5 (1972).
"Samuel M. Chapin," 8 CALIF. WESTERN L. REV. 185 (1972).
"Environmental Problems of the Oceans: the Need for International Controls," 1 ENVIRONMENTAL LAW 149 (1971).
"In Honor of Chief Judge Stanley H. Fuld," 71 COLUM. L. REV. 531 (1971).

BIBLIOGRAPHY

"Pollution: an International Problem Needing International Solution," 7 TEX. INT. L. J. 1 (1971).
"Conservation of Man," 19 J. PUB. L. 3 (1970).
"Managing the Docket of the Supreme Court of the United States," 25 RECORD 279 (1970).
"Press and First Amendment Rights," 7 IDAHO L. REV. 1 (1970).
"Some Dicta on Discrimination," 3 LOYOLA U. L. REV. (L.A.) 207 (1970).
"Federal Courts and the Democratic System," 21 ALA. L. REV. 179 (1969).
"Dedication to Chief Justice Earl Warren," 48 NEB. L. REV. 3 (1968).
"Future Lawyer's Role in Solving Local and International Problems," 1 U.S.F.V. L. REV. 101 (1968).
"Juvenile Courts and Due Process of Law," 19 JUV. CT. JUDGES 9 (1968).
"Discurso," 27 REV. C. ABO. P. R. 485 (1967).
"A Role of the Governments of the World in Establishing a Rule of Law Instead of Force," THE CHANGING ROLE OF GOVERNMENT. Vol. IV, No. 1, West Georgia College Studies in the Social Sciences, Carrolton, Ga. 1965, pp. 3-17.
"Forward to Mr. Justice Black, a Symposium," 65 YALE L. J. 449 (1965).
"Law Reviews and Full Disclosure," 40 WASH. L. REV. 227 (1965).
"Phil S. Gibson," 2 L. IN TRANS. Q. 129 (1965).
"Rule of Law in World Affairs," 40 WASH. L. REV. 673 (1965); 13 KAN. L. REV. 473 (1965).
"In Honor of Adolf A. Berle," 64 COLUM. L. REV. 1371 (1964).
"Bill of Rights and the Free Society: an Individual View," 13 BUFFALO L. REV. 1 (1963).
"Bill of Rights is Not Enough," 38 N.Y.U. L. REV. 207 (1963).
"In the Classroom and the World, a Reach for Far Horizons: a Tribute to Wesley A. Sturges," 18 U. MIAMI L. REV. 1 (1963).
"Judge Charles E. Clark," 73 YALE L. J. 1 (1963).
"Right of Association," 63 COLUM. L. REV. 1361 (1963).
"Wesley A. Sturges: in Memoriam," 72 YALE L. J. 639 (1963).
"Karl N. Llewellyn," 29 U. CHI. L. REV. 611 (1962).
"Law and the American Character," 37 CALIF. S. B. J. 753 (1962).
"Lawday, U.S.A.," 36 CONN. B. J. 4 (1962).
"Lawyers of the Peace Corps," 48 A.B.A.J. 909 (1962).

"The Supreme Court Years: Tribute to C. E. Whittaker," 40 TEX. L. REV. 742 (1962).
"Arizona's New Judicial Article," 2 ARIZ. L. REV. 159 (1960).
"Public Trial and the Free Press," 2 P. E. A. L. Q. 54 (1962); 46 A.B.A.J. 840 (1960); 33 ROCKY MT. L. REV. 1 (1960).
"Supreme Court and its Case Load," 45 CORNELL L. Q. 401 (1960).
"Vagrancy and Arrest on Suspicion," 70 YALE L. J. 1 (1960).
"In Forma Pauperis Practice in the United States," 2 N. H. B. J. 5 (1959).
"Legal Institutions in America," LEGAL INSTITUTIONS TODAY AND TOMORROW, edited by M. Paulsen. 1959. pp. 274-278.
"Means and the End," 1959 WASH. U. L. Q. 103 (1959).
"On Misconception of the Judicial Function and the Responsibility of the Bar," 59 COLUM. L. REV. 227 (1959).
"Role of the Lawyer," 12 OKLA. L. REV. 1 (1959).
"Hazards to Liberty," 7 DECALOGUE 1 (1957).
"Jerome N. Frank," 10 J. LEGAL ED. 1 (1957).
"Jerome N. Frank," 24 U. CHI. L. REV. 625 (1957).
"Durham Rule: a Meeting Ground for Lawyers and Psychiatrists," 41 IA. L. REV. 485 (1956).
"Interposition and the *Peters* Case, 1778-1809," 19 F.R.D. 185 (1956); 9 STAN. L. REV. 3 (1956).
"Bill of Rights, Due Process, and Federalism in India," 40 MINN. L. REV. 1 (1955).
"In Memoriam: George H. Dession," 5 BUFFALO L. REV. 3 (1955).
"Some Antecedents of Due Process," 39 A.B.A.J. 851 (1953); 2 KAN. L. REV. 1 (1953); 13 LAW. GUILD REV. 145 (1953); 28 NOTRE DAME LAW. 497 (1953).
"Honesty in Government," 4 OKLA. L. REV. 279 (1951).
"Recent Trends in Constitutional Law," 30 ORE. L. REV. 279 (1951).
"Tennessee Across the World," 21 TENN. L. REV. 797 (1951).
"Underhill Moore," 59 YALE L. J. 189 (1950).
"The Human Welfare State," 97 U. PA. L. REV. 597 (1949).
"Stare Decisis," 21 OKLA. B. A. J. 294 (1950); 49 COLUM. L. REV. 735 (1949); also published by the Association of the Bar of the City of New York (Benjamin N. Cardozo lecture), 1949.
"Democracy Charts its Course," 1 U. FLA. L. REV. 133 (1948).
"The Dissenting Opinion," 8 LAW. GUILD REV. 467 (1948).

"Law in Eruption: a Concept of Lawyers' Duty in a Time of Change," 34 A.B.A.J. 674 (1948).
"Max Radin," 36 CALIF. L. REV. 163 (1948).
"Procedural Safeguards in the Bill of Rights," 31 J. AM. JUD. SOC. 166 (1948).
"Harlan Fiske Stone—Teacher," 35 CALIF. L. REV. 4 (1947).
"Chief Justice Stone," 46 COLUM. L. REV. 693 (1946).
"The Lasting Influence of Mr. Justice Brandeis," 19 TEMP. L. Q. 361 (1946).
"The Free Society—at Home and Abroad," 4 LAW. GUILD REV. 1 (1944).
"The Bar's Responsibility," 17 TENN. L. REV. 49 (1941).
"The Lawyer and the Public Servant," 26 A.B.A.J. 633 (1940).
"Pre-Trial Procedure," 26 A.B.A.J. 693 (1940).
"Improvement in Federal Procedure for Corporate Reorganizations," 24 A.B.A.J. 875 (1938).
"Scatteration v. Integration of Public Utility Systems," 24 A.B.A.J. 800 (1938).
"The Lawyer and Reorganizations," 1 NAT. LAW. GUILD Q. 31 (1937).
"Legal Problem of Control over Protective Committees for Municipal and Quasi-Municipal Obligations," 2 LEGAL NOTES ON LOCAL GOV'T 81 (1936).
"The Lawyer and the Federal Securities Act," 3 DUKE B. A. J. 66 (1935).
"Directors Who Do Not Direct," 47 HARV. L: REV. 1305 (1934).
"Protective Committees in Railroad Reorganizations," 47 HARV. L. REV. 565 (1934).
"Federal Securities Act of 1933," (with G. E. Bates), 43 YALE L. J. 171 (1933).
"Landlords' Claims in Reorganizations," (with J. Frank), 42 YALE L. J. 1003 (1933).
"Some Effects of the Securities Act upon Investment Banking," (with G. E. Bates), 1 U. CHI. L. REV. 283 (1933).
"Stock 'Brokers' as Agents and Dealers," (with G. E. Bates), 43 YALE L. J. 46 (1933).
"Symposium on Credit for the Urban Employee," 42 YALE L. J. 473 (1933).
"Wage Earner Bankruptcies—State v. Federal Control," 42 YALE L. J. 591 (1933).

"A Factual Study of Bankruptcy Administration and Some Suggestions," (with J. H. Marshall), 32 COLUM. L. REV. 25 (1932).
"The Hastings Bill and Lessons Learned from the Bankruptcy Studies," 7 J. N. A. REFEREES BANK. 25 (1932).
"Secondary Distribution of Securities, Problems Suggested by *Kinney v. Glenny*," (with G. E. Bates), 41 YALE L. J. 949 (1932).
"Some Functional Aspects of Bankruptcy," 41 YALE L. J. 329 (1932).
"Business Failures Project—an Analysis of Methods of Investigation," (with D. S. Thomas), 40 YALE L. J. 1034 (1931).
"Business Failures Project—a Problem in Methodology," 5 J. NAT. ASSOC. REFEREES IN BANKRUPTCY 142 (1931); 39 YALE L. J. 1013 (1930) (with W. Clark & D. S. Thomas).
"Equity Receiverships in the United States District Court for Connecticut, 1920-1929," (with J. H. Weir), 4 CONN. B. J. 1 (1930).
"Functional Approach to the Law of Business Associations," 23 ILL. L. REV. 673 (1929).
"Insulation from Liability through Subsidiary Corporations," (with C. M. Shanks), 39 YALE L. J. 193 (1929).
"Vicarious Liability and Administration of Risk," 38 YALE L. J. 584 (1929).

Book Reviews

Lewis, A., *The Supreme Court and How It Works.* N. Y. TIMES BK. R. Pt. 2, p. 2 (6 November, 1966).
Handlin, O. M., *The Dimensions of Freedom.* N.Y. TIMES BK. R. p. 3 (22 October, 1961).
Cohn, E., *The Predicament of Democratic Man.* N. Y. TIMES BK. R. p. 5 (1 October, 1961).
Eisenstein, L., *The Ideologies of Taxation.* N.Y. HERALD TRIBUNE Sept. 24, 1961, § 6 (Books), at 13 col. 1.
Cohen, Felix, S., *The Legal Conscience: Selected Papers of Felix S. Cohen.* N. Y. TIMES BK. R. p. 3 (19 February, 1961).
Loss, L., & Cowett, E. M., *Blue Sky Law.* 73 HARV. L. REV. 1235 (1960).

Jennings, W. I., *Approach to Self-government.* 32 TUL. L. REV. 788 (1958).
Berle, A. A., Jr., *Twentieth Century Capitalist Revolution.* 103 U. PA. L. REV. 1108 (1955).
Quindry, S. E., *Bonds and Bondholders, Rights and Remedies, with Forms.* 2 Vol., 34 COLUM. L. REV. 1391 (1934).
Samuel, H. B., *Shareholders' Money.* 34 COLUM. L. REV. 787 (1934).
Berle, A. A., Jr., *Cases and Materials on Corporate Finance.* 17 VA. L. REV. 625 (1931).
Mulla, Sir D. F., *Law of Insolvency in British India.* 40 YALE L. J. 840 (1931).
Radin, M., *Lawful Pursuit of Gain.* 44 HARV. L. REV. 1164 (1931).
Clark, R. E., *Treatise on the Law and Practice of Receivers.* 2d ed., 39 YALE L. J. 592 (1930).
Beale, J. H., *Cases on the Measure of Damages.* 3d ed., 38 YALE L. J. 698 (1929).
Britton, W. E., *Cases on the Law of Bankruptcy.* 24 ILL. L. REV. 121 (1929).
Crane, J., *Cases on Damages.* 38 YALE L. J. 608 (1929).
Holbrook, Evans & Aigler, *Cases on Law of Bankruptcy.* 2d ed., 37 YALE L. J. 685 (1928).
Joslyn, L. E., *Students' Manual of Bankruptcy Law and Practice.* 22 ILL. L. REV. 347 (1927).
Clark, B. B., *New York Law of Damages.* 2 Vol., 26 COLUM. L. REV. 780 (1926).

Forewords and Introductions

Foreword to *Symposium on the Denver Public Defender*, 50 DENV. L. J. 1 (1973).
Preface to *Symposium on Law and Technology*, 45 SO. CALIF. L. REV. 1 (1972).
Foreword: Computerization of Government Files: What Impact on the Individual?, 15 U.C.L.A. L. REV. 1371 (1968).
Foreword to *Symposium on Right to Counsel*, 45 MINN. L. REV. 693 (1961).
Foreword to *Symposium on the S.E.C.*, 28 GEO. WASH. L. REV. 1 (1959).

New Law Review, 3 UTAH L. REV. 1 (1952).
Foreword to *Symposium on World Organization*, 55 YALE L. J. 863 (1946).

Casebooks

CASES AND MATERIALS ON BUSINESS UNITS, LOSSES, LIABILITIES, AND ASSETS (with Shanks, C.M.). Chicago: Callaghan & Co, 1932.
CASES AND MATERIALS ON THE LAW OF CORPORATE REORGANIZATION (with Shanks, C. M.). St. Paul, Minn.: West Publishing Company, 1931.
Reviewed:
Blackstock, L. G. 10 TEXAS L. REV. 396 (1932).
Crimmins, J. M. 7 NOTRE DAME LAW. 132 (1931).
Dewing, A. S. 45 HARV. L. REV. 1138 (1932).
Dodd, E. M. Jr., 17 CORNELL L. Q. 317 (1932).
Evans, A. E. 20 KY. L. J. 188 (1932).
Finletter, T. K. 80 U. PA. L. REV. 624 (1932).
Harvey, R. S. 20 GEO. L. J. 571 (1932).
Johnson, S. 18 VA. L. REV. 472 (1932).
Kline, J. V. 41 YALE L. J. 1255 (1932).
Peppin, J. C. 20 CALIF. L. REV. 347 (1932).
Shapiro, W. H. 6 ST. JOHN'S L. REV. 197 (1931).
Swaine, R. T. 32 COLUM. L. REV. 402 (1932).
2 DET. L. REV. 144 (1932).
CASES AND MATERIALS ON THE LAW OF FINANCING OF BUSINESS UNITS (with Shanks, C. M.). Chicago: Callaghan & Co, 1931.
Reviewed:
Payne, P. M. 18 VA. L. REV. 593 (1932).
Root, E., Jr. 41 YALE L. J. 481 (1932).
CASES AND MATERIALS OF THE LAW OF MANAGEMENT OF BUSINESS UNITS (with Shanks, C. M.). Chicago: Callaghan & Co, 1931.
Reviewed:
Isaacs, N. 41 YALE L. J. 150 (1931).
O'Keeff, A. J., Jr. 5 SO. CALIF. L. REV. 176 (1931).

Table of Cases

Tax Cases

Alison v. United States	35
Allen v. Trust Co.	37
Arrowsmith v. Commissioner	31-33, 37, 64, 123, 134
Bercaw v. Commissioner	69
Bilder, Commissioner v.	27
Bingler v. Johnson (Supreme Court)	68
Bingler v. Johnson (Court of Appeals)	68
Bogardus v. Commissioner	50, 51
Central Tablet Manufacturing Co. v. United States	xi, 139
Clifford, Helvering v.	15-17, 19, 29, 34, 39, 49, 124, 133, 134
COMMISSIONER v. — See Name of Taxpayer	
Correll, United States v. (Supreme Court)	60, 70-71, 122, 125
Correll v. United States (Court of Appeals)	71
Cory Corp. v. Sauber	52
Davis, United States v. (Supreme Court)	72-73, 125
Davis v. United States (Court of Appeals)	73

Davis v. United States (District Court) 72
Dobson v. Commissioner 50-51
Duberstein, Commissioner v. 50-51, 59, 129
Equitable Life Assurance Society v. Commissioner 33-34
Estate of Bosch, Commissioner v. 71-72
Estate of Noel, Commissioner v. (Supreme Court) 136
Estate of Noel v. Commissioner (Court of Appeals) 136
Estate of Noel v. Commissioner (Tax Court) 136
Federal Power Commission v. Memphis
    Light, Gas & Water Div. 42
Gambrill, Helvering v. 19
General American Investors Co. v. Commissioner 38, 41-42
Generes, United States v. 65-67, 71, 92, 93, 121, 128, 134
Gilmore, United States v. 49, 128-129
Glenshaw Glass Co., Commissioner v. 3, 38, 41
Gregory v. Helvering 48
Griffiths, Helvering v. 19
Guggenheim v. Rasquin 19
Harmon, Commissioner v. 13, 28, 30, 31, 32, 35, 37, 64, 122, 134
HELVERING v. – See Name of Taxpayer
Idaho Power Co., Commissioner v. xi, 139-140
Kaiser, United States v. 51, 59, 128-129
Keefe v. Cote 72, 73
Kerr v. Commissioner 72
Knetsch v. United States 44, 46-49, 59, 64, 92, 133-134
Korpan, United States v. 37
Lake, Inc., P.G., Commissioner v. 35, 42-43, 49
Lester, Commissioner v. 52, 58, 59, 67, 121, 134
Lewis, United States v. 13, 30-32, 37-38, 134

TABLE OF CASES 201

Lewyt Corp. v. Commissioner 35
Lucas v. Earl 30
Maguire v. Commissioner 13-15, 17, 19, 29, 34, 124
Merchants National Bank v. Commissioner 36
Nash v. United States 42-43
National Alfalfa Dehydrating Co., Commissioner v. xi, 139
Olympic Radio & Television, Inc., United States v. 34
Patrick, United States v. 44
Peurifoy v. Commissioner 13-33
Phelps v. Commissioner 72-73
Poe v. Seaborn 28-30, 134
Powell, United States v. 67-68, 122
R. J. Reynolds Co., Helvering v. 17
Reynolds, Helvering v. 17-18, 19
Riley Investment Co., J. E. v. Commissioner 9-10, 12, 13, 17, 31, 33, 58-59, 125
Robertson v. United States 33, 36
Rudolph v. United States (Supreme Court) 54-58, 59, 66, 127, 129
Rudolph v. United States (District Court) 57
Ryan v. United States 68
Scaife Co. v. Commissioner 12-13, 17, 31, 33, 58-59
Skelly Oil Co., United States v. 63-65, 66, 67, 73, 74-75, 92, 121, 122, 127, 128, 134
Snow v. Commissioner xi, 139
Southwest Exploration Co., Commissioner v. 74-75
Stanton v. United States 50-51
Stewart, United States v. 19-23, 64, 125
Stidger, Commissioner v. 68-70, 121-122, 127, 128
Sullivan, Commissioner v. 38, 39, 40, 41

Tank Truck Rentals Inc. v. Commissioner   38, 39, 40, 41
Tellier, Commissioner v.   41
UNITED STATES v. — See Name of Taxpayer
Virginian Hotel Corp. v. Helvering   19, 23-26, 31, 38, 124-125
Wood, Helvering v.   15

Corporate Insider Regulation Cases

American United Mutual Life Insurance Co. v.
   City of Avon Park   79-81
Anderson v. Abbott   83
Blau v. Lehman   87-88, 90, 92-93
Brown v. Gerdes   82-83
Caplin v. Marine Midland Grace Trust Co.   80, 88, 92-93
Connecticut Ry. & Lighting v. Palmer   81
Emil v. Hanley   81
Feder v. Martin Marietta Corp.   91
General Protective Comm. v. SEC   84-85
General Stores Corp. v. Shlensky   83-84, 87
Leiman v. Gutman   82-83
Pepper v. Litton   80, 81
Randall, United States v.   93-94
Rattner v. Lehman   88
Reliance Elec. Co. v. Emerson Elec. Co.   90, 92-93
SEC v. Drexel Co.   85, 87
SEC v. Medical Comm. for Human Rights   62-63
SEC v. New England Slec. System   88-89
SEC v. United States Realty & Improvement Co.   84
Smith v. Sperling   84-85

TABLE OF CASES 203

St. Joe Paper Co. v. Atlantic Coast Line R.R.   84-85
Superintendent of Ins. v. Bankers Life
    & Casualty Co.   88-90
Swanson v. Traer   84-85
UNITED STATES v. — See Name of Respondent

Labor Cases

Boeing Co., NLRB v.	105
Carpenters Local 60 v. NLRB	95
Electrical Workers Local 761 v. NLRB	105
Excelsior Underwear Inc.	104
Express Publishing Co., NLRB v.	102
Guss v. Utah Labor Bd.	94-95
H. K. Porter Co. v. NLRB	103
Machinists Lodge 35 v. NLRB	101
Marine Workers, NLRB v.	106
NLRB v. — See Name of Respondent	
Nash-Finch Co., NLRB v.	100-101, 104
News Syndicate Co., NLRB v.	95
Operating Engineers Local 825, NLRB v.	100
Packard Motor Car Co. v. NLRB	96
Republic Steel Corp. v. NLRB	96, 124-125
Retail Clerks Local 1625 v. Schermerhorn	94-95
Rutter-Rex Manufacturing Co., J. H., NLRB v.	105
Strong, NLRB v.	103-104, 105
Teamsters Local 357 v. NLRB	95, 100, 103
Textile Workers Local 1029, NLRB v.	106
Textile Workers Union v. Lincoln Mills	99
Travis v. United States	94-95

Typographical Union v. NLRB 95
Universal Camera Corp. v. NLRB 105
Wyman-Gordon Co., NLRB v. 104-105, 121

Welfare Cases

Carleson v. Remillard 113
Dandridge v. Williams 108, 110-112
Hopkins v. Cohen 107, 108
Jefferson v. Hackney 108, 113
King v. Smith 111, 112, 113
Lewis v. Martin 112
New York State Dep't of Social Services
   v. Dublino 107
Richardson v. Belcher 113
Richardson v. Perales 108, 113
Richardson v. Wright 106-107
Social Security Board v. Nierotko 106-107
Wyman v. James 114-115, 121, 123
Wyman v. Rothstein 106-107

Miscellaneous Cases

Ballard, United States v. 132
Dennis v. United States 132
Poulos v. New Hampshire 132
Public Utilities Comm'n v. Pollack 122
UNITED STATES v. — See Name of Respondent
Wunderlich, United States v. 123
Zorach v. Clauson 132